Mismeasuring Schools' Vital Signs

This book helps school and district leaders avoid the pitfalls that await those making sense of their school's data. Whether you're interpreting achievement gaps, graduation rates or test results, you're at risk of reaching a mistaken judgment. By learning about common errors and how they're made, you'll be ready to choose safer, surer paths to making better sense of the wealth of data in your school or district. The authors help educators build better evidence, see conclusions more clearly and explain the data more persuasively.

Special features include:

- "Questions to Spark Discussion" in each chapter encourage school site, district leaders and board trustees to apply each chapter's content to their own situations.
- Data visualizations, together with the authors' interpretations, will help you learn how to do visual analysis (and reach the right conclusions).
- Practical tips provide clear guidance.
- Supplemental resources can be found at the book's website, https://www.k12measures.com, including interactive data visualizations and analytic exercises to help you learn a concept by "doing."

Steve Rees is Founder and current President of School Wise Press consultancy. He is also the leader of its K12 Measures team.

Jill Wynns is an urban education policy expert and a 24-year veteran of the San Francisco Unified School District (USD) Board of Education.

Other Eye On Education Books Available from Routledge
(www.routledge.com/eyeoneducation)

First Aid for Teacher Burnout: How You Can Find Peace and Success, 2nd Edition
Jenny Grant Rankin

Becoming an International School Educator: Stories, Tips, and Insights from Teachers and Leaders
Edited by Dana Specker Watts and Jayson W. Richardson

Trailblazers for Whole School Sustainability: Case Studies of Educators in Action
Cynthia L. Merse, Jennifer Seydel, Lisa A.W. Kensler, and David Sobel

Get Organized Digitally!: The Educator's Guide to Time Management
Frank Buck

Creating, Grading, and Using Virtual Assessments: Strategies for Success in the K-12 Classroom
Kate Wolfe Maxlow, Karen L. Sanzo, and James Maxlow

How to Make Data Work: A Guide for Educational Leaders
Jenny Grant Rankin

Teaching Practices from America's Best Urban Schools: A Guide for School and Classroom Leaders
Joseph F. Johnson, Jr., Cynthia L. Uline, and Lynne G. Perez

Rural America's Pathways to College and Career: Steps for Student Success and School Improvement
Rick Dalton

A Guide to Impactful Teacher Evaluations: Let's Finally Get It Right!
Joseph O. Rodgers

The Strategy Playbook for Educational Leaders: Principles and Processes
Isobel Stevenson and Jennie Weiner

Unpacking Your learning Targets: Aligning Student Learning to Standards
Sean McWherter

Strategic Talent Leadership for Educators: A Practical Toolkit
Amy A. Holcombe

Working with Students that Have Anxiety: Creative Connections and Practical Strategies
Beverley H. Johns, Donalyn Heise, Adrienne D. Hunter

Implicit Bias in Schools: A Practitioner's Guide
Gina Laura Gullo, Kelly Capatosto, and Cheryl Staats

Mismeasuring Schools' Vital Signs

How to Avoid Misunderstanding, Misinterpreting, and Distorting Data

Steve Rees and Jill Wynns

Routledge
Taylor & Francis Group

NEW YORK AND LONDON

Cover image: photomontage by Nikki Mitchell and William Georges

First published 2023
by Routledge
605 Third Avenue, New York, NY 10158

and by Routledge
4 Park Square, Milton Park, Abingdon, Oxon, OX14 4RN

Routledge is an imprint of the Taylor & Francis Group, an informa business

© 2023 Steve Rees and Jill Wynns

The right of Steve Rees and Jill Wynns to be identified as authors of this work has been asserted in accordance with sections 77 and 78 of the Copyright, Designs and Patents Act 1988.

All rights reserved. No part of this book may be reprinted or reproduced or utilised in any form or by any electronic, mechanical, or other means, now known or hereafter invented, including photocopying and recording, or in any information storage or retrieval system, without permission in writing from the publishers.

Trademark notice: Product or corporate names may be trademarks or registered trademarks, and are used only for identification and explanation without intent to infringe.

Library of Congress Cataloging-in-Publication Data
Names: Rees, Steve (Data analyst), author. | Wynns, Jill, author.
Title: Mismeasuring schools' vital signs : how to avoid misunderstanding, misinterpreting, and distorting data / Steve Rees, Jill Wynns.
Description: First Edition. | New York : Routledge, 2023. | Includes bibliographical references and index.
Identifiers: LCCN 2022012847 (print) | LCCN 2022012848 (ebook) | ISBN 9781032183411 (Hardback) | ISBN 9781032225265 (Paperback) | ISBN 9781003272915 (eBook)
Subjects: LCSH: Educational evaluation—Data processing. | Educational indicators.
Classification: LCC LB2822.75 .R434 2023 (print) | LCC LB2822.75 (ebook) | DDC 379.1/58—dc23/eng/20220701
LC record available at https://lccn.loc.gov/2022012847
LC ebook record available at https://lccn.loc.gov/2022012848

ISBN: 978-1-032-18341-1 (hbk)
ISBN: 978-1-032-22526-5 (pbk)
ISBN: 978-1-003-27291-5 (ebk)

DOI: 10.4324/9781003272915

Typeset in Optima
by Apex CoVantage, LLC

To my brother Richard Rees, and my father-in-law, Allan Goldstein, both of whom guided me wisely and patiently through the debates about analytic methods in the fields of psychology and intelligence.

Steve Rees

Contents

List of figures, sidebars and tables	viii
Preface: the two paths that led us to write this book	xi
About the authors	xxiii
Acknowledgments	xxv

	Introduction: the human cost of mismeasurement	1
1	What is mismeasurement and how does it occur?	6
2	Twisting test results and missing sound evidence of learning	35
3	The hidden hazards of interpreting graduation rates	81
4	Gaps mismeasured, misattributed and misunderstood	106
5	Logic errors when identifying and evaluating English learners	165
6	Mistaken ways of measuring money, buildings and people	195
7	Reducing barriers to progress at every level	233
	Index	249

Figures, sidebars and tables

Figures

1.1	Illustration of the many interested parties taking stock of a school's vital signs	15
2.1	Comparison of a standard calculator (left) with the interface provided to students taking the Smarter Balanced math test (right)	42
2.2	Body-mass index for boys of different ages	47
2.3	College going rate of Class of 2018	51
2.4	Frequency distribution of 2016 California CAASPP/SBAC math results of fourth and eighth graders	53
2.5	Smarter Balanced report to parents of a student's results, 2016	56
2.6	Second graders' scores on two reading tests	60
2.7	Cross-sectional view of math Smarter Balanced scores for students in a hypothetical K–5 elementary school district	67
2.8	Quasi-longitudinal view of math Smarter Balanced scores for students in a hypothetical K–5 elementary school district	69
2.9	Six elements you should know about any assessment interpretation that claims to measure progress	70
4.1	A multicausal model of influences at work on kids in school	110
4.2	Suspension rates of students by ethnicity for 16 districts, 2019	118
4.3	Suspension rates of students by ethnicity for 16 districts, 2019	120
4.4	Scores of white and Latino/Hispanic eighth-grade students on the National Assessment of Educational Progress from 1990 to 2019	128

Figures, sidebars and tables

4.5	Student subgroup results by score level on Smarter Balanced English language arts test (2019), Washoe County, Nevada School District	136
4.6	Average test scores vs. socioeconomic status in Bloomfield School District, Indiana, and Warren Consolidated Schools, Michigan	141
4.7	Gap in average test scores between white and Hispanic students in Bloomfield School District, Indiana, and Warren Consolidated Schools, Michigan	142
4.8	Gap in average test scores vs. school poverty between white and Hispanic students in Bloomfield School District, Indiana, and Warren Consolidated Schools, Michigan	144
4.9	Average students' test scores vs. socioeconomic status in Aldine, Texas, and Rosemount-Apple Valley-Eagan, Minnesota	145
4.10	Gap in average test scores between white and Hispanic students in Aldine, Texas, and Rosemount-Apple Valley-Eagan, Minnesota	146
4.11	Gap in average test scores vs. gap in school poverty between white and Hispanic Students in Aldine, Texas, and Rosemount-Apple Valley-Eagan, Minnesota	147
4.12	Average students' test scores vs. socioeconomic status in Charlottesville City Public School District, Virginia, and Chico Unified School District, California	149
4.13	Average students' learning rates vs. socioeconomic status in Charlottesville City Public School District, Virginia, and Chico Unified School District, California	150
4.14	Gap in average test scores between white and Hispanic students in Charlottesville City Public School District, Virginia, and Chico Unified School District, California	152
4.15	Gap in learning rates between white and Hispanic students in Charlottesville City Public School District, Virginia, and Chico Unified School District, California	153
5.1	EL students making progress toward proficiency, Class of 2024 over five years: Napa Valley USD alone	181
5.2	EL students making progress toward proficiency, Class of 2024 over five years: Napa Valley USD and 15 similar districts	182

5.3 EL students making progress toward proficiency, Class of 2024 over five years: Napa Valley USD and Fairfield-Suisun USD — 183

5.4 Class of 2024, ELs reclassified as fluent-English-proficient students over five years: Smarter Balanced test results, Napa Valley USD and 15 similar districts — 185

5.5 Never EL (English-only) and reclassified English-fluent students' scores on SBAC, math 2019, grades 3–8 — 187

5.6 Never EL (English-only) and reclassified English-fluent students' scores on SBAC, English language arts, 2019, grades 3–8 — 189

6.1 Teachers retained at district since 2015 — 223

Sidebars

1.1 How an extraordinary principal almost became a casualty in the accountability wars — 12

2.1 How every state once claimed its students' scores were above average — 48

2.2 California's misleading K–12 dashboard could lead to closure of the wrong schools — 63

3.1 School push-out: What is it? — 90

3.2 When grad rate problems land your high school in the accountability doghouse — 99

5.1 Making the right decision may require bending the rules — 175

6.1 Enabling elementary teachers to teach their best subject all day long — 218

6.2 When dead ex-employees get paychecks, position control is out of control — 222

7.1 Dr. Ritu Khanna: an assessment director who teaches leaders how to think about test results — 242

Tables

3.1 Cumulative impact of 15 percent annual student turnover on a single graduating class cohort over four years — 82

Preface: the two paths that led us to write this book

 Steve Rees

My path started when my son, Ben, reached school-age in 1983. Because I lived in San Francisco, a city that *required* parents to choose schools, his mother and I had to select his elementary school. A desegregation challenge by the NAACP led to an agreement with the city's school district to let a federal judge named William H. Orrick decide how kids would be assigned to schools. After a brief and successful experiment with letting parents choose schools, Judge Orrick decided that the era of the district assigning kids to schools was over. He ruled that parents would now choose schools. In 1984, with over 70 elementary schools within the compact 49 square miles that comprise San Francisco, the choice put the burden of responsibility directly on parents' shoulders.

I felt the weight of that burden and started a search that combined classroom observations with data analysis. Luckily, Judge Orrick had ordered the district to gather and publish data that went far beyond what other California districts were required to share. In addition, the district had put a man in charge of their research and evaluation division who gladly shared with citizens the data he compiled at the judge's behest. Bob Harrington was in harmony with the spirit of the judge's orders, and he welcomed public interest in the data his team harvested. Being both a gentleman and a Democrat, as well as a division leader of considerable diplomatic skill, he welcomed me and others like me into the deep end of the data pool. This welcome was a dozen years before the worldwide web became the publishing platform for data like these.

I jumped into the search fully, just as most of my friends did. With schools of many flavors within a mile of anyone's home, certainly one

Preface: our two paths

would be worth trying. My ex-wife and I, after visiting a half-dozen schools and spending a half-dozen days poring over school stats, found a school nearby that looked promising: Buena Vista Elementary. When the day to apply arrived, we got up at 4 a.m., took a lawn chair, a thermos of coffee and blanket, and went down to sit in line. As luck would have it, our mission proved successful. Our son was admitted (first-come, first-served) and had a great experience. We fit into the school's community easily. Our daughter followed five years later.

This turned out to be a formative experience. It revealed differences in values among friends. It shaped the friendships and habits of minds of our kids, of course. But it also sparked a deep interest in me that blossomed into a life choice about 10 years later to leave my profession, magazine publishing, and turn toward making sense of schools' vital signs. If there were guidebooks like *Zagat's Guides* to help people choose a restaurant, why weren't there books to help parents choose schools? If a brother from another planet were to land in America in 1995 and survey the printed matter that was designed to help people make choices, that extraterrestrial would find *Zagat's Guides* to help diners, the *Racing Form* to help horse-racing fans place their bets, movie guides, college guides, city guides and more. But nowhere would our extraterrestrial visitor find school guides. Would he conclude from this that people didn't care as much about choosing schools as choosing where they went for dinner?

In 1995, I decided to test that notion and started a publishing company to publish guides to public schools in major California cities. This experiment in school information led us to soon turn toward the worldwide web, where we published county-by-county rankings of California's elementary, middle and high schools, not unlike *Zagat's Guides'* rankings. We soon licensed them to the *L.A. Times* and their syndicate for wider distribution. In addition, we built a software engine that generated reports in English and Spanish about each school in California (nearly 10,000). The popularity of these reports with parents, home buyers, realtors, teachers and principals seeking new assignments, combined to help us reach the promised land of financial self-sufficiency, but too slowly. So in 1999, I turned our resources to help those running California schools and districts create and publish school accountability report cards. Since 1988, California required that district leaders publish reports about their schools that contained data galore and include descriptive writing by principals. By cobbling together attendance data, test scores, suspension stats and more with principals' observations, district leaders presumed this would satisfy citizens' need to know. The reports looked like Little League newsletters. Since those were the early days of desktop publishing, this was no surprise. But the informality of the writing, amateurish desktop design and clip art made this a rather unserious response to the public's serious concerns. The lightweight nature of those school accountability reports, as they were called, was in contrast to the heavy weight of responsibility parents felt in choosing schools.

In truth, parents and others wondered what exactly was the quality of educational services their school district was creating. With no less than 40 percent of the state budget dedicated to funding public schools and community colleges, this large a share of public funds required more serious answers than a light-spirited four-page newsletter. In 1998, the California state testing program had just resumed. Before that, local districts selected their own testing firms. Some didn't bother to test their students at all. But when the results were delivered, districts distributed reports to parents only about their own kids. The school-level and district-level reports often stayed under lock and key in the desk drawer of an assistant superintendent. This practice of concealing results only fueled the public's skepticism.

That was the year that I turned my small company's resources fully to the task of helping school and district leaders tell their schools' stories professionally. Because a new curriculum had been introduced that all districts would follow, at the same time that the California Standards Tests became a requirement, all schools and districts found themselves on common ground. Teach to the same standards. Give students in each grade level 2 through 11 the same tests. Then put the results before the public and let the chips fall where they may. I felt this made for a publishing challenge I wanted to tackle.

The opportunity I found most compelling was the freedom to interpret test results somewhat differently than the California accountability system required. We could meet the requirements of law line for line. But we could also go beyond its minimal requirements and use more fully the wealth of data being harvested by the California Department of Education. We created county-specific and school-level specific benchmarks so a middle school principal could see how her school in Fresno County was doing compared to other middle schools in the county. We published college-going data gathered by the underappreciated California Postsecondary Education Commission. We discovered data about libraries and published that. We

Preface: our two paths

guided principals to write about facets of their programs that the public cared about. Then our editors polished principals' writing so no one had a reason to be embarrassed.

What soon followed was the start of the No Child Left Behind (NCLB) era. Federal legislation became law in 2001. Soon all states had to shape up, in some respects more fully than California required. Even with its aspirational goals—all children proficient by 2014—the federal regs gave states room to decide how to present the facts. California, with its Academic Performance Index (API), distilled students' test results (and high schools' graduation rates) into a single three-digit score. For those looking for a simple measure of "better schools," the Academic Performance Index became their compass. Real estate agents loved it when the numbers were good and ignored it when they weren't. California officialdom kept a firm hand on the technical measures that went into the Academic Performance Index, but it left districts room to exercise freedom to present their facts as they saw fit.

I led our team into the freedom zone, where we made the most of interpreting those results in ways more truthful, more understandable and more relevant to parents' concerns. We did this for about 240 districts over 14 years, publishing reports in English and Spanish that got read, on average by about one-third of the families enrolled in our client districts. But I was also pleased to learn that more than 80 percent of the principals we surveyed told us that our reports showed them something new about their schools. To reveal any aspect of a school to a principal for the first time, a school whose staff and students she knew well, was a tribute to our ability to build evidence and interpret it, and to our method of framing facts in a comparative context.

But what I've found troubling, 20 years into this post-NCLB phase of the school accountability era, are four flaws: (1) relying on a method of interpreting test scores that does more to describe the students than the school; (2) missing the opportunity to use state longitudinal data systems to look at multiyear growth of the same students over time; (3) ignoring the imprecision of test results, especially in smaller schools and districts; and (4) disregarding context when analyzing gaps in achievement or opportunities to learn. In surveying many states for this book, I was surprised to see so many commit one or more of those errors.

One factor, above all, led us to write this book. We shared the hope that some school and district leaders, as well as school board trustees, will use the freedom they've got to measure what matters to them, and do so in ways that avoid the errors we've identified in this book. The good news is that social scientists have made much progress in developing methods of squeezing sound meaning from data. You're free to follow their lead. We'll point you in directions we think are promising. If you don't like your state's way of making sense of your schools' vital signs, we urge you to break for the freedom zone and report results as you see fit, in addition to the way your state requires. Just keep in mind the carpenters' watchword: measure twice, cut once.

Jill Wynns

In the 24 years that I served on the San Francisco USD Board of Education, I evolved from a parent who trusted her gut on almost everything related to schools (even my own children's education) to a policy-maker who always searched for more information, more data and especially more help to interpret data and to understand the meaning of that data. It is not that I started out deliberately ignoring facts, but rather that data was not readily available or explained to parents or even school board members.

When I started to look for a kindergarten for my oldest son, the conventional wisdom among middle-class parents in San Francisco was that only a few "alternative" elementary schools were good enough for our kids and that, certainly, no neighborhood schools in diverse neighborhoods were. In fact, even though I went through a months-long process of visiting schools and doing research, my son landed in a really good San Francisco public school largely based on luck. I took a chance on a nice school in a nice neighborhood across town from my home. It reminded me of the public schools my siblings and I went to in New York State, cheerful, pleasant, fun. Kids were learning and seemed to be enjoying school. Like most parents, I didn't know what else to look for. Even though the district had a complex and inequitable process, circumstances allowed my son to get into what turned out to be a wonderful school for him and for our family.

My family's dedication and investment in that public school, along with similar commitments by many other families, helped make it better, more connected to the community and more popular. These kinds of efforts were replicated by thousands of families across the city. San Francisco public schools, like most American public schools, struggled to meet rising

Preface: our two paths

expectations for all students with declining resources, but the upward trajectory continued over time.

We formed a community coalition and passed five local bond measures for new and modernized facilities, a local sales tax for schools, two parcel taxes and a landmark set-aside of city dollars for the school district and universal preschool. Community support was profoundly improved. Even the newspapers softened their relentless negative coverage and "gotcha" attitude. Partnerships with the city government, business groups and community-based organizations became the hallmark of the school district. Test scores rose and the district developed new data sources. But the information on which the district relied remained indecipherable to most of the public, largely, I think, because the district failed to explain it or clarify how it was used.

How did I learn to understand educational data? Most importantly, how did I learn what questions to ask about the data that would actually help me understand the meaning of our data? The first person to explain to me what the scores on standardized tests meant was the principal of my son's elementary school. We had a Parents' Club meeting to help parents understand test reports. This was quite unusual at the time. The principal explained how standardized test scores, both those of our individual children and of the school, could teach us something about how we were doing. She pointed out that the scores showed groups of questions that tested knowledge and skills in a variety of areas in both English and math. She emphasized that teachers and parents should read the results carefully because they would help us to understand our students' strengths and weaknesses. I left that meeting feeling like I had learned something important about how schools worked.

Later, when I started attending school board meetings and parent advisory committees, I learned that my school district, the San Francisco Unified School District, was testing students every year and had been for years. This did not seem unusual to me. As a former public school student, I had taken a battery of standardized tests every year as a child. A few years earlier, as part of the ongoing settlement of a desegregation lawsuit brought by the NAACP, the district had agreed to begin longitudinal studies of student test scores, comparing each student's achievement year to year, and to disaggregate the scores by ethnic groups, English fluency and socio-economic status. The purpose was to compare the results for students in the schools "targeted" for desegregation to the rest of the schools in the district.

Preface: our two paths

I did not understand how unusual this was, in the late eighties, to collect and study this achievement data for the purpose of evaluating student learning for different groups of students. At that time, this information was being used for what seemed to me to be a noble purpose: to improve the educational experience and success of students who were not traditionally doing well in school or were presumed to be "disadvantaged." This was my first lesson in how school data analysis was practiced.

When I was elected to the school board in 1992, my tenure in local, state and national education policy-making (1993–2016) was during the age of standards-based reform and the enormous expansion of testing. It was also the era when school boards, districts and schools were urged to make data-driven decisions to hold teachers, administrators, schools and districts accountable. California developed a state accountability system based on extensive state standards and annual testing, and regulations requiring growth from year to year.

My understanding of the technical aspects of standardized testing and data analysis grew steadily as I pursued my training and professional development as a board member. I learned in training offered by the California School Boards Association. I embraced state leadership, was a member of the Delegate Assembly for my entire 24-year tenure, served for 14 years on the Board of Directors and served as president in 2012. I was also active in the National School Boards Association's Council of Urban Boards of Education and was elected to their National Steering Committee for 11 years. I also regularly attended the Council of the Great City Schools conferences and served on their Board of Directors and task forces. I listened to many data directors and administrators recount how they were analyzing their data and how they made judgments about achievement.

It was at one of these conferences that I felt like a bolt of lightning had struck when I listened to a history of the development of norm-referenced tests, heard about their development for the purpose of identifying those who were not fit for military service and began to understand the impact of this type of testing on public schools. These tests worked well for sorting students but did not assess the effectiveness of teaching or identify the needs of individual students. The racial and socioeconomic segregation I had seen was suddenly visible to me as a consequence, in part, of testing. I just wanted to jump up and say, "Wait. Why are we still doing that?" Sometimes I did and was seen as too outspoken, even troublesome, but I began to search for more knowledge about testing data and its use.

Preface: our two paths

I had the chance to learn a lot about the movement for test-based accountability and to interact with experts and policy-makers who were shaping this direction for the federal government. I listened to and met with Secretaries of the U.S. Department of Education, and their senior staffs and advisors. I also met with legislative staff members, the people writing the bills that would change the relationship between local school districts and the federal government.

Within a few years, a federal test-based accountability system, part of No Child Left Behind, was mandated for every state, trying to combine both state authority to have their own standards and using tests that allowed each state's schools to be compared to every other school in their state.

Now all aspects of school reform were framed by testing data. This was not a neutral conversation. It seemed to me that we were always fighting a battle about the purpose of enhanced testing. The battle intensified and limited the ability to engage in any neutral dialogue about the models being developed and used, or the analysis that followed the testing.

Trust in public schools declined. Elected school boards were accused of causing this failure, of being uncaring, incompetent and merely defenders of the status quo, including inherent racism in the system. That was really hard to respond to. It was a version of "When did you stop beating your wife?" I know that most school board members are incredibly dedicated and hardworking public servants and that public schools were struggling without adequate resources, making genuine efforts to improve instruction, raise the skill levels of their teachers and staff and address the challenges faced by their students, and making steady, incremental progress.

Particularly troubling was the insistence that snapshots of data taken each year, and viewed at each grade level, were all that mattered. Accountability systems that measured growth of the same students over time were dismissed as inadequate. The federal government insisted that all schools and all students must meet an absolute standard by a certain time, regardless of where they began, regardless of their circumstances, regardless of the resources available in their state or district.

We did not include the achievement of the same students year to year, or their learning rates. We compared them to students in the same grade the next year and subsequent years. For policy-makers, it did not help us to plan carefully or to identify trends and patterns to which we could respond. We needed better tests to measure this year-to-year growth, and better vantage points from which we could view the results of the same students over longer periods of time.

The more I explored the intersection between test score data and accountability agendas, the more I realized that data was often distorted when used to build lopsided evidence to support political agendas. I saw this not so much as a fight against these agendas with which I disagreed, but as a commitment to inquiry, to understanding the evidence and learning the meaning of the data. This led me to think more about the data that I was seeing from our own schools and district, and particularly about the methodology used to analyze information, seek to understand the implications of emerging trends and suggest policy based on what the data reveals.

Deepening my understanding of the practices used in data gathering and data analysis helped me to grow my knowledge base. I think that this helped me to expand my thinking. I have not given up my political position regarding policies and practices based on what I view as faulty data-based analysis, but I welcome a climate surrounding school accountability that is not quite so hot, not quite so polarized and more open to discussion. That is what I hope that this book can encourage. I have lived through this period where there seemed to be a minimum of serious discussion of what questions we were trying to answer, and insufficient scrutiny of the methods of data gathering and analysis. Posing questions for research and improved understanding of the relationship between the data being analyzed and the conclusions reached are essential for educators working in every role in the school improvement process.

What to expect

Who this book is for

The readers we have in mind are those brave enough to lead or govern districts and schools, and those striving to step up to those responsibilities. We also have in mind policy people, journalists, advocates, active parents, education reformers and teachers who share a concern with the quality of the evidence about how schools are doing. Reputations (and more) ride on that evidence. Finally, we hope that graduate students in schools of education find this book to be a practical bridge from their studies to their next workplace.

Preface: our two paths

Readers who may feel a bit out of their element in a numbers-intensive environment are going to feel at home here. Our approach relies much more heavily on visual representations than on tables of numbers. While mathematical approaches to identifying patterns offer great insight to those capable of applying quantitative methods, it is not an approach we take in this book. You'll soon see that our analytic methods are mainly visual and logical.

What you'll find in each chapter

Chapter 1 looks at the ways that people take stock of human activity in schools, and at the many ways that they can stray into the error zone. We make a case for the value of critical examinations of mistakes. This is a common path to knowledge in other fields. Why isn't it a common practice in education, a profession where "best practices" seem to be fashionable? We also advance our ideas about the transformation of data to knowledge. You may be surprised to discover that we don't pay much attention to data in and of themselves, but rather pay attention to the building of evidence and the reasoning that leads people to draw conclusions.

Chapter 2 is about the misinterpretation of test results, looking at errors of commission, omission and judgment. We discuss disregard of a test's purpose, the misunderstanding of what a test might measure, the degree of imprecision and uncertainty inherent in that measure, the choice of the wrong metric, the disregard of spread and over-attentiveness to central tendency and more. We look closely at the mismeasurement of growth, which is so central to evaluation of student-level, school-level and district-level progress. You'll learn about the myth of Lake Wobegon, and the history of misunderstanding of norms on national tests. Plus, you'll find tips and guidelines to help you avoid the hazards that are prevalent in the assessment landscape.

Chapter 3 is centered on the challenge of interpreting graduation rates. Within the world of high schools, all the technical smarts in the world won't help those who lack street smarts. The converse is equally true. For those who think it's a relatively easy, straightforward matter, I urge you to proceed with care. Deceptive data sparkles like fool's gold on the surface. You can pick them up and think you're holding the real thing, but good luck using them to pay for your groceries.

Chapter 4 is focused on the mismeasurement of gaps, both gaps in student achievement and gaps in opportunities to learn. The underlying questions driving gap analysis are often about bias and fairness, whether students have been treated equally. We argue that while disproportionate results alone aren't sufficient to prove bias is at work, we believe that evidence of bias can, indeed, be discovered if you are willing to work hard to define and analyze the results with care. We offer a case in point: teacher-assigned grades. With equal treatment of students so high on so many districts' list of values, we ask why measuring unequal treatment isn't done with greater deliberation. Toward the end of this chapter, you'll find the exemplary work of the Stanford Educational Opportunity Project, which has advanced the art and science of gap measurement by a quantum leap.

Chapter 5 is about the mismeasurement of students we call English learners but should probably be calling "emerging bilingual" students. The semantic confusion itself (aren't all early elementary students learning English) is a clue to the miscounting and illogic that warp the appraisal of their progress. This chapter also examines the inexcusable inaccuracy that has become common practice when identifying students who appear to be English learners, as well as the sizable hurdles put in the way of those students when they are ready to be reclassified as English-fluent.

In Chapter 6, we examine the peculiar ways that education leaders measure money, buildings, land and people. These four resources are quite valuable yet are too often measured in ways that distort their value. In the case of people, most school districts don't evaluate their teachers in any meaningful way. In an organization that delivers a human service, failing to understand who your best teachers of emerging readers might be, or your best middle school math teachers, leaves district management with a terrible blind spot. The misunderstanding of money is evident in many ways. We explore the concepts missing from so many district business offices: measures of the cost of services per-student, cost-effectiveness of programs, cost-benefit analysis, and measures of the impact beyond three years of spending decisions.

Chapter 7 offers what may be a surprisingly positive measure of hope. We believe that facing the errors endemic in the management of schooling can indeed lead to improvements. We recommend changes to every level of the system: pre-service education, credentialing programs, professional development, state departments of education and testing firms. There's plenty of blame to go around, and the good news is that there's a corresponding bundle of praise to be earned by those who learn some new moves and get measurement-savvy.

The flavors of content you'll find

We've tried to provide many handles on information throughout the book. Anecdotes of great stories appear as sidebars. Skip them if you like. Or read them as you encounter them. They provide a change of pace, without interrupting the flow of the chapter. Suggestions of smart things you can do appear as tips. (A pointing finger marks these.)

For those who may be interested in applying what you've read to real-world questions, we've provided guiding questions at the end of each chapter. Some are for school board trustees, some for district leaders and others for principals. Many are scenarios that should spark discussion.

In the same spirit, we've created a website (https://www.k12measures.com) that extends the content of the book in three ways. First, you'll find interactive versions of many of the data visualizations that appear in the book. The fun of playing with these is one reason to click over to the website. But another reason is that you can find additional guidance to help you learn how to do exploratory data analysis. We'll be adding analytic exercises and object lessons to help you gain confidence as you build competence in making sense of visual evidence.

Second, the site contains additional content for each chapter. This will include essays and blog posts we write, as well as new resources as we discover them. Magazine articles, journal articles, books and more will get our attention as we offer week by week new installments of what will become an annotated bibliography.

Third, you will have an opportunity to send us your questions. It's not just our generosity, but our self-interest at work. It's our way of extending our ability to learn from the questions you ask. If enough readers take an interest in this Q&A, we'll establish the technical functionality for an online community conversation.

Finally, the endnotes and references are a bridge to the scholarly work of others that may be useful. We did this, not solely to give credit where credit is due, but because we consider ourselves to be bridge-builders, connecting you to useful knowledge. When we cite a work, it's in the interest of pointing you in a promising direction.

About the authors

Steve Rees

When he started School Wise Press in 1995, Steve Rees brought to education leaders a publishing team that could help them make sense of their schools' vital signs and communicate it.

He led his company to build award-winning accountability reports to a professional standard, serving 240 California districts. His writing has appeared in *Education Week, EdSource* and the *San Francisco Chronicle*. And he has been a frequent presenter at conferences of California education leaders.

In 2014, he launched the K12 Measures team and turned their talents toward building visual analytic expressions of schools' and districts' vital signs. He has since written and delivered curricula to enhance the skills of education leaders interpreting test results, building evidence from data and using it wisely.

He attended public schools in the San Francisco Bay Area and attended UC Santa Cruz. In 2017, he moved from San Francisco, where he had lived for 47 years, to New York City. He is the happy father of two, and grandfather of three.

Jill Wynns

Jill Wynns served on the San Francisco USD Board of Education for 24 years. She is an expert

About the authors

on state and federal education issues, California school finance, urban education and governance, charter schools, privatization of public schools, school health programs, healthy food in schools, arts education and labor-management cooperation.

She is a former President of the California School Boards Association and served as Chair of the California Cities, Counties and Schools Partnership. She was a long-term member of the Steering Committee of the Council of Urban Boards of Education of the National School Boards Association and served on the Board of Directors of the Council of the Great City Schools.

Jill is a consultant to Funding the Next Generation, a project of the California Endowment that provides support to local communities in California seeking local funding for children's services and schools. She led campaigns that raised more than a billion local dollars for San Francisco public schools.

Jill holds a BA in humanities from New College at Hofstra University in New York and studied at Harvard and Wiks folkhogskola in Balingsta, Sweden. She is the mother of three children who attended San Francisco public schools and the grandmother of five.

Acknowledgments

Thanks to Sean F. Reardon and The Educational Opportunity Project at Stanford University for their permission to use Figures 4.6 through 4.15 in Chapter 4. To explore these images interactively, visit the Educational Opportunity Explorer site at: https://edopportunity.org/.

Steve Rees

I'd like to acknowledge the exceptionally valuable help provided by many who reviewed this manuscript. David Osborne provided the guidance of a veteran author, helping me always keep the reader in mind. Readers have been spared many tangents because of his watchful eyes and good judgment. His keen eye for a weak link in an argument enabled him to flag questionable assertions and always led to improved writing. His book, *Reinventing America's Schools*, about the charter movements in New Orleans, Denver, and Washington, D.C., encouraged me to pay attention to the details that make good stories come alive.

I also want to thank Phil Morse for his comments on the mismeasurement of students who are learning English. Thanks, as well, to Tom Barrett for his comments on the assessment chapter. In prior years, Phil and Tom also taught me a lot about assessment, when they were part of a short-lived assessment consultancy I launched in California.

Thanks to Eric Zilbert, who recently retired from his leadership position at the California Department of Education, where he ran the assessment group. Eric has generously shared his views with me on many occasions over the past 12 years, fielding technical questions of all sorts. His open-door

Acknowledgments

policy has encouraged me to knock when I needed a psychometrician's guidance when wrestling with key technical concepts.

Special thanks to Henry Levin, whose guidance on all things economic helped my thinking evolve fuller and faster. A friend and recently retired high school teacher in New York City, Lynn Yellen, vetted the chapter on graduation rates. In addition, Matt McElroy helped improve the clarity of the chapter on gaps misunderstood. Thanks to both of you.

I also am grateful for the help of Josh Schultz, Deputy Superintendent of Napa County Office of Education in California, and Tony Wold, a business leader in several California districts, for their comments and critiques of the chapter on money, land and buildings, and people. I highly value the help they've provided, based on their knowledge of the work of district business management and human resources.

I'm especially grateful to Glen Webb, recently retired from Morgan Hill USD, California, Superintendent Barbara Nemko of Napa County Office of Education and Superintendent Fred Navarro of Newport-Costa Mesa, California. They've given me the chance to learn at their sides as my team and I served them as analytic partners.

Thanks to my colleagues, too: Greg Smith, who was the architect, designer and engineer who built many of the data visualizations that fill this book; Michael O'Neill, who is an educator of educators, and who has coached me in becoming a better workshop leader and presenter; and Stephen Gervais, whose modeling skills and geospatial analysis talents have taught me a great deal. I tip my hat in gratitude to Jenny Rankin, whose energy and encouragement led me to tackle this book. And kudos to Nikki Mitchell and Will Georges, whose creative talents appear on the cover.

And thanks, too, to my coauthor, Jill Wynns, whose ideas are sharp, whose b.s. detectors are well tuned and whose experience as a school board leader is vast. I'm especially grateful for her reservoirs of patience as we dared to write this book together.

Finally, I tip my hat to my wife and partner, Elizabeth Goldstein, whose generosity of spirit and patience gave me the gift of time I needed to bang my thoughts into publishable form. I was lucky to find her ready to pull me out of the clouds and back to terra firma on more than a few occasions. And my gratitude to my friend, Peder Jones, for encouraging my interest in how school districts are managed, and for his wise guidance along the way.

Jill Wynns

I would like to acknowledge and thank Dr. Ritu Khanna, who taught me how to look at data and to discover what it might reveal, as well as for her time in a wonderful discussion we had in preparation for this book.

I particularly want to recognize my coauthor, Steve Rees, whose interest in working with me, a policy and governance-focused person, on a book about data and analysis, has given me the opportunity to share a part of my experience that informed much of my work. He is the primary writer of this work, but it is the product of our discussions and shared experiences over many years, as well as intense work during this past year. The insights he gained working with school districts and data experts were extremely helpful to me as a school board member and remain so today.

Of course, I want to thank and acknowledge my family for their support during my long career, including the writing of this book.

Introduction
The human cost of mismeasurement

This book isn't just about numbers. It's about what happens to students, teachers and parents because leaders have misunderstood or misused numbers. Frankly, this book is really about people, and the things they do to each other using numbers badly.

If we were writing about the vital signs of patients in hospitals, mismeasurement would be easier to document, and its consequences more visible. Nurses might give medication to patients in the wrong dosage. Patients at home might fail to take their pills or take them twice. Doctors might misdiagnose patients' illnesses. Or a doctor might misunderstand the meaning of a lab test because he or she doesn't understand the probability of a false positive or false negative result. Manufacturers of intubation equipment might not sterilize valves or tubing. Drug companies might misunderstand the meaning of their clinical trials. Doctors might discharge patients too quickly, only to see them return days later. In every case, someone is harmed by mismeasurement, and that harm causes someone to suffer.

In the school world, harm caused by mismeasurement takes a form that is less visible, and less well documented. But it is no less real to those who feel the pain, and those who are close to them. The pain it causes will range from large to small. When a student's mastery of math is higher than his teacher realizes, and he is retaught something he already knows well, that student may be frustrated, annoyed or resigned. His time will be wasted as he is retaught something he knows, and his capabilities underestimated. A different sort of pain results when a student is misidentified as an English learner despite having equivalent mastery as his monolingual peers. That

DOI: 10.4324/9781003272915-1

Introduction

student may get routed into English language development classes for three, four or five years until an enlightened teacher realizes the original error and corrects it. The cost to the student: missed classroom opportunities and the demoralization that may result from being misunderstood. The cost to the district: wasted instructional time.

Diagnosing the reason for a student's difficulties with subject matter content or skill development is the teacher's challenge, just as diagnosing the cause of a patient's pain is a doctor's responsibility. In the medical world, scientific advancements in knowledge of diseases' causes, test instruments and research have enabled doctors to improve their diagnostic judgment. Some hospitals have embraced decision-support technology to augment the diagnostic judgment of their medical teams. In the school world, teachers have not yet enjoyed similar improvements. District investment in better assessments, and the skills of those who interpret them, has been slow even as investment in storage and retrieval of data has been high.

The use of sound evidence, analytic methods and good judgment to improve the diagnosis of barriers to learning has been rare. Even in the face of dyslexia, progress has been far too slow. This neurological disability that makes it hard to read for the 7–15 percent of the students who were born this way can be detected. Yet as of March 2022, only 39 states require dyslexia screening today. In districts that do not screen for dyslexia, students are simply marched through reading instruction until they fail to read. This becomes the diagnostic method in too many districts. The cost to students: lost time and an erosion of their self-confidence as learners. The cost to districts: wasted instructional time and demoralized teachers.

What about the harm to students who can't graduate because they can't pass algebra? Is the student not allowed to walk the stage and earn a diploma and a handshake because he didn't try? Or was his failure to pass algebra due to math instruction in fifth grade by a teacher who was not in command of math skills himself, leaving half of his students struggling with fractions, decimals and equivalents? If you can't handle fractions, how can you master algebra? Diagnostic tests would have turned up that student's skill deficits. If a district doesn't license those diagnostic assessments and leaves teachers to make do with the curriculum-embedded tests they already have in hand, these teachers will have lacked the instrument needed to detect skill deficits. The cost to the student: not graduating high school, starting life with a barrier to better jobs. The cost to the district: wasted instructional time.

Districts and schools also suffer institutional pain from the mismeasurement of their vital signs. During the era of No Child Left Behind, the reputations of schools and districts would rise and fall based on aspirational targets dubbed Adequate Yearly Progress goals. The goals were based on year-to-year changes in students' test scores, and the pursuit of a future state of grace where all students attained scores in math, English language arts and science that were above the magic line set by experts, the line of "proficiency" or "meeting standard." If your students' scores fell, on average, below that line, for three years in a row, your schools' teachers could be reassigned, or your principal transferred. If students' scores remained below the line for five years, the school could be closed or turned over to others who would be free to restaff it and design new programs.

Charter schools, too, have suffered from the misuse of vital signs at the do-or-die moment of their renewal authorization hearings. The charter that charter schools operate under in most states requires periodic review and reauthorization, often every five years. In those charters, founders make commitments to attain results. If those results aren't met, the authorizers have grounds to not renew their charter. Good authorizers have used evidence wisely when considering a charter school's right to operate another five years. The "weeding of the garden," as some have called it, is a healthy process if the right vital signs are measured properly and viewed from the right perspective. But this process can stray into the decidedly unhealthy zone if the state's view of vital signs is askew. California is one state where that is a prominent problem, due to a combination of logical and statistical flaws. In Chapter 2, you'll find an account of Ánimo Ellen Ochoa Charter Middle School in East Los Angeles, which almost lost its right to operate despite its students learning at a pace one-and-a-half to two times faster than their peers statewide.

In Chapter 7, you'll read about the dilemma faced by school board members of San Francisco USD, who faced the pressure of federal regulations requiring them to transfer a high school principal as a result of students' test scores. The school was in the second year of a turnaround, and the new principal responsible for its success was an all-star, recruited by the district to tackle a tough assignment. The board questioned the interpretation of the evidence presented by the U.S. Department of Education and won a waiver. Other districts were not as fortunate and lost leadership talent because of accountability rules that twisted test results and graduation rates into mismeasurements of school effectiveness.

You'll read in Chapter 6 about the Indianapolis Archdiocese Schools, who with the help of assessment expert John Schacter and his analytic team, found a way to improve the working conditions for elementary school teachers in the higher grade levels, who prospered when they were freed up to teach their best subject to the students they did best with, all day long. No surprise, evidence of their students' learning took a sharp turn up as a result.

This book is a call to education leaders to put numbers to work and reason in command in the cause of better educational experiences for both students and teachers. So many fields are abandoning old approaches based on tradition alone and welcoming insights from the proper measurement of important things. It happened years ago in baseball. Billy Beane, the manager of the Oakland A's baseball team in 2002, demoted his scouts' recommendations and promoted the statistical analysis of emerging talent. Those statistical methods of identifying talent were the work of Bill James, who first broached his ideas in book form in 1977. So, those ideas took about 25 years to root and bear fruit. Most teams now have a stat-head and a data collection staff in the front office.

It happened years ago in medicine. Dr. Warren Warwick, a pediatrician, conducted a study for the Cystic Fibrosis Foundation, in search of the variability of outcomes of the 117 hospitals that treated patients with cystic fibrosis (CF) at that time. Dr. Leroy Matthews at Fairview-University Children's Hospital, in Minneapolis, led the pack by far, showing in 2003 that their patients were living 47 years past their initial diagnosis, compared to the national average life expectancy of CF patients of 33 years. His exceptional practices, which included inventing a new way to cough and a mechanical vest that pounded patients' chests, were only identified when Dr. Warwick gathered comparative evidence.[1]

If two tradition-bound professions like baseball and medicine can evolve by bringing evidence-based empirical thinking forward, isn't it time for the profession of education management to do the same? Perhaps you'll be the leader to carry this hope to the table where decisions are made. We hope this book provides some inspiration for you to do just that.

Note

1. Atul Gawande, "The Bell Curve," *New Yorker*, December 6, 2004, www.newyorker.com/magazine/2004/12/06/the-bell-curve. Atul Gawande—surgeon, MacArthur Fellow, associate professor at Harvard Medical School and the Harvard School of Public Health, and author—has written extensively about the growth of evidence-based medicine in several books, including *The Checklist Manifesto* (2011) and *Better: A Surgeon's Notes on Performance* (2007). His essays appear often in the *New Yorker* magazine, where he is a staff writer. His stories of the place of measurement and the power of attentiveness to detail are inspiring accounts of the improvement process in the most human of sciences.

What is mismeasurement and how does it occur?

What is mismeasurement? It's not an everyday term in the school world, after all. But it is commonly used in other fields and professions. When we use the term "mismeasurement," we mean an error that occurs when gauging the quantity or quality of behavior, attitudes or other human events. Mismeasurement includes misunderstanding the size or meaning of something, which in turn may lead to errors in judgment. Given how much data educators have been collecting over the past several decades, it shouldn't be surprising that some of them have been measured incorrectly. But where in the process have those errors occurred? Who has made them? How consequential are they?

We don't expect errors when an event is recorded in a database, or when simple student-level events like attendance are assembled into a body of evidence (attendance statistics). We expect those to be routine, free of bias and free of errors. But accidents occur in the act of observation, in the recording of events and in the act of human judgment. All three steps are full of human effort, including human bias, and are susceptible to error.

Our definition of mismeasurement also includes misunderstanding the *meaning* of something. We expect people to disagree about the interpretation of measures of organizational vital signs, especially when the reputation of a school or district depends on it. We also expect differing interpretations to emerge from the same body of data. Attendance statistics, for instance, used to be viewed as simply the percentage of days that students attend school. Now you'll often see attendance data viewed from the vantage point of chronic absentee rates—the percentage of students who are absent more than 10 percent of school days. Other analysts reframe attendance data to isolate those days missed that are adjacent to holiday breaks, or to exclude excused absences. New meaning may emerge from each reframed point of view.

So, mismeasurement as we use it is more than a recording error or the use of the wrong measuring tool. Mismeasurement also includes misinterpretation. It may be making a mountain out of a proverbial molehill. Or it may be ignoring the mountain altogether. We consider mismeasurement to include errors of human judgment. In between the act of counting something and reporting that result is a lot of reasoning. To begin examining the soundness of that reasoning, let's create a typology of mismeasurement.

Three types of mismeasurement: errors of commission, omission and judgment

The most obvious way to measure something incorrectly is to count it poorly. These are *errors of commission*. If you are counting attendance, it could result from a human error, like an attendance clerk mistakenly keystroking a day's attendance at one school. Or it could result from a spreadsheet formula that sums only 28 of the 30 or 31 days of a month, producing an incorrect monthly summary. Or the error could result from a troubled data upload from your district to the state. I should mention the rare intentional error, a site administrator who falsifies her school's attendance for the day to avoid scrutiny by the district office team. These are the easy cases, because they involve counting things that are unambiguous and are also either present or absent.

A less obvious way to mismeasure something is to not count it at all. If that something is money, mismeasurement of this type could result from a policy that allows PTA or PTO funds to go directly to a school site without being passed through the general fund. Or it could result from a chart of accounts that has no place to note money spent on translation services for parents. If that's the case, you will be unable to gauge what your cost of serving a multilingual community has been. A chart of accounts that fails to allocate costs to specific school sites is another example. When the U.S. Department of Education requires that districts disclose school-level expenditures, those states that had the foresight to include a category for the site that benefited from an expenditure saved themselves hundreds of hours of catch-up bookkeeping.

What is mismeasurement?

Failing to note the first language fluency of students who are not yet fluent in English is another example. The way you'd educate a child who enters school reading chapter books in Spanish and whose parents attended college is different from the way you'd educate a child who begins school without knowing the letters of the alphabet, who hasn't been read to and whose parents left school after eighth grade. Another example: the students whose gender identity or affectional preference isn't noted because these are considered private matters. As a result, we don't have statistics about the dropout rate of gender-ambiguous or gay students. All these are examples of *errors of omission*.

The third category of mismeasurements is *errors of judgment*. This can include cases of interpretive judgment that are poorly connected to the evidence. Or they may be judgments that rest on flawed logic. Of course, many people can draw different and valid judgments from the same body of evidence. But all judgments are not created equal. Some just can't hold water because they're already filled with holes.

Let's identify opportunities for errors of all three types, using test scores as an example. Let's consider a teacher-created quiz at the end of the week, based on a week of instruction, focused on a chapter in a textbook every student was assigned to read. The students are fifth graders, and the subject is science. The purpose of the test is simply to check for understanding. The test includes just 10 questions. How could a teacher make mistakes with a test so short and whose purpose is so simple?

There are many opportunities for mismeasurement here. First, *errors of omission*. The chapter of that science book was dedicated to photosynthesis. Did the teacher's 10 questions cover all the key dimensions of photosynthesis? The short nature of the test required that the teacher select some dimensions and omit others. Was a key aspect not tested? This process of selecting subtopics or standards is a type of sampling. It's unavoidable. Were the questions testing a student's ability to recall something she read, or explaining her understanding of a process? Tests can aim for a depth of knowledge that's low, middle or high. Large-scale tests that are computer adaptive are built from item banks that offer a range of depth of knowledge for each question. Modest quizzes with fewer than 15 questions can't do that.

Second, let's consider *errors of commission*. This teacher's writing skills weren't great, so two of the 10 test questions were awkwardly phrased. This made the questions hard to understand. In fact, one of those two awkward questions could be interpreted in two distinct ways. This would lead students to choose not one, but two of the four multiple choice options as the correct answer. But because the teacher didn't recognize the awkward syntax of the two questions, she wasn't able to see that students who did read and understand the chapter might select a different answer as correct.

Third, let's give two examples of *errors of judgment*. The teacher scored the quiz and tallied a summary of her 30 students' results. Here are those results. What does she conclude?

Answered all 10 correctly	2 students
Answered 9 correctly	5 students
Answered 8 correctly	5 students
Answered 7 correctly	3 students
Answered 6 correctly	5 students
Answered 5 correctly	5 students
Answered 4 correctly	3 students
Answered 3 correctly	2 students

Her first observation is that her students have a pretty divergent understanding of photosynthesis. She concludes that the week of instruction "worked" more or less for the 15 students who answered seven or more questions correctly, and that it didn't "work" for the 15 students who answered six or fewer questions correctly. She believes that if her classroom instruction was effective for the top half of the class, then the bottom-scoring half of the class must have either not read the textbook or not paid attention during class. She resolves to review the unit with all 15 of the bottom-scoring students the following week.

But this teacher has not taken note of the variation in reading skills and English fluency among her students. So, she's interpreted the quiz results in error, by neglecting evidence that some of her students' wrong answers are a result of weak command of academic English and lagging reading skills. In this fifth-grade class, 15 of the 30 students were struggling readers. They were between one to two-and-a-half grade levels behind in their reading comprehension skills, and their Lexile scores matched the lagging comprehension scores. The reading resource teacher was working with 10 of them in Tier 2 multitiered system of support—what used to be called remediation or response-to-intervention. Another five students were English language learners, scoring intermediate on their state's

What is mismeasurement?

English language development test. Until she can interpret the students' answers within the context of students' reading skills and command of academic English, she is prone to errors in judgment about the meaning of the test results.

Frequency of mismeasurement of test results

How often might teachers make mistakes interpreting test results? More often than you might think. It turns out that the rate at which teachers draw the wrong conclusions is closely related to the quality of the reports that convey test results. Thanks to Jenny Rankin, a California scholar, author and speaker, this question of teachers' errors of interpretive judgment was the topic of her 2013 doctoral dissertation.[1] She designed a six-page questionnaire about the California Standards Tests and enlisted 211 teachers to respond. The questionnaire presented test results as data tables and as charts, and it asked teachers what those data meant. The format was multiple choice, and the questions were quite straightforward. No trick questions. No complex data. Just common reports that were faithfully representative of the reports being used by about 300,000 teachers in California at that time. About half the teachers were given reports that included reasonably well-documented versions of the reports, and the other half were given reports without those supports.

When Rankin tallied the results, she discovered that teachers made *correct interpretations about half the time* (48 percent to be exact) when they enjoyed the use of an interpretive guide, footers to explain the meaning of column heads and an abstract to introduce the assessment and its purpose. When the control group interpreted results without any of these supports, *teachers correctly interpreted results about one-ninth of the time* (11 percent).[2]

The theory she was testing was that improvements in the report designs would significantly improve the rate of correct inferences. The good news was that her hunch was strongly affirmed by her experiment. Teachers' rate of correct interpretation using all forms of support improved by a factor of four. The bad news is that even with these supports, they made correct interpretations only half the time. Her research revealed that investing in higher quality reporting has a huge impact on teachers' interpretations and that even at best, teachers' judgments were flawed half the time. It is this aspect of the mismeasurement of schools' vital signs that this book will examine in greatest depth.

Jenny Rankin's startling findings are also a reminder that the numbers do not speak for themselves. The low regard in the school world that is all too often given to the presentation of quantitative information invites misperception of the evidence. Rankin, who before becoming an author and scholar was an assessment administrator in Saddleback Valley USD, California, saw how much harm resulted from teacher misinterpretation. After her dissertation was complete and her degree awarded to her, she wrote a book that codified for educators the standards they should expect: *Standards for Reporting Data to Educators: What Educational Leaders Should Know and Demand*.[3] She was acutely aware of the human factor that goes into building evidence of student learning. We are going to do the same.

But the federal rulebook for sizing up school and district effectiveness during the No Child Left Behind (NCLB) era deserves attention, as well. The federal legislation called for states to decide how to realize the result the NCLB laws called for: identifying the schools that were lagging the most and doing something to improve them. The states took the federal regulations that defined Adequate Yearly Progress (AYP), applied them to their own tests (mostly given in the spring) and curricular standards and came up with an unavoidably complex set of rules for interpreting test results that were both hard to understand and riddled with logic errors. The very American notion that all children should be able to reach the promised land of proficiency if their schools provided effective instruction led to aspirational goals that by 2012 led the Obama administration to approve waivers from the consequences of failing to attain Adequate Yearly Progress for 26 states. Why? The landscape was covered with schools that had not brought enough of their students into the promised land of proficiency. It was no longer surprising for a district of six schools to have four that had failed to make AYP, and for two of those four to have fallen into the dreaded zone of Program Improvement, where they would have to let students attend other schools, reassign teachers and perhaps the principal, or in the most extreme cases, turn over management of the school to another organization or close it entirely.

How an extraordinary principal almost became a casualty in the accountability wars

By Jill Wynns

Burton High School in San Francisco is the pride of the Bayview district, a traditionally African American neighborhood. It was created as a small school as part of the legal settlement of our desegregation consent decree and led by a legendary principal, beloved by many parents and students. She was definitely a principal who ruled with an iron hand, a commanding style of leadership that was welcomed by the parents in this community. The results at Burton were often very good for those who responded well to this authoritarian style of school administration, but it was clearly not for everyone. The school had a very high turnover of teachers, as well as students.[4] Its teaching corps required an annual supply of new, inexperienced teachers whose futures depended on the principal's good evaluations.

When she retired after more than 20 years at Burton, student achievement began to decline. It was hard to find administrators who would take charge there, and hard, as well, to persuade teachers to stay. I was on the district's board in those years, and in our ongoing efforts to reform our district, we alternated between supportive and punitive forms of accountability. On the punishing end of the spectrum was what we called "reconstitution"— replacing the entire staff, which led to mostly poor results. This generated a lot of tension between schools and "downtown." We hired a new superintendent to change that culture.

Recruiting and training new site leaders was one of our most important and most difficult strategies. We recruited promising candidates from outside the district and retained the University of California at Berkeley to train our internal candidates. At Burton, we hired new principals a few times, both inside and outside hires. None of them were successful. Some were overwhelmed by the complexity of growing a small school, and others were daunted by leading a staff that was not stable or used to working together.

The most important thing was getting the chemistry right. Eventually, we did find the principal we wanted. Bill had come from the charter world to our district. By the time he had been there for two years, we had been able to see improvement and positive momentum at Burton.

In the meantime, the Obama administration's Race to the Top and other efforts were requiring obedience to their formula for school improvement.

Title I schools that were identified as Program Improvement schools if they had not shown adequate increases in test scores, including Burton, were subject to sanctions. There was a list of "interventions" and some of them were required. At Burton, there was already a longer school year, smaller classes, academies, and special professional development. But what was inescapable was the federal demand that we remove the principals of schools like Burton that were in the advanced stages of Program Improvement. For Burton, the school board and the administration, this was a terrible blow. We felt like we had finally gotten this key leadership component right. But if the school's new leader couldn't create the increase in test scores that the Program Improvement rules demanded (increases that were not possible), the federal regs required that he had to go.[5]

The members of the Board of Education that I was part of were often at odds with each other. But on this issue, we managed to work together with the superintendent to win a waiver to keep our principal-of-choice at Burton and resist that arbitrary federal regulation that had nearly undercut our hard work. We were unwilling to allow our progress to be stopped.

We worked together, gathering the evidence of the impact of the changes at the school. The California Department of Education was responsible for implementing the intervention program, so we had to persuade them to request a waiver of this requirement to remove a successful principal. We made a special presentation to the U.S. Department of Education, gathered years of evidence and appealed to everyone we knew, including the U.S. Secretary of Education, before the waiver was granted. This time, the story had a happy ending. In the years that followed, I kept on advocating for a case-by-case response to federal and state accountability enforcement to spare other principals the ordeal that Burton's principal endured.

The statistical calculations built into the byzantine rules for Adequate Yearly Progress and Program Improvement worked in one respect. They did catch schools where students weren't learning much at all. But those calculations also snagged schools that were doing fine, and some that were actually doing great, as well. This overidentification problem (high rate of false positives) was driven by many contributing factors beyond aspirational goals of legislators. One of those factors was the measurement of student achievement by the level of their scores, rather than by their rate of learning gains. If a student were to start school at kindergarten two grade levels

What is mismeasurement?

behind his peers and made one-and-a-half years of progress each year, he would catch up by fourth grade. But each year of that student's remarkable progress would not have counted until he reached the mark of proficient, according to the rules of AYP. Imagine a school full of kids who start school behind grade level. The calculation of AYP would have been blind to their progress until they crossed the magic line into the land of proficiency. The second big factor contributing to the flaws in the NCLB era accountability system, advanced persuasively by Jim Popham, is that the big, standardized state tests were never designed to measure instructional effectiveness.

The steps to building evidence and interpreting its meaning

To err is human. So, let's look at the human factor in the building of judgments about schools' vital signs (see Figure 1.1). Indeed, building is what we are doing. This view is common to many fields. Consider Sherlock Holmes's sense of the raw material needed to build evidence: "Data! data! data!" he cried impatiently. "I can't make bricks without clay."[6]

I see five steps in this process: (1) observation, (2) recording that observation as data, (3) gathering data together to build a body of evidence, (4) viewing those data from a vantage point, and (5) inferring an opinion or judgment from the evidence. At every step, human effort is involved, and it is fallible.

Observing

Education data are created by humans, observing the interaction of other humans in school. We consider some things worthy of observation, and we disregard others. Choices are unavoidable. Everything is not equally noteworthy.

Recording data

Observations become data when they are recorded. In the old days, they were notes in what was often called a "cume file." These days, they are

What is mismeasurement?

Figure 1.1 Illustration of the many interested parties taking stock of a school's vital signs

Everyone is observing and measuring some part of the school. But they are doing so separately. School is an ensemble of human relations. How are they going to relate one dimension of measurement with another? How do the vital signs of the whole school come together in this fragmented evaluation?

Art: Robert Neubecker

keystrokes entered into a student information system or an electronic gradebook. Both words and numbers are data. Occasionally, data are mistaken for facts, something true beyond doubt, beyond bias, beyond question. This gives facts undeserved power. Are the facts recorded as binary, simply present or absent? Or are the facts recorded on a scale?

Building evidence

Then humans organize those data. They structure them, sort them, filter them, transform them, append other information to them and assign attributes to them. This gives them a particular shape, and it will serve a specific purpose. It may be to meet a reporting responsibility, or answer a question posted by the executive cabinet or the board or argue in favor of funding or defunding a program. Evidence is built from bricks made of data, joined by mortar, which is logic, usually designed to persuade others. Like all things that are built by humans, evidence can be built well or built poorly. It can both reveal and conceal patterns that matter.

Viewing data from a vantage point

We have reasons to view the evidence from our own vantage point. A community advocate has a place to stand and an angle from which to view the evidence that is distinctly different from that of the school board trustee. A reporter has yet another place to stand, with a distinct vantage point of her own. The teachers union has yet another vantage point on the matter. Well-built evidence may serve some, but it will rarely serve all. But for those who build evidence, they would do well to anticipate the differing interests of all those who pay it attention, and the different vantage points from which it will be viewed.

Drawing inferences

It's quite common for scientists to disagree about the meaning of evidence. Doctors who examine the same patient and analyze the same test results will disagree on the diagnosis. In the social sciences, disagreements about the meaning of evidence abound. In these fields, the disagreements are rich material. They are signs of minds at work. But in the world of K–12, why do we hear so little debate about the meaning of evidence? At the cabinet meetings of district leadership, why is there often such quick agreement about what the data mean when the evidence itself is so ambiguous? This step is perhaps the most human of all. It requires reflection, conversation and imaginative leaps. As a result, it is the step most prone to errors in human judgment. For this reason, it deserves the greatest degree of scrutiny.

The point of this is to establish that human judgment is involved at every step, from recording data, to validating data as correct, to building evidence, and to reaching inferences. When we think about the mismeasurement of schools' vital signs, we should remember that we are in the realm of uncertain things, imprecise measurements and fallible human judgment.

How errors are introduced

Being alert to the opportunities for error is the first step in helping you become a wiser interpreter of schools' vital signs. To help you avoid the hazards of mismeasurement, let me share with you four factors that contribute to the grander problem. These are semantic sloppiness, innumeracy, low level of assessment literacy and poor design of visual representations of data.

Semantics

At times we are a bit loose with our words. In the interest of brevity, we may choose a common term that's easier to remember than a longer, more exact term. Consider this example: using "poverty" to describe students who qualify for meal subsidies. In fact, a student is entitled to reduced-price meals if his family earns less than 1.85 times the federal poverty standard. A family of four, sharing a household income of $48,470, meets that test because in 2020, the federal poverty threshold was $26,200 in the 48 states (excluding Alaska and Hawaii where that threshold is $32,750 and $30,130 respectively). Or we choose terms that have become archaic. My friend in the construction trades tells me that carpenters still call framing lumber a 2" x 4" even though it measures 1–1/2" x 3–1/2". Or we get lazy and forget that English language arts tests aren't the same as tests of reading skills alone. So, when asked how third-grade students score in reading, we quickly and incorrectly offer up their Smarter Balanced Assessment Consortium (SBAC) or Partnership for Assessment of Readiness for College and Careers (PARCC) English language arts scores.

What is mismeasurement?

The measurement terms themselves have been misused so often that one must wonder why. Perhaps it's due, in part, to two problems coinciding. First, we Americans suffer collectively from low levels of quantitative literacy. Second, few of us have ever been taught the rules for how to write about numbers. Thankfully, those rules have been clarified by author and research professor Jane E. Miller. Her work was published by the University of Chicago Press in 2004 and is titled *The Chicago Guide to Writing about Numbers*. It is now in its second edition. This venerable academic publishing house first published this work as a companion to its respected *Chicago Manual of Style*, now in its seventeenth edition. The language of numbers is not a language we're really taught. No surprise, the author explains she was moved to write this book because

> I have seen poor communication of numeric information at all levels of training and experience, from papers by undergraduates who were shocked at the very concept of putting numbers in sentences, to presentations by business consultants, policy analysts and scientists, to publications by experienced researchers in elite, peer-reviewed journals.

In brief, she encountered this lack of command of the language of numbers so frequently that she believed that a guide was sorely needed.

Quantitative illiteracy (innumeracy)

Far too many suffer from the curse of low levels of quantitative literacy. Personal experience may provide anecdotal evidence. Ever heard a friend confess, almost with pride, that he's never been good at math? Or can you recall someone saying, after making a public *faux pas* with numbers, "Oh, I'm more of a people person than a numbers person." (When did those become mutually exclusive attributes?) If you still doubt this assertion, I suggest you read the first few chapters of John Allen Paulos's book, *Innumeracy: Mathematical Illiteracy and Its Consequences*. It's a short book in which he makes a convincing case for the wide reach of this affliction.

How widespread is innumeracy? About 54 million adult Americans were unable to do arithmetic with whole numbers and percentages, derive reasonable estimates, or interpret simple statistics in text or tables, according to the Program for the International Assessment of Adult Competencies.

That's about 26 percent of Americans, those between the ages of 16 and 65. About 16 million were unable to complete one-step tasks involving counting, sorting or identifying elements of simple graphs. Americans also rank low in quantitative literacy when compared to other countries in the Organisation for Economic Co-operation and Development (OECD). A study published in 2016, based on the 2012 and 2014 results of an international study called the Program for the International Assessment of Adult Competencies, showed American adults between the ages of 16 and 65 scoring in the lower half. Of 23 countries in the study, 16 of them scored higher than the U.S. Most dramatic was the share of Americans who scored at the bottom range in quantitative skills: 28 percent versus the international average of 19 percent. Also worth noting was that the score of Americans in literacy skills was considerably higher than their numeracy scores. Just seven countries scored significantly higher than the U.S. in literacy.[7]

This is not a problem suffered solely by those who haven't gone to college. Educators, scientists and economists are not immune to this affliction. In the field of medicine, mistaken interpretations of the relative risks and benefits of a treatment have plagued many doctors. Misinterpretations of clinical trials have resulted from a belief in the magic power of "statistical significance" and a discounting of the size of the effect of a treatment. Authors Stephen T. Ziliak and Deirdre N. McCloskey, in their book *The Cult of Statistical Significance: How the Standard Error Costs Us Jobs, Justice, and Lives*, present the case of Vioxx, a popular painkiller from Merck, as an example of this innumeracy weak spot. The clinical trials led to five reported deaths among users of Vioxx, and only one death among those in the control group, which was using Naproxen. Because the difference in these fatality rates were under the 5 percent threshold established by tradition as the line separating "statistical significance" from "statistical insignificance"—the possibility that the result was due to chance—the drug was allowed by regulators to go into production. They made this decision despite the evidence of a 5-to-1 ratio of deaths between those taking Vioxx and those in the control group.[8] Merck conducted this clinical trial in the year 2000, and by 2003, Vioxx earned $2.5 billion in sales. Merck took the drug off the market in September 2004, after a deluge of reported heart attacks and deaths. By August 2005, the company faced 4,200 lawsuits. The medical journal *Lancet* years later published research that estimated that 88,000 people suffered heart attacks as a result of taking Vioxx and that 38,000 of them had died. The trials turned up evidence that Merck had also hidden data about three additional heart attacks during the clinical trial. But the point is that the 5-to-1 ratio of bad effects in the Vioxx panel compared to the control panel was sufficient in and of itself to halt the trials.

The efforts of Ziliak and McCloskey to end the misuse of statistical significance eventually proved persuasive. In March 2019, the American Statistical Association, in a remarkable moment, took a stand renouncing the use of p-values, the test of statistical significance. The entire issue of their journal, *The American Statistician*, was dedicated to the end of the use of p-values, and 43 statisticians contributed their own essays in rallying around the flag. The journal's editors drove a spike in its heart by saying they no longer wanted to see tests of statistical significance in the papers submitted. And they did so in terms that were decidedly not academic. Their guidance to fellow statisticians, referring to the use of p-values was blunt:

> Don't. Don't. Just . . . don't. . . . Don't say "statistically significant." The ASA Statement on P-Values and Statistical Significance stopped just short of recommending that declarations of "statistical significance" be abandoned. We take that step here. We conclude, based on our review of the articles in this special issue and the broader literature, that it is time to stop using the term "statistically significant" entirely.[9]

If statisticians could misuse mathematical methods of such fundamental importance, how fallible might the rest of us be in every field? Surely, this was a humbling moment for those who are statisticians, and those who practice statistics in other fields.

Assessment illiteracy

James Popham, considered by many to be the Jedi master of assessment, has written about the prevalence among educators and administrators of a low level of assessment literacy. He has written about this frequently, but perhaps most passionately in his short book, *Unlearned Lessons: Six Stumbling Blocks to Our Schools' Success*.[10] In Chapter 6, titled "Abysmal Assessment Literacy," he excoriates his fellow educators for their assessment knowledge deficits:

far too many current classroom teachers and at least some school administrators truly do not know they need to possess a modicum of assessment knowledge, nor do they know what it is that they need to know about educational assessment.

He continues to explain that it's not their fault, exactly. Rather, he points to the failure of their pre-service education and to the deficiencies of their in-service professional development.

Popham goes on to explain his sense of the breadth and depth of educator resistance to testing itself:

> because tests are the chief tools teachers must use to determine whether their instruction actually works, we would expect that the nation's educators would be genuinely conversant with educational testing. But are they? . . . Put simply, most of today's educators know almost nothing about educational assessment. . . . For many educators, "test" is a four-letter word, both literally and figuratively—an opaque and off-putting term.[11]

Coming from Popham, who taught educational measurement for nearly 30 years at the University of California, Los Angeles Graduate School of Education and Information Studies, and whose speaking appearances at conferences gave him frequent contact with administrators and teachers, he ought to know. Popham explains why outrage should be a more common response to discovery of this profession-wide deficit.

> How would you feel if, upon becoming seriously ill, you were being treated by a doctor who didn't understand such medical fundamentals as the normal range of blood pressure, cholesterol, or blood sugar? If you weren't outraged by your physician's lack of familiarity with such basics, you should be.

James Popham reached this conclusion about "abysmal" levels of assessment literacy after dedicating most of his five decades of work in the field to raising that level among educators. He has written more than 25 books on the subject. In 2002, the National Council on Measurement in Education recognized him with its Award for Career Contributions to Educational Measurement. He's a former president of the American Educational Research Association. This certainly adds weight to his harsh evaluation of this weak link in the chain of knowledge needed by those in the education management profession.

What is mismeasurement?

Design of visual representations of data

The problems of innumeracy and semantic sloppiness are compounded by defective design skills. When Excel put charting capability in the hands of everyone who was ready to enter the row-and-column world of numbers, it became an amateurs' field day. So much power in the hands of so many people so ill-prepared to use it correctly led to a deluge of deformed data representations. Three-dimensional bar charts that distorted the true size of things. Pie charts that couldn't be read. Color palettes that caused color-blind people to misread the results. Tables with indecipherable column heads. Reports issued with no user guides. Inadequate footnotes failing to note key assumptions. Axes on graphs poorly labeled. Scales of axes distorted to exaggerate or diminish the value displayed. The list is long.[12]

The ease with which any person with a computer can create a visual representation of data is impressive. In the hands of a skilled person, this power advances our understanding of the meaning inherent in the numbers. But in the hands of amateurs, it makes possible the rapid reproduction of gibberish.[13] Information design is a discipline. It is taught to people who communicate for a living. Its principles are universal and practiced by professionals all over the world in similar ways. But those design principles should also be mastered by people given responsibility for communicating a school's or district's vital signs. You wouldn't let a person present a slide deck at a public board meeting without being sure they could write well, and chunk their ideas into pieces, representing them on slides. If they're presenting data, you'd want to be sure they understand how to design the visual representation of evidence so its meaning is clearly communicated to an audience.

In the K–12 world, the ignorance of psychometric fundamentals, mixed with low levels of numeracy, combined with lack of skill in the design disciplines was a recipe for dangerous dishes. Many who consumed these meals got sick and didn't know it. This led to many half-baked misrepresentations, eaten all too quickly by too many K–12 leaders who were even more confident that they were well nourished by "data."

Many shared the blame for spreading this mess far and wide. State education agency leaders had the authority to do the greatest harm. Too many of them told testing firms to design reports that simplified results to red, yellow and green. Lacking confidence in educators' abilities to understand imprecision, almost every state told testing firms to design their reports without indicators of imprecision, the unavoidable fuzzy factor that is part of every test. Those little stem-and-whisker plots were considered too challenging for educators to understand. So, they disappeared, and in their place was a prevalence of stop-and-go color palettes—a sea of red, yellow and green.

One state agency whose logic errors and design flaws have been particularly consequential is the California Department of Education. Their accountability dashboard has taken measures of many vital signs and transformed them into colors. The loss of scalar measures is worsened by their disregard of imprecision when interpreting test results. To this they add a basic logic error when interpreting gaps. Their rule for gap measures calls for comparing any student subgroup to the "all students" group, a puzzling departure from the common convention of comparing subgroups to each other (e.g., boys to girls). The logic error is that you cannot compare a part of something to the whole it is part of. The collateral damage that has resulted from these mistakes and many more is both large in scale and in the degree of harm. One consequence is reputational damage to a school or district. Other consequences include school and district planning teams wasting time and money pursuing remedies to things that aren't really a problem and failing to improve real problems that are not noted by the dashboard.[14]

Yes, lack of skill in design was a contributing factor to the mismeasurement of schools' vital signs. But it was the confluence of factors that led to the erosion of meaning of the evidence itself. Errors of judgment in education have this in common with human errors in other fields: engineering, medicine, aviation, finance. It is rarely one factor that causes a failure. It is a combination of factors that usually share one other human foible: an excess of self-confidence.

Methods to minimize risk of misjudging evidence

All too frequently, sound evidence is interpreted poorly. The cause is as likely to be flawed logic as it is the use of the wrong technical method. Throughout this book, you'll find many examples of mistakes of both types. So, at the start, let's put in your hands two methods we've found to be valuable for their practicality and their understandability: comparative effectiveness and practical benefit. Both provide approaches to thinking about evidence you will find useful.

Comparative effectiveness

This is a method of inquiry that grew up in the field of medicine. The National Academy of Medicine defines comparative effectiveness research as

> the generation and synthesis of evidence that compares the benefits and harms of alternative methods to prevent, diagnose, treat, and monitor a clinical condition or to improve the delivery of care. The purpose of CER is to assist consumers, clinicians, purchasers, and policy makers to make informed decisions that will improve health care at both the individual and population levels.[15]

In essence, this method aims to determine the degree to which an intervention works best for which patients, in comparison to other alternative treatments, while also considering relative risks and benefits, costs and circumstances surrounding that treatment. Comparative effectiveness research includes random controlled trials but also includes many other research designs that are less formal and less exact.

Indeed, this method was one of the foundational ideas of the Dartmouth Atlas of Health Care, which studied the regional variations and disparities in medical treatments, patient outcomes and costs. As the evidence base for outcomes improved, including the creation of risk-adjusted measures of outcomes, other organizations applied comparative effectiveness methods to determine which hospitals had the best and worst outcomes for identical procedures. States created agencies to monitor comparative effectiveness of doctors, clinics and hospitals. A nonprofit journalism venture, ProPublica, created an analysis of comparative effectiveness of hospitals and surgeons in performing eight high-stakes elective surgeries, including knee replacement, hip replacement, cervical (neck) spinal fusion and gall bladder removal using laparoscopic methods. This project was just one part of their "Vital Signs: Know More About Your Doctor" effort.

The benefits of this method of inquiry in medicine have been dramatic. Forensic analysts working for insurance companies have used it to detect Medicare fraud. Patients have used it to avoid surgeons and hospitals where the complication rates look to be too high. One reporter, working with ProPublica, told the story of how one patient, a man who went to the emergency room because of heart trouble, decided to turn down a doctor's recommendation for a coronary angiogram and a stent, based on a third doctor's opinion based on analysis of outcomes. In this article, "When Evidence Says No, But Doctor Says Yes," the reporter explains the patient avoided a treatment that had no evidence of benefit, but which carried a risk of heart attack for one of every 50 patients.[16]

Because the delivery of health care and schooling share many attributes, I expected that with so many researchers working in the field of education (the American Education Research Association includes about 25,000 members) and so many kids in school (about 56 million in the U.S. in 2020, about five million in Canada, about 7.25 million in the United Kingdom as of 2016), there would be an education equivalent of the Dartmouth Atlas of Health Care project that looked at variations in education programs, results and costs. I searched and discovered my expectations were ill-founded. No equivalent yet exists.

However, the work of John Hattie follows in this tradition. His book, *Visible Learning*, compares the effect size of 138 "treatments" designed to improve student outcomes. Using over 800 studies that he turned into a large evidence base of comparative effectiveness, he rank-ordered those "treatments" (really, just things educators have turned to in the effort to improve student outcomes). Half fell below an effect size of 0.40, which he called the "hinge point." In the book, he comments on each of these factors and arrays their relative effect on what he calls a barometer of influence. His point is to direct practitioners toward those choices that are above the hinge point, which show above-average effect.

Hattie affirms the power of comparative effectiveness in opposition to the "what works" approach. In his own words:

> Almost everything works. Ninety percent of all effect sizes in education are positive. . . . When teachers claim they are having a positive effect on achievement or when a policy improves achievement this is almost a trivial claim: virtually everything works. One only needs a pulse, and we can improve achievement.[17]

I believe Hattie is also advancing his ideas in opposition to the popular "best practices" approach. In other fields, with clear standards for

What is mismeasurement?

exemplary methods and where outcomes are observable, best practices are more defensible. But in education, the phrase is usually a way to dress up a favored way of teaching, or a method of organizing learning, and bestowing on it a magical quality. The next time a colleague tells you something is a "best practice," ask how he or she knows this to be true. Perhaps it's a good idea. But what makes it best? Is it always best? For everyone? At what cost? Even if you identify the practices common to the most successful teachers of writing in middle school, simply copying those practices doesn't add up to the "best practice." If life were that simple, teaching and managing learning would be a cookbook of the best ingredients and the best way to combine them for the best results. This is silly. But it is a reductionist phrase that often hides both a lack of knowledge and sloppy thinking.

Hattie acknowledges, somewhat unhappily, at the start that his meta-analysis is limited to one measure of effect, students' test scores. He names the many other consequences of the time students spend in school and makes clear he values them highly. But lacking measures of effect for any other factors, he makes the best possible use of the data he has in hand. Only in passing does Hattie mention that his approach puts aside the relative cost of the "treatments" he reviews. The cost-benefit view is not his bailiwick, but it is, of course, a member of the family of comparative effectiveness methods. If you are a district leader or a school board member, you'll be making budget decisions that always carry with them the question, "Is this the best use of the funds for the purpose we have in mind?" Or more to the point, "Is the benefit we're expecting to create with these funds for those students being purchased by us at the lowest cost?" (For more about the economics of comparative effectiveness, see Chapter 6 on the work of Henry Levin, Fiona Hollands and their Center for Benefit-Cost Studies of Education.)

Practical benefit

An accomplished scholar and creator of a program for helping lagging learners do better, Stanley Pogrow is an advocate of a down-to-earth use of a particular variety of comparative effectiveness. He calls his method practical benefit. He juxtaposes his notion in opposition to a statistical concept—statistical significance—that is much used and abused, although now officially dead, buried by the American Statistical Association in March 2019.[18] For Pogrow, it is not just a method of inquiry but also a criterion for judging the quality of evidence. Practical benefit is also a concept he raises as an alternative to effect size alone. In a readable article he wrote for the journal *The American Statistician*, Pogrow makes the case against effect size, a position that has raised a fair number of objections, in turn.[19]

Here's how he defines it. "Practical benefit is defined as the likelihood that action taken on the basis of a given research finding will produce clearly noticeable and highly desirable benefits for your school(s)."[20] He is guiding practitioners to wade through mountains of research, selecting only those that meet his criteria for evidence. The method he champions pays high regard to the practical limits of site and district leaders: limited time, limited range of choices, limited funding.

He makes the case for the power of simple, descriptive statistics about the "treatment" under consideration: the unweighted, unadjusted mean or median; standard deviation; and effect size. He boldly encourages readers to disregard all other statistics and evaluate whether the size of the intended improvement and its local impact (likelihood of being effective on your students in your environment) indicate it's worth switching from your current choice to this alternative. He calls this the three-number system. While you may find his guidance about disregarding other statistics to be too bold, his intent is to guide people to a decision that is smart and actionable, without being distracted along the way.

The resistance to evidence and empirical methods

What goes into forming human judgment, the final step in the process of making sense of any observation? These elements include, first, the *quality of thinking* by those responsible for reaching an interpretation. This includes their logical reasoning skills and their arithmetic skills. Second, the interpretation team also shares a theory that determines the *point of view* from which they observe the facts. A third element is the *reason for the measurement* itself. In other words, what evidence is the measurement expected to provide, and to what degree is that evidence well suited to answer that question?

As we apply these criteria throughout this book, I hope you'll begin to wonder why the decades-long pleas to teachers and education leaders to practice data-driven decision-making have been so useless. Those pleas to "just use data" rested on a notion that the data would speak for themselves. Perhaps some believed the data held magical properties that would point everyone in the right direction. Did the proponents of data-driven decision-making think that tests were so revealing and the scores so unambiguous that the actions educators should take could be reduced to a red-yellow-green traffic light? Or were they not attentive to the varied quality of human judgment that had to make sense of test results? *How one uses data* is the determining factor.

Before you read further, I want to offer an additional precaution. Bluntly stated, education is a profession where empirical methods have not yet taken root. Regrettably, there is little debate about evidence-based practices within the school world as there is in the fields of medicine, clinical psychology[21] and professional baseball. Those debates are signs of a healthy profession. But in education, there are few signs of a debate. There are simply those who rally around the flag they call data-driven decision-making, and those who disagree with them. These two camps, in the education research world, mainly shout at each other. The parallel in the teacher-practitioner world is the now lopsided shouting match between those who defend testing and those who oppose it.

Perhaps this is a sign that the education profession itself has not really matured at the same pace as other fields. That's the question that John Hattie poses at the end of his seminal book, *Visible Learning*. This quote is preceded by a reference to the debates within medicine about evidence-based practices.

> The evidence-based revolution [in medicine] came through repugnance and pressure from groups that were adversely affected by the poor quality of service in the medical profession. Maybe legal cases about equity in outcomes across various ethnic groups, poor service by teachers, clinical trials of new educational treatments, and a set of international standards and expectations for outcomes from schooling may be the catalyst for change and improvement in education. More of the same is certainly not the answer. The key question is whether teaching can shift from an immature to a mature profession, from

opinions to evidence, from subjective judgments and personal contact to critique of judgments.[22]

Links to extend your reading and interaction

The following link will carry you to additional resources, writing and dialogue about the topics discussed in this chapter. We welcome your comments and continued exploration. You'll find it on the following page on the book's website: https://www.k12measures.com/ch1

Questions to spark discussion

District leaders

1. Think back to your administrative credential courses and write down the quantitative analysis skills you learned. Then list the analytic reasoning skills you learned. Did you learn to distinguish high-quality from low-quality evidence? Did you learn how to identify the "noise" from the "signal" in data? Did you learn that assessments always contain imprecision and uncertainty and that both are measurable? With this in mind, redesign your administrative credential requirements. What do you wish, in retrospect, that you'd been taught? What would you put on the list of less relevant bodies of knowledge you'd rather not have invested time learning?

2. Can you recall ever debating the interpretation of test results for the district you're leading now, or in a district you've worked in the past? On a scale that ranges from dogmatic to open, where do you believe your district leadership team sits when it comes to debating alternate interpretations of assessment evidence? If you've been lucky enough to enjoy a lively debate of differing interpretations, did the discussion encourage others to venture their opinions?

Principals and other site leaders

3. Think of all the decisions your teachers are making, especially about student mastery of subject matter and skills. Do you believe they have evidence of reasonable quality to determine who has and hasn't learned a particularly important standard? For an elementary school teacher in charge of a first-grade class, what is the quality of evidence she uses to group students by reading skill?

4. What evidence do you have to evaluate your teachers? What portion of that evidence is from your observation of classroom teaching? What portion comes from evidence of learning? What is the quality of both types of information? If you use assessments of students as evidence of instructional quality, how exactly are you interpreting that? Does your interpretation factor in the degree of imprecision of those assessments and their degree of uncertainty?

School board trustees

5. Given the prevalence of sloppy practices interpreting education evidence of all kinds, what policies might you put in place that would restrict worst practices? Consider the professional requirements for principals. Consider the professional development course work that might make up for educational deficits in the past.

6. How much investment in professional development of your site leadership would be justified, relative to the risk of harm resulting from errors of professional judgment that would result from innumeracy at that level (cost/risk ratio)? Consider the cost/benefit of improved use of student and teacher time, of learning gains attained by more students at a faster pace.

Notes

1. Jenny Rankin, "Over-the-Counter Data's Impact on Educators' Data Analysis Accuracy" (Ph.D. diss., Northcentral University, 2013). https://www.proquest.com/dissertations-theses/over-counter-datas-impact-on-educators-data/docview/1459258514/se-2.

2. A helpful summary of Jenny Rankin's study and the central experiment that revealed high rates of teachers' misjudgment of the meaning of test results can be found in the December 2013 issue of a newsletter, *California Council on Teacher Education*. In an article titled "Remedying Educators' Data Analysis Errors with Over-the-Counter Data," she explains her central thesis and her hopeful conclusion. http://ccte.org/wp-content/pdfs-newsletters/ccte-news-2013-winter.pdf.

3. Jenny Rankin, *Standards for Reporting Data to Educators: What Educational Leaders Should Know and Demand* (New York: Routledge, 2016).

4. The greater the rate of student turnover, the lower the suitability of the federal accountability rules. The marking of progress (what the federal rules attempted to measure) presumed a stable student body that would reflect the yearly investment of instruction, compounded over time.

5. The federal accountability rules for high schools were exceedingly complex during the No Child Left Behind era. The way that California implemented them was daunting. Here is a summary. To avoid the vortex of doom called Program Improvement, a high school had to attain Adequate Yearly Progress (AYP). Doing that in California required threading the needle—meeting all five of the following criteria: (1) 90 percent of students who took the California High School Exit Exam had to score at or above proficient in English/language arts, and 89 percent had to do the same in math; (2) 95 percent of eligible students (oddly, it was tenth graders who took this exit exam) had to take these tests; (3) every sizable subgroup of students (including special education and English learner students) also had to meet or beat that same proficiency mark; (4) the school had to attain a certain score (770) on California's own accountability system called the Academic Performance Index; and (5) the school had to attain a 90 percent graduation rate or satisfy alternate improvement criteria. If a school failed to make Adequate Yearly Progress, it fell into the gears of the Program Improvement (PI) machinery. Exiting PI was rare. Each year that a school remained in PI, the consequences became more severe. Years one and two of PI required that the district offer students

transfers to other schools and tutoring. Years three and four required that the district reassign least effective staff and perhaps the principal. Year five required the most severe corrective actions, which could include replacing all or most of the school's teachers, turning the school over to another organization to manage, or closing the school altogether. By the time No Child Left Behind (NCLB) was 10 years old, so many schools had fallen into Program Improvement that it was neither surprising nor embarrassing to learn your school had joined the crowd. By 2013, the Obama administration had granted waivers from NCLB enforcement to 26 states. By the end of 2015, Congress passed, and President Obama signed into law, a successor to NCLB, the Every Student Succeeds Act, which gave states more flexibility to define their own approaches to improving schools where student achievement continued to lag.

6. Sir Arthur Conan Doyle, "The Adventure of the Copper Beeches," in *The Adventures of Sherlock Holmes* (London: George Newnes Ltd., 1892).

7. B. D. Rampey, R. Finnegan, M. Goodman, L. Mohadjer, T. Krenzke, J. Hogan, and S. Provasnik, *Skills of U.S. Unemployed, Young, and Older Adults in Sharper Focus: Results From the Program for the International Assessment of Adult Competencies (PIAAC) 2012/2014: First Look* (Washington, DC: National Center for Education Statistics, U.S. Dept. of Education, 2016). https://nces.ed.gov/pubs2016/2016039rev.pdf.

8. Stephen T. Ziliak and Deirdre N. McCloskey, *The Cult of Statistical Significance: How the Standard Error Costs Us Jobs, Justice, and Lives* (Ann Arbor: University of Michigan Press, 2008), 28–31.

9. Ronald L. Wasserstein, Allen L. Schirm, and Nicole A. Lazar, "Moving to a World Beyond $p<0.05$," *The American Statistician* 73, no. supp. 1 (March 2019), 1–19, https://doi.org/10.1080/00031305.2019.1583913.

10. James Popham, *Unlearned Lessons: Six Stumbling Blocks to Our Schools' Success* (Cambridge: Harvard Education Press, 2009), 125–6.

11. Ibid.

12. Ben Jones, *Avoiding Data Pitfalls: How to Steer Clear of Common Blunders When Working with Data and Presenting Analysis and Visualizations* (Hoboken, NJ: John Wiley & Sons, 2020).

13. The work of Edward R. Tufte has been articulate and thorough, both in defining the design principles that are the foundation of the field of data visualization, and in critiquing abuses of those principles. His first four books, all published by Graphics Press in Cheshire, Connecticut, are *Envisioning Information* (1990), *Visual Explanations* (1997), *The Visual*

Display of Quantitative Information (2001) and *Beautiful Evidence* (2006). His website holds a rich collection of visual treats and intelligent writing about the craft of building visual evidence. www.edwardtufte.com/tufte/.

14. Steve Rees has written a summary of the range of flaws with the California dashboard, which was published in June 2020 on the website of ED100, a nonprofit organization dedicated to making sense of California schools. https://ed100.org/blog/california-school-dashboard-has-broken-gauges. He has also written many blog posts offering more specific critiques of the California accountability dashboard. These were published on the website of his company, School Wise Press, between July 2018 and June 2020. https://schoolwisepress.com/category/dashboard/.

15. *Initial National Priorities for Comparative Effectiveness Research* (Washington, DC: National Academies Press, 2009). https://doi.org/10.17226/12648.

16. David Epstein and ProPublica, "When Evidence Says No, But Doctor Says Yes," *Atlantic*, February 22, 2017, www.theatlantic.com/health/archive/2017/02/when-evidence-says-no-but-doctors-say-yes/517368/.

17. John Hattie, *Visible Learning: A Synthesis of Over 800 Meta-Analyses Relating to Achievement* (New York: Routledge, 2009), 15–16.

18. Wasserstein, Schirm, and Lazar, "Moving to a World Beyond p<0.05," 1–19.

19. Stanley Pogrow, "How Effect Size (Practical Significance) Misleads Clinical Practice: The Case for Switching to Practical Benefit to Assess Applied Research Findings," *The American Statistician* 73, no. supp. 1 (March 2019): 223–34, https://doi.org/10.1080/00031305.2018.1549101.

20. Stanley Pogrow, *Authentic Quantitative Analysis for Education Leadership Decision-Making and EdD Dissertations: A Practical, Intuitive and Intelligible Approach*. 2nd edition. (Tecumseh, MI: International Council of Professors of Educational Leadership, 2017), xvi.

21. Paul E. Meehl in 1954 published what he later called "my little book" asserting that statistical analysts could diagnose schizophrenia in patients with greater accuracy than the psychiatrists who were treating them. He published this claim in a book titled *Clinical Versus Statistical Prediction: A Theoretical Analysis and a Review of the Evidence*. This started a roaring fire of heated debate within the profession of psychology, a debate that has evolved but has never been settled.

22. John Hattie, *Visible Learning: A Synthesis of Over 800 Meta-Analyses Relating to Achievement* (New York: Routledge, 2008), 258–9.

References

Hattie, John. *Visible Learning: A Synthesis of Over 800 Meta-Analyses Relating to Achievement.* New York: Routledge, 2008.

Jones, Ben. *Avoiding Data Pitfalls: How to Steer Clear of Common Blunders When Working with Data and Presenting Analysis and Visualizations.* Hoboken, NJ: John Wiley & Sons, 2020.

Meehl, Paul E. *Clinical Versus Statistical Prediction: A Theoretical Analysis and a Review of the Evidence.* Minneapolis: University of Minnesota Press, 1954. https://doi.org/10.1037/11281-000.

Paulos, John Allen. *Innumeracy: Mathematical Illiteracy and Its Consequences.* New York: Hill and Wang, 1989.

Popham, James W. *Unlearned Lessons: Six Stumbling Blocks to Our Schools' Success.* Cambridge: Harvard Education Press, 2009.

Rampey, B. D., R. Finnegan, M. Goodman, L. Mohadjer, T. Krenzke, J. Hogan, and S. Provasnik. *Skills of U.S. Unemployed, Young, and Older Adults in Sharper Focus: Results from the Program for the International Assessment of Adult Competencies (PIAAC) 2012/2014: First Look.* Washington, DC: National Center for Education Statistics, U.S. Dept. of Education, 2016. https://nces.ed.gov/pubs2016/2016039rev.pdf.

Rankin, Jenny. "Over-the-Counter Data's Impact on Educators' Data Analysis Accuracy." PhD diss., Northcentral University, 2013. https://www.proquest.com/dissertations-theses/over-counter-datas-impact-on-educators-data/docview/1459258514/se-2.

Rankin, Jenny. *Standards for Reporting Data to Educators: What Educational Leaders Should Know and Demand.* New York: Routledge, 2016.

Tufte, Edward R. *Envisioning Information.* Cheshire, CT: Graphics Press, 1990.

Tufte, Edward R. *The Visual Display of Quantitative Information.* Cheshire, CT: Graphics Press, 2001.

Wasserstein, Ronald L., Allen L. Schirm, and Nicole A. Lazar. "Moving to a World Beyond $p<0.05$." *The American Statistician* 73, no. supp. 1 (March 2019): 1–19. https://doi.org/10.1080/00031305.2019.1583913.

Ziliak, Stephen T., and Deirdre N. McCloskey. *The Cult of Statistical Significance: How the Standard Error Costs Us Jobs, Justice, and Lives.* Ann Arbor: University of Michigan Press, 2008.

Twisting test results and missing sound evidence of learning

Education may be the only field where opponents of testing have a stronger voice than those who defend it. Is there a debate within the pharmaceutical industry where people either favor or oppose clinical trials? Do members of the medical profession favor or oppose CAT scans or MRIs? Of course not. In those fields, arguing against evidence itself would be equivalent to championing ignorance. The discussion in these fields is not *whether* to test, but *how* to test, *whom* to test, *when* to test, *which* test to use and at *what cost*. Those in the education profession are stuck in a cruder pro-con argument about testing.

The anti-testing forces seem to have the strongest voice at this moment, and it's not just due to the pandemic-related interruption of state-level assessments. There are just too many districts where "test" is still a four-letter word. The teacher unions have taken a stand in opposition to testing, saying it intrudes on instruction. The National Center for Fair and Open Testing known as FairTest urges people to "just say no to standardized tests" and provides guidance on opting out.[1] Surprisingly, the testing companies are not speaking up to defend testing except when reporters call them for comment in the face of criticism. Those who have spoken up in favor of better-quality tests used more wisely are scholars like James Popham and Howard Wainer, professional organizations, policy centers, education reform groups and equity advocacy organizations like the Education Trust. In the public square, these defenders' voices are at this time not as forceful as critics' attacks.

Be aware that we're in a high-stakes and highly politicized conflict. The higher the stakes, the more deformed test results are likely to become. I'm also concerned about the degree to which people's self-interests are wrapped up in the interpretation of students' test results. Real estate agents need to reassure prospective home buyers that the schools in town are doing just fine. Local employers need to reassure prospective recruits with families that their local schools will do a fine job educating their children. Of course, principals and superintendents want to bring good news to their school board members, and the easiest way to do that is with test scores that are trending up-up-up. With so much at stake for so many, it's no wonder that deriving sound evidence from test results is a challenge.

But that challenge isn't just a result of the political use of test results as ammunition, or the inherent complexity of the evidence. Popham, in an article in *Educational Leadership* magazine,[2] asserted that it would take administrators only a dozen hours or so reading one of his books in a study group to gain a reasonable level of assessment literacy. With such a modest effort required to compensate for this knowledge deficit, Popham caused me to wonder whether the cause might be self-interest, the fear that evidence captured in test results might reveal mistaken board policies, mistakes by adults when classifying students or errors in selecting curricula. If so, what is the remedy?

Test scores have unfortunately become the proxy for school and district effectiveness. In states that have a more elevated approach to interpreting test results, they at least use growth measures rather than achievement levels as the proxy, a modest improvement. Popham makes a persuasive case against the use of tests for this purpose in this article from the journal *Phi Delta Kappan*.

> But tests capable of providing score comparisons aren't necessarily tests that should be used to evaluate schools or teachers. Such evaluative applications of educational assessment, although similar in some ways to comparative applications of educational assessment, are fundamentally different. However, increasingly America's educators are being evaluated on the basis of their students' performances on tests that were created to yield comparative score interpretations rather than to measure instructional quality. This is a terrible mistake.
>
> This mistake is being made because of an erroneous but pervasive belief by Americans that schools are responsible for the knowledge and skills students display when responding to achievement tests. In some instances,

this is accurate. Instruction in schools is responsible for certain skills and bodies of knowledge that are measured by today's achievement tests. . . . To what extent is a student's performance on a traditional achievement test attributable to what was taught in school rather than what was brought to school? For many of today's achievement tests, we just can't tell.[3]

His article continues to explain three of the reasons for his opposition. First, too many standards result in tests that often assess things students haven't been taught. Second, he explains that these state tests were not designed to accurately distinguish between test takers who have been taught well and test takers who have been taught badly. Instructional effectiveness is at the center of school effectiveness. If that isn't captured in state test scores, then inferring school quality from those scores is likely to lead to a flawed conclusion. Third, he explains that these state assessments are built to distinguish students' results from each other. Questions that make it into these assessments are those that about half of the students in the test panel answer correctly. Those questions that everyone answers correctly don't distinguish one student from another.

Let's advance your ability to identify mistaken assertions about the meaning of test results. Our quest, after all, is to help you fine-tune your error-detectors, so you can disregard false evidence and flawed conclusions, and regard sound evidence and reasonable conclusions more fully. We've created a taxonomy of mistaken assertions, a gallery of errors, based on the belief that once you've seen what a mistake looks like, you'll have an easier time spotting it the second time around. Let's use the simple categories from Chapter 1: *errors of commission, errors of omission* and *errors of judgment*.

We've taken more than statewide standardized tests into consideration. This taxonomy of errors is applicable to interim assessments, diagnostic assessments, minimum competency tests and more.

Errors of commission

This is a group of errors where someone does something wrong. It may be an error in administering a test, using a test for the wrong purpose, mismatching evidence to the question they're trying to answer, building test questions that contain bias, presenting a question poorly to the test-taker or programming errors in the branching logic of a computer-adaptive test. There are many errors of this type, but in the interest of sanity, let's review eight of them.

Wrong purpose

This is a case of a test used for the wrong purpose. This type of error was becoming so common in the No Child Left Behind era that the American Psychological Association published a new set of Standards for Educational Assessment in 2014 that featured this "wrong purpose" problem front and center.[4] One such example would be relying on an interim math assessment for diagnostic purposes. Diagnostic assessments are highly specialized, delivering many items on very specific concepts that may be highly dependent on each other (the ed-jargon term is "scaffolded"). Diagnostic assessments can determine where in a ladder of knowledge or skill a student may have a missing rung or two. Interim assessments are designed to measure growth, not identify missing skills or misunderstood concepts. They can be stretched to do that, of course. But the quality of the diagnostic information from an interim assessment is going to be lower than the quality of information about skill deficits you'd gather from a diagnostic assessment.

Wrong instrument

Choosing the wrong test results in a mismatch of the evidence to the question it was intended to answer. If we were discussing weather forecasts, the parallel would be the use of a thermometer rather than a barometer to determine whether rain was imminent. For example, if your district wanted to test reading fluency of its first graders and selected a test that only measured a student's ability to comprehend sentences, but didn't pay much attention to phonemic awareness, you'd miss the most important information needed to estimate students' emerging reading skills.

Another example would be the use of a high school exit exam to gauge students' readiness for college. High school exit exams test minimal competency. They are designed to measure students' abilities to pass the lowest threshold possible. In California, the math part of the high school exit exam

aimed at measuring mastery of eighth- or ninth-grade algebra skills. That has modest relevance to a student's readiness for college, but it doesn't come close to providing evidence of higher-level math skills that the SAT or ACT have provided for decades.

Wrong students

This is an error of a basic sort—testing the wrong students. Unfortunately, this happens all the time with students who are considered English language learners. Forgive me if what you are about to read seems insultingly simple. But I need to be blunt. Giving a math test in English to a student who cannot yet read English is not going to tell you anything about his or her mastery of math. If the student can't understand the questions, what is the point of giving the test to that student? This is a problem many assessment firms appreciate, so they've developed Spanish language versions of their assessments. If you ask a student which version of the test she'd prefer to take—Spanish or English—you give the student her best chance at displaying what she knows. But too many district administrators have been less alert to this opportunity. The result is a mess. Not only is the individual student's command of the subject matter-at-hand effectively not evaluated, but the low score that results leads a teacher to think the student's level of knowledge and skill is lower than it may really be. On top of that, the results for the class, the grade level, the school and district become clouded. The more students who are tested who are not yet able to read and write academic English, the more clouded the aggregate test results become.

Errors of test administration

When and where districts determine that a test should be given is no small matter. When are students most awake, alert and attentive? Well, it's probably not first thing in the morning. If a high school is telling students to take significant tests at 8 a.m., how many students will be groggy? If a district assessment director schedules their spring interim assessment in the same week as their state's standardized test, students will certainly show signs of test fatigue. If an elementary school teacher gives a reading test that will shape placement decisions before kids have had breakfast, some of those kids will be distracted by their growling stomachs. If the gardening crew is mowing outside the classrooms where students are taking tests, the noise will be a distraction for some portion of those students.

How students take a test also factors into their scores. When pencil-and-paper tests were the universal way that students rendered their answers, we could assume that all students were more or less equally capable of holding that pencil and bubbling in a Scantron form. But when computers supplanted pencils and Scantron forms, the range of students' abilities to provide their answers suddenly increased dramatically. A student's familiarity with the keyboard itself is a big factor. Did you teach your kids to type? Did you buy software to help your kids do so? The convention for turning ideas into words on a Q-W-E-R-T-Y keyboard is how we expect students to write. But by what age do we expect them to be functionally capable at the level needed to answer test questions? (Of course, a student's facility with a mouse device is less likely to vary.)

Where students take tests and under what conditions also introduces opportunity for errors to occur. The coronavirus pandemic led many test publishers to scramble, devising ways to deliver tests to students working at home. The quest was a noble one. How could a test a student takes at home, out of sight of teachers and perhaps parents, deliver estimates of mastery close to what proctored exams taken in a classroom deliver? It's not difficult to imagine that a curriculum-embedded assessment might succeed, delivering a set of review questions at the end of a chapter, to check for understanding. But could an interim assessment do that, an assessment that requires uninterrupted Internet connectivity so its computer-adaptive engine can fetch the next question? The Northwest Evaluation Association (NWEA) offered remote testing about 100 days after the mid-March 2020 shutdown of most of schools. Its test questions change as its computer intelligence analyzes a student's answers, adjusting the next question to fit the depth of that student's knowledge and skills, based on analysis of his prior answers. To what extent did the computer adaptive engine work for students at home?

Well, their clients gave tests to millions of students. But what portion of students in those districts didn't take the remote version of the NWEA's Measures of Academic Progress (MAP) assessments? And for those who did take it, to what degree did their responses differ from the test they would have taken in school on computer equipment they used regularly in a classroom with fellow students? Did the time they spent on those tests taken at home differ from the time they spent on the test when given at school? Did the usual distractions of home influence their answers? To what extent did students take those tests without turning to older siblings or textbooks for help with answers?

We'll have to wait for NWEA's research people to try answering these tough questions.

Errors in test design or item construction

On occasion, those who design academic assessments for a living make mistakes. Those errors can occur in the phrasing of the test questions themselves. At times, those errors are due to cultural blind spots. For example, a question that includes a reference to snow wouldn't make sense to a lot of students in the southeastern United States. But test designers are also capable of making mistakes when they design how those questions meet the student on a screen. The twin disciplines called UI-engineering (user interface) and UX-engineering (user experience) are complex. To be good at both, technology companies invest in teams of specialists and that talent is expensive. When assessment firms went on a talent search, they faced a tight labor market for UI and UX engineers. One consequence when the Smarter Balanced assessments debuted in 2015 was confusing user interfaces. One publisher and author of math textbooks and tools, Steven Rasmussen, was astonished when he reviewed the Smarter Balanced math test sample questions. Here's what he wrote in March 2016:

> Unfortunately, the Smarter Balanced tests are lemons. They fail to meet acceptable standards of quality and performance, especially with respect to their technology-enhanced items. They should be withdrawn from the market before they precipitate a national catastrophe. . . . What I found shocked me. This analysis of mathematics test questions posted online by Smarter Balanced reveals that, question after question, the tests:
> - Violate the standards they are supposed to assess;
> - Cannot be adequately answered by students with the technology they are required to use;
> - Use confusing and hard-to-use interfaces; or
> - Are to be graded in such a way that incorrect answers are identified as correct and correct answers as incorrect.

Twisting test results

If the technology-enhanced items on the Smarter Balanced practice and training tests are indicative of the quality of the actual tests coming this year—and Smarter Balanced tells us they are—the shoddy craft of the tests will directly and significantly contribute to students' poor scores.[5]

While he mentions flaws of several kinds, the second and third bullets in Steve Rasmussen's list point to design errors. Because he is a publisher of math textbooks (Key Curriculum Press), inventor of math tools (Geometer's Sketchpad) and an author himself, he knows the complexity of interface designs and the challenge of understanding the experience of the user. Translating a paper-based test question into an interactive computer-based question is complicated. He doubted that the test developer had time to do this right.

His 34-page memo of April 2015 was neither shy nor lacking in detail. An example of incompetent design he describes is an interface to enter numbers using a mouse. That interface transposes the placement of keys on a calculator but comes close to appearing to be a calculator. The meaning of other keys containing arrows is ambiguous. In fact, this is not a calculator at all but a way to input numbers into their proper fields, doing what a student would normally do with a keyboard or keypad (see Figure 2.1).

Rasmussen flags a bundle of problems: five buttons in the top row, four of them arrows; keys are numbered in a sequence that differs from

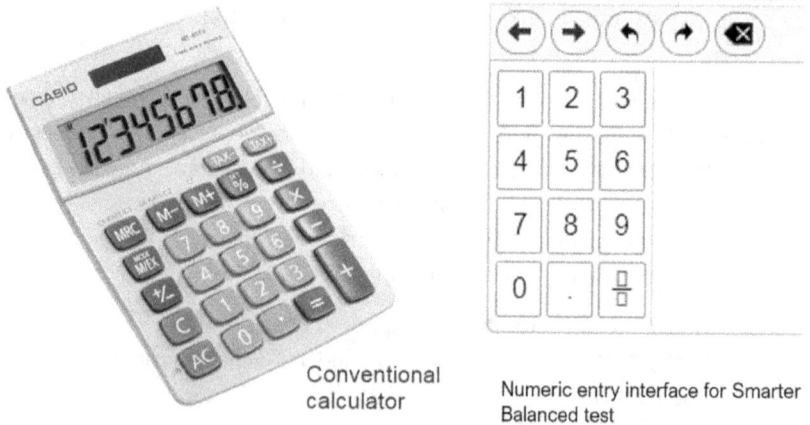

Conventional calculator

Numeric entry interface for Smarter Balanced test

Figure 2.1 Comparison of a standard calculator (left) with the interface provided to students taking the Smarter Balanced math test (right)

that of a calculator (convention has calculators with keys numbered 7–8–9 in the top row, 4–5–6 in the middle row, and 1–2–3 in the bottom row); the right-most key on the bottom row looking like a subtraction sign, but not behaving like one; and the device allows for a student to input more than one decimal point. Noting how many mistakes the test designer made on this screen-based tool alone, Rasmussen wonders how they could possibly design intelligent interfaces for other tools. In essence, he faults bad craftsmanship and weak quality controls, and assigns blame to both the companies that created the tests and the state agencies that fielded them.[6]

Rasmussen's paper contains comments from math educators and leaders of their associations that share a critical appraisal of the quality of both the Smarter Balanced and PARCC math assessments at every grade level. While their objections vary in tone and intensity, they all share an embrace of the Common Core math standards, and a fear that low-quality assessments would spark a public rejection of the standards themselves.

Errors in test sensitivity and specificity

Some tests just aren't good at measuring what they're supposed to measure. The most common form of this error is a test that is not sensitive enough to determine with reasonable confidence and accuracy whether a student needs extra help. If the test is a screening test, it is likely to miss kids who should be flagged for help or further testing. Tests whose purpose is to screen kids who may be dyslexic, for example, are supposed to discriminate between students who may be lagging because they may be dyslexic and those who are lagging for other reasons. Dyslexia is a neurological disorder that is often described as an information processing problem. It makes it hard for students to turn letters into sounds that they recognize as words, and it reveals itself in a pattern that is, to some degree, different from that of a non-dyslexic student has who is struggling with reading. This is not easy to do. Diagnosing it requires putting together a range of evidence, and the screening test's role is to contribute to the evidence of those who are possibly dyslexic from those who are not, and produces a measure of risk (not a diagnosis). It is one step in a series of steps that lead to a diagnosis. If a screening test is given to 100 kindergartners and 100 first graders, and 80 of the kindergartners and 70 of the first graders test positive (many screening tests for dyslexia only return a yes/no result), then the screener hasn't done a good job. We can say this because dyslexia experts believe that the incidence of dyslexia in the general population is between 5 and 17 percent.[7] The incidence rate among boys is understood to be two to three times higher than among girls. If a screening test can't get reasonably close to the number of students who are likely to be dyslexic, what use is it?

Wrong unit of measurement

The states each have their own favored metrics and vocabulary when describing tests and test results. Some favor threshold boundary measures (e.g., the percentage of students who were "proficient" or "met or exceeded standard"). Some favor measures of central tendency (average scale score). Others use scale scores to measure how far above or below a mark of "meeting standard" students scored. All these approaches are fine, as long as their meaning is kept intact. But reporting the percentage of students meeting standard is far different from reporting students' average scale score.

This is not a semantic quibble. I'm urging you to fit the evidence to the question you're trying to answer. At the same time, I encourage you to form your questions with care. Different units of measurement and different methods of deriving them are best matched to specific questions.

"Did this year's fifth graders, as a whole, score higher on their math test than last year's fifth graders?" This question requires the average scale score for the test, because that measures the results of all students. You'll need those results for two years of fifth graders, of course. But is that really your question? This is called a cross-sectional view. If you're the sixth-grade math teacher in the middle school where last year's fifth graders will be enrolling next year, that may be a starting point for your planning. But you'd also want to know the shape of the distribution—what we'll call the "spread"—of all students' scores. This would be more helpful to the middle school math teachers because they'd see how many incoming students are scoring above and below grade level, and how far from grade level they're scoring. If one-fourth of the class is scoring two grade levels below where they should be, they would know to prepare lots of help.

"Did this year's fifth graders make as much progress as they did in the prior year?" That's an entirely different question. In this case, you're comparing the same kids' results over time—this year's fifth graders to their scores as fourth graders in the prior year. This is called a longitudinal measure if it truly looks at the same kids across time. It is one of the ways to measure growth, and it has the advantage of being direct, simple to explain and easiest to understand. The metric you'll need is the average or median scale score, because that's the one measure that describes how all kids scored. Ideally, you'd also relate that median scale score to the factor that tells you how far results spread from that midpoint. That is the standard deviation, and it tells you in scale score points how far from the median 68 percent of students' results fall (34 percent lower and 34 percent higher than the median scale score). The larger that number, the greater the spread or variation in students' results.

"What percentage of our third graders were reading at or above the state standard?" In your state, this may be called the "proficient" level or simply "meeting standard." But it is a line drawn by psychometricians, informed by subject area experts, and it is essentially an informed guess. A lot of smart people invest a lot of time in drawing that line wisely. But it is, in the end, a human judgment and is therefore fallible. By the way, this is a threshold boundary measure, and it describes only what some of your students have scored. It does not describe all students' results, not does it tell you what they've scored. It only describes the portion of students whose scores have crossed a line.

It may matter a great deal in your state's accountability system, and your school board may care most about this. If your school board asks you to report the percentage of third graders reading below grade level based on your state's assessment, make sure of two things. First, make sure that your test results *actually measure reading*. An English language arts test includes some questions designed to estimate reading skill. But you'll need to pull the reading sub-test out of the larger test. Hopefully, you'll have other tests you give to estimate your students' reading skills, and if so, you can add those results to your answer. Second, include in your answer the *degree of imprecision* in the answer, and if you can, your degree of confidence in that answer. Later in this chapter, in the section on errors of omission, you'll learn more about these two factors that are always present in every test of human knowledge and skill. Acknowledging imprecision and uncertainty and sharing your knowledge of the size of them both is always the best course.

Twisting test results

Wrong benchmark or norms

A benchmark provides you something to compare against. It provides meaning to measures of all kinds. In fact, benchmarks provide a context that's essential if we are to make sense of a measurement. Norms, often expressed as grade-level norm tables, are an example of a benchmark. Without benchmarks, all you've got are a bunch of numbers (what stat-heads call descriptive statistics). For this reason, benchmarks deserve your attention.

Consider you are taking your 10-year-old son to a routine pediatrician appointment. The physician's assistant will weigh your child, measure his height and tell you the results. You probably knew both facts already. But you want to know what they mean. When your child's pediatrician arrives, you're likely to ask, "How do his height and weight look to you?" And the doctor is likely to offer a reply like this. "Compared to other boys his age, he's right in the zone we consider to be normal—between the 50th and 75th percentile." And if your pediatrician is a good explainer, she'll take down a body-mass index chart suitable for boys around that age and show you where your child's body-mass index puts him relative to other boys. The benchmark in that body-mass index chart was an aggregate derived from hundreds of thousands of measurements. Imposed on it may have been judgments of experts who drew threshold boundaries around "normal" that allowed for some variance in height and weight combinations. Those human judgments, together with the aggregation of lots of other kids' measurements, give you reference points that enable you to answer your question.

Here is an example of an age-and-body-mass index chart for boys, from 2 to 20 years old (see Figure 2.2). The chart contains explanations for four hypothetical 10-year-old boys whose heights and weights results in a body-mass index ratings of 13, 18, 21 and 23. They combine objective measurement of height and weight and age with human judgment. What constitutes a healthy range of weights for a boy who is 13 and is a certain height? At what point is a boy's weight unhealthy, and when is a boy so heavy that he is deemed to be obese?

Test results are normed in a similar manner. They combine measures of skill and knowledge with human judgment about its meaning. If you're evaluating the PSAT results of your eighth graders, you'll be able to reference a norm table provided by the College Board, the organization that owns the PSAT and the SAT and the AP program. It should enable you to help a student figure out how she did compared to other kids who took the PSAT.

Twisting test results

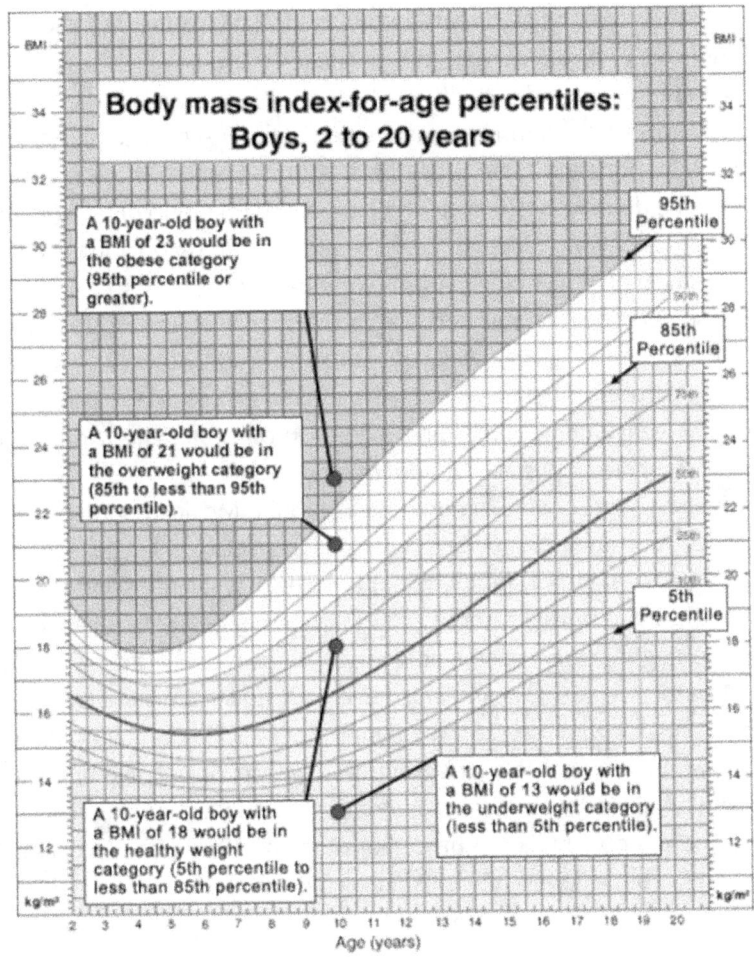

Figure 2.2 Body-mass index for boys of different ages
A body-mass index chart for boys between the ages of 2 and 20. The chart shows four examples of boys whose height and weight put them in four categories: underweight (bottom), healthy (second from bottom), overweight (third from bottom) and obese (top). Body-mass index is a measure of the relationship between a person's height and weight.
Source: Centers for Disease Control

The test publishers deliver many things of value to districts and state departments of education. Some, like test items—the questions and multiple-choice options themselves—are tangible. You can see them and evaluate their quality. Others are less tangible or more abstract and are more difficult to evaluate. Norms belong in this latter category. When most test publishers deliver results, they evaluate each student's result, each class's result, each grade level's result, each school's and district's result, against norms. Those norms can be created both for scores and for growth. If you are a principal, you better have a firm grasp of those norms. To what degree do those students in the national norm group differ from your students? How many students' scores went into them? How long ago were the tests given on which those norms were based?

These questions are key, because the norm may be the most important factor when someone evaluates your students' results. Even if that person is examining your students' year-to-year growth, he or she will also want to know how your students are doing relative to other students. And for that purpose, the norm group is that pool of other students.

What if your school is in a town close to the Mexican border, and 45 percent of your students are classified as English learners because they are Spanish speakers and becoming fluent in English? If the norm group is representative of the students in the U.S., then only 9 percent of the students in that norm group are like your students in this way. Is this the norm group you'd like to compare your students to? If your students were all in a hardscrabble, rural part of the U.S., with nine out of 10 kids getting subsidized meals, would you favor a norm group that was representative of the U.S. as a whole, where five out of 10 students nationally are getting meal subsidies? You'd probably like to have more localized benchmarks available, ones that fit your students' circumstances more closely.

How every state once claimed its students' scores were above average

In the era of the 1980s and early 1990s, long before you could discuss states sharing common education standards and common assessments, each state made its own choice of test instruments. The companies that built those assessments invested in building panels of tens of thousands of students whose scores served as a benchmark or norm, against which all other students would be scored. These resulted in national percentile rankings that revealed to parents that their child's score was higher than some percentage of other students in the nation. Assembling those norm groups and deriving scores representative of students nationally proved to be costly. So, testing companies invested in renorming as infrequently as possible, which turned out to be every seven to nine years.

That's a long time between renorming efforts. As students and teachers became more familiar with these tests, students' scores climbed. "Score creep" entered the vocabulary. Eventually, so many states' education chiefs were boasting that their kids had scored above average (meaning above the average scale score of the norm group), that the claims started looking implausible. Indeed, some were. In 1988, a West Virginia doctor, J.J. Cannell, got hopped-up about this and researched every state's claims. He couldn't find a single state that reported its students' scores to be below average. His anger at the false claims of state education leaders led him to write a book, *How Public Educators Cheat on Standardized Achievement Tests: The "Lake Wobegon" Report*.[8] His book caught the attention of Edward Fiske, lead education reporter for the *New York Times*, who covered it on February 17, 1988, in a story headlined, "Standardized Test Scores: Voodoo Statistics?" This article boosted Dr. Cannell's visibility, and he soon went on the talk-show circuit. The spark of J.J. Cannell's "Lake Wobegon Report" started a national wildfire. One result was a loss of credibility of education leaders and the tests they relied upon. But a beneficial result was that a lot of superintendents started paying more attention to the norms used by the testing companies they'd hired.

☞ **Tip:** if your district has licensed interim assessments, take a close look at the technical manual describing the norm tables. In addition to finding information about the scale measure itself, you should be able to answer these questions: How long ago were the tests taken on which the norm tables were based? How many students' results were included in the sample, both overall and at each grade level? Has the test publisher weighted the results to match a national profile of U.S. students? Have they calculated norms for growth as well as of scores? Ask your test publisher if they offer subgroup level norms (by gender, ethnicity, etc.). Then ask them if they could give your state's unadjusted state level average scale scores for every grade level and subject tested. This would at least enable you to answer state-specific questions like this: "How are our elementary kids doing in math compared to other kids in our state?"

Twisting test results

One solution to what may be a substantial difference between the students included in the national or state norms and your students is to benchmark your results against schools or districts with *students most like your own*. You can do-it-yourself by searching for schools or districts whose students resemble your own in the three ways that most directly affect their readiness and ability to learn: parent level of education (most powerful effect), English language fluency and participation in the free-and-reduced-price meals program. Feel free to add other criteria to your matched set of similar schools or districts. You might include attributes of your school or district: grade levels served, funding, number of students enrolled. You might favor including community factors: geographic location, rural/suburban/urban, household income. Find no less than five schools or districts to build a context to frame your own results. Do not merge them into one phantom entity but instead keep them separate. As you proceed with your analysis, you'll find this comparative context will help you to see your own school or district in a different light. Best of all, you'll be able to say, "Well, compared with the five districts with students most like ours, here's how we're doing." That shows you know where your district or school stands.

In Figure 2.3, you'll find an example of a comparative view of the college-going rates of the Class of 2018 from a California school district compared to 15 districts whose students are highly similar to their own. Leaders in this district, Morgan Hill USD, were able to show their board, staff, parents, community leaders, realtors and journalists that four districts with students highly similar to their own sent more kids to college in that graduating class, and 11 sent fewer. The top two districts sent about 5 percent more students to college in the Class of 2018. Using leaderboards or ranked bar graphs to show the degree of difference, as well as the rank order, makes it possible for people to make sense of these key facts and share them with others. If instead of this comparison, Morgan Hill's leaders shared that 65 percent of the Class of 2018 went on to enroll in college, that number would hold less meaning and be less easily remembered. The value of creating a set of highly similar districts for comparison purposes is quite high. It is a norm group of your own construction. The rewards for this do-it-yourself approach are high.

Twisting test results

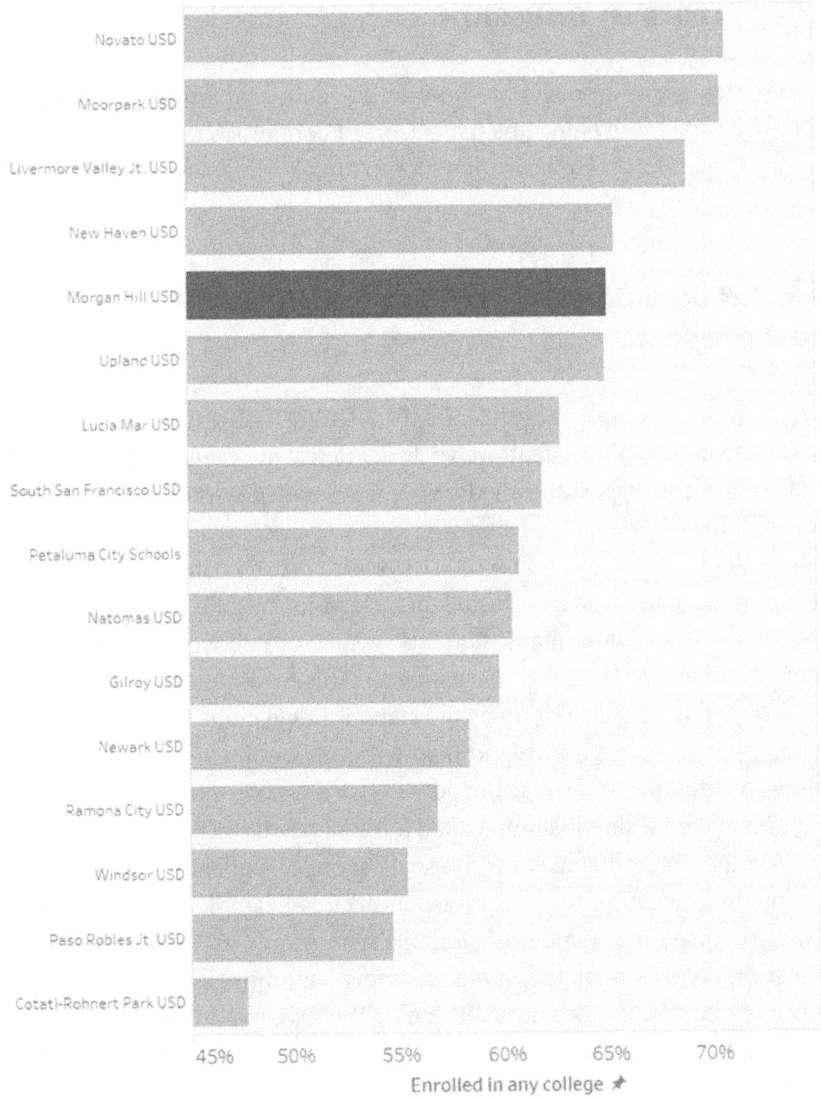

You'll find a link to a live version of this visualization at the following web page: https://www.k12measures.com/ch2/#fig2.3

Figure 2.3 College going rate of Class of 2018

    Leaderboard comparing rate at which Morgan Hill's students in the Class of 2018 enrolled in college, compared to students in 15 similar districts. Cohort defined as those enrolled as freshmen four years prior.

Source: K12 Measures. © School Wise Press

Errors of omission

The mistakes that result from choosing to ignore information can sometimes be even more damaging than errors of commission. This type of error is rarely intentional. However, that doesn't make it any less egregious.

The overemphasis on averages and the blind spot of spread

We have all become so accustomed to seeing test results expressed as a single number that I fear we've lost interest in everything else. Let's stop seeking averages and medians and instead ask for a picture of the whole thing—the *entire set of results of all students who took a test*. The whole thing would give you a picture of the *spread* of results. This would reveal how many students' results are close to the midpoint or median, for instance, and how many students' results are above and below that mark and how far from that mark they sit. This measure of spread is often represented in statistical form as the standard deviation. This just tells you what range of scores above and below the midpoint captures about two-thirds of test-takers' results. But let's rely on visual representations and express that on a simple graph called a frequency distribution.

On the horizontal axis sits the scale score of students' results. Values are omitted because they are irrelevant to this example. On the vertical axis, you'll see the number of students who scored at various points on the scale. What's depicted, then, is simply the number of students who scored at each point on the scale score. The example in Figure 2.4 is for the California version of the Smarter Balanced Assessment Consortium (SBAC) math test, which California dubbed the California Assessment of Student Performance and Progress (CAASPP), given in 2016. About 480,000 fourth graders' scores and about 480,000 eighth graders' scores are accounted for.

The curve representing fourth graders' results is the one with the higher peak and the narrowest spread separating the left and right tails of the curve. Those mark the lowest and highest obtainable scale scores. The symmetry of the curve reflects that about as many fourth graders scored below the midpoint as above, and at about the same rate.

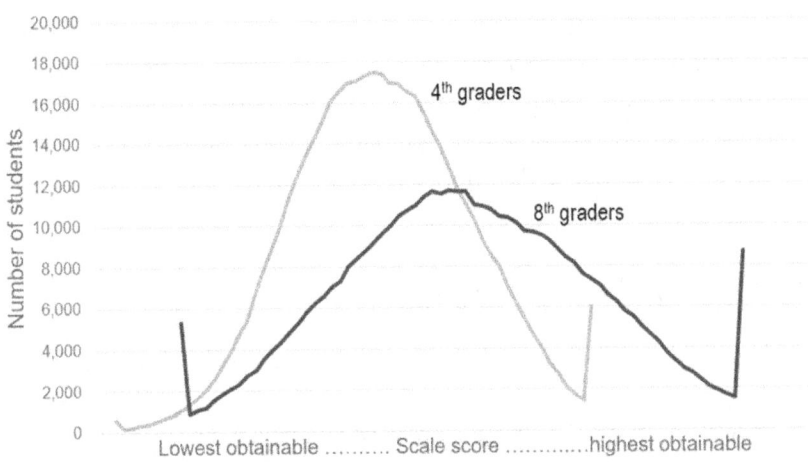

Figure 2.4 Frequency distribution of 2016 California CAASPP/SBAC math results of fourth and eighth graders

Frequency distribution showing the number of students who attained every possible score on the California version of the SBAC in math in 2016.

Source: Eric Zilbert, California Department of Education

But now compare the shape and spread of fourth graders' results to those of the eighth graders. The peak of the curve for eighth graders is lower, and the feet of its curve are much farther apart. It's spread so wide that I can almost feel the pain of being a student on the left tail, a student whose math skills are lagging far behind his peers. Imagine the challenge of being the math teacher to eighth graders and coping with students who are so far behind. The hardship for both lagging students and those expected to teach them is visible here. The challenge for leading math students and their teachers is also in full view.

Note the upward spikes at the end of the right tail of both the fourth and eighth graders' results? That represents the number of students who obtained the highest possible scale score on this test. This provides a picture of the limits of what that test was able to measure, a factor that may be even more relevant when taking stock of achievement gaps. Take a closer look at the height of the eighth graders' curve on the right tail of the distribution. That spike tells us that about 9,000 students attained the highest possible score on the test that year. It's about three-fourths as high as the peak (mode), a score attained by about 12,000 students. Because the test was only designed to measure mastery of grade-level standards, we don't get to see how much higher they would have scored if more difficult questions had been presented to them. In brief, we're seeing the limits of what this test is measuring. This is the power of seeing the whole picture in a frequency distribution graph. We are jarred awake from the sleepy state we've been lulled into by the tyranny of averages.

The blind spot of imprecision

Let's consider the inescapably fuzzy nature of test scores. When we test kids, we're trying to gather evidence of something that exists out of sight, somewhere between their ears. Whatever their test scores reveal, it can only be an estimate of what they know. The good news is that the psychometricians have a pretty good handle on the degree of imprecision, on the size of the fuzzy factor. The bad news is that in most districts and states, only assessment directors get the benefit of this information.

Imprecision is not a mistake. It's the unavoidable result of the limits of test instruments, and of the limits of what a student can show what she knows during a test lasting less than an hour. The good news is that the size of the imprecision is known, and that's why sharing knowledge of that imprecision is so important. *It's key to interpreting the meaning of a score.* Once you know it, you can bracket the student's reported score by the amount of imprecision (what I prefer to call the "fuzzy factor"). That bracketed band contains a range of possible scores. If you can see that range of possible scores, then you can take it into account when you're interpreting the meaning of a score, be it for a student, a school or a district.

This "fuzzy factor" varies for every test, based on the number of questions on the test, the type of questions and their degree of difficulty. And it also varies based on the number of test events you're interpreting. If you're interpreting one student's score on the Smarter Balanced assessment, which has a range from about 2000 up to about 3000 scale score points, a student's score commonly has a "fuzzy factor" of between +/− 24 to +/− 50 scale score points, depending on the number of questions answered. When a teacher is rapidly sorting students into those "meeting" and "not meeting" standard, this degree of imprecision can easily affect the teacher's sorting decision. It is common for students in the middle two levels in California's system to straddle a boundary line, providing *no exact answer to the question, "Did she or did she not meet standard?"*

States' varied approaches to disclosing imprecision

Each state department of education has its own way of communicating individual students' test results to their parents. These reports reveal not just their skill in making sense of the meaning of test results, but also the degree to which they trust parents to handle the complexity that's unavoidable when estimating what students have learned. The litmus test is whether these parent reports include any reference to score imprecision, and if they do, how it's presented. New Mexico's state department of education does a good job of telling parents that scores are imprecise. In Texas, Illinois, Maryland, California, Ohio, Indiana, Florida and many other states, the parent reports make no mention of imprecision. In my search for states that did reveal the "fuzzy factor" to parents, I discovered that California did reveal this imprecision in the first two years (2015 and 2016). However, in 2017 and subsequent years, all signs of imprecision had disappeared, a regrettable decision, and one which still awaits an explanation.

As you can see in Figure 2.5, the "fuzzy factor" was represented in the report districts mailed to parents, visible as stems-and-whiskers above and below the dot, which was the student's reported score. No surprise, it's large enough to cross the line between the middle two levels of mastery. This report was created by the Smarter Balanced consortium and distributed by the California Department of Education. It intentionally provided an example of a student whose results crossed the threshold boundary separating Levels 2 and 3. Interestingly, the text that accompanied this didn't account for the ambiguity of results. Just for reference, the SBAC's technical manual reveals that the classification accuracy rate in these middle two bands (Levels 2 and 3) is about 70 percent. In other words, just seven out of every 10 kids whose scores land in the middle two bands will be classified correctly as having either met the standard or scored below the standard.

If your state uses the tests offered by the other consortium, the Partnership for Assessment of Readiness for College and Careers (PARCC), its scale score ranges from 650 to 850. With only 200 points on the scale, the size of the "fuzzy factor" will seem to be smaller because it will appear in single digits. But in fact, the relative degree of imprecision in the PARCC assessments is about the same as that contained in the SBAC assessments.

Twisting test results

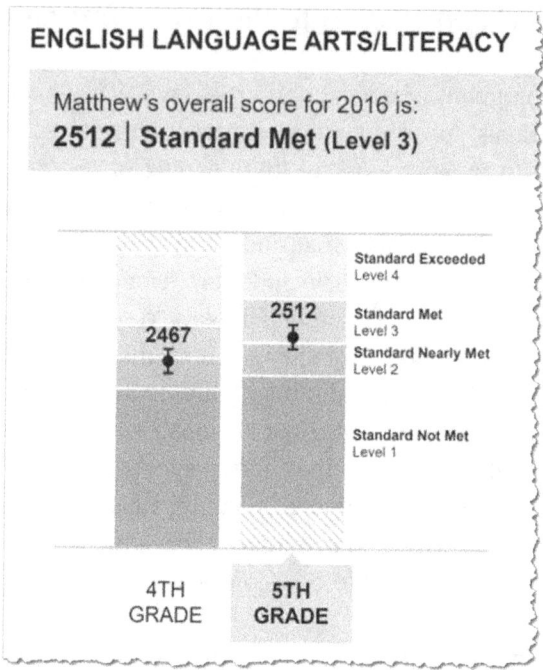

Figure 2.5 Smarter Balanced report to parents of a student's results, 2016
A rare example of a 2016 Smarter Balanced report intended for parents, which shows how much imprecision is captured in the student's reported score. These parent reports stopped including the stem-and-whisker expressions of imprecision the following year.
Source: Smarter Balanced consortium, 2016

The NWEA MAP interim assessments, however, delivers results with a somewhat smaller "fuzzy factor." Using a scale that runs from about 100 to 400 (measured in something called Rasch units), their tests customarily show imprecision of about +/− 3 scale score points for a student who has completed all the test questions. Relative to the two big state assessments, this is a somewhat smaller degree of imprecision at the student level. No surprise, the NWEA MAP assessment was specifically designed to measure individual student growth. The CAASPP and PARCC assessments were designed to measure the degree of school- and district-level success at meeting grade level standard, a much different purpose.

If you want to infer growth from two administrations of the same test, you must account for the imprecision of both the prior and current scores. The "fuzzy factor" when measuring growth amplifies, because both measurement at both points in time include imprecision.

When you're analyzing groups of students' scores, then the degree of imprecision is reduced. The more observations, the lower the "fuzzy factor." Here's one example from a district we've worked for in California. When analyzing 76 students in a grade level, their state assessment results, the CAASPP, reflected +/– 13 scale score points of imprecision. A grade level of kids in a larger school, containing 260 kids, reflected +/– 7 scale score points of imprecision. An entire school, with 624 kids tested, saw its "fuzzy factor" reduced to +/– 5 scale score points. This degree of imprecision can, indeed, affect a California school's accountability standing.

The blind spot of uncertainty

There's still more to the "fuzzy factor." The psychometricians also know the probability of a student's "true score." (Yes, that's a technical term, referring to the range of possible scores.) It is customary for assessment firms to set that probability level at 68 percent. This turns out to be the equivalent of +/– 1 standard deviation, which puts 34 percent of the results to the right of the median line, and another 34 percent to the left. All this means is that roughly two-thirds of the time, a student's "true score" will fall within that range. The rest of the time, it will fall outside it.

If this sounds familiar, it may be because you're remembering the footnotes at the bottom of political polls. Those footnotes tell readers the four things they need to know to interpret the result: the number of people polled, how they were selected, the error margin (the degree of imprecision) and the confidence interval (degree of uncertainty). When likely voters are polled, and 48 percent of them are for Joe Gladhand and 45 percent are for Lizzy Borden, if the margin of error is +/– 5 percent with a confidence 90 percent, you cannot conclude that Joe Gladhand is leading. He might be lagging. But at least newspaper publishers and the political polling services they subscribe to trust that the reader is capable of interpreting imprecision and uncertainty. That has led to the convention of the explanatory footnote beneath every display of polling results. It is an industry standard, taught in journalism schools and included in the Associated Press's *Style Guide*. Readers are served well by those publishers who follow these guidelines, and those readers who ignore the small print below those polling table results do so at their own peril.

Do education leaders at the state and district levels have equally stringent standards for reporting test results? Yes, the standards are clearly established for testing in the *Standards for Educational and Psychological Testing* (2014).[9] Three organizations share the responsibility of authorship and hold the copyright jointly: the American Psychological Association, the American Educational Research Association and the National Council on Measurement in Education. In March 2021, they even made the 2014 edition available free in PDF format. In addition, in 2016, Jenny Rankin published a book that defined the standards for quality reporting of education data. That book, *Standards for Reporting Data to Educators*,[10] was based on her years of experience both as an assessment leader in Saddleback Valley USD, California, and as cofounder of a company, Illuminate-Ed, that was in the business of providing test reporting and data services to school districts. These two volumes enable anyone to know the dos and don'ts of testing and reporting test results.

One reason why teachers and parents rarely see the imprecision of test scores, I suspect, is a long-standing distrust by state education leaders in the ability of parents, teachers, principals and district leaders to make sense of the complexity inherent in educational testing. Testing firms, responding to state contract specifications, take an unfortunately passive role all too often and don't defend the higher standards they know should be applied to state testing contracts. This distrust is evident in the prevalence of red, green and yellow in so many state assessment reports. These attempts to turn test results into something that "even a teacher could understand" is a sign of not just mistrust. It is a sign of surrender.

The challenge of multiple measures: triangulating on readers' skills

There is a short list of skills that schools promise to develop in every student. This short list begins with the ability to read. Despite the centrality of reading to learning, the two state-level assessments—SBAC and PARCC—weren't designed to measure reading skills closely. They were designed to provide estimates of students' mastery of grade-level standards at the school and district levels. Consider the number of questions alone. Just 14 to 16 of the 40 to 43 questions in the Smarter Balanced English language arts test given to third graders are focused on reading. If a district wants to know whether its kids are learning to read at a point in time early enough to matter, it would need to use interim assessments or early literacy assessments designed to do just that. The skills these tests measure include decoding, vocabulary and phonemic awareness, the key elements that make reading comprehension possible.

The good news is that many districts have licensed tests that do measure the emerging reading skills of students in grades K–2 and higher. Teachers rely on these tests when deciding whether to refer a student for help. That help may be in the form of a reading specialist who works with smaller groups of struggling readers, bringing more personalized help their way. Educators used to call this reading remediation. While that term is out of fashion, two other terms refer to contemporary methods for making this decision: response to intervention (RtI) and multitiered systems of support (MTSS). The rate at which students are referred out of the classroom (called Tier 2 referrals in the MTSS system) is the thing to watch. That referral rate is an indicator that may customarily wander between 5 and 10 percent. When that rate strays from 10 toward 15 percent, consider that to be a yellow flare in the sky. It may signal trouble that the mainstream reading program itself—its method and the workbooks and teachers guide and training—is not working. It may signal trouble that the teachers delivering that reading program are not effective. Or it may signal that neither the program nor the teachers delivering it are succeeding. When the referral rate reaches or exceeds 15 percent, imagine a red flare. That painful moment is the time to admit that too many students aren't learning to read.

If you want to evaluate how effectively your district is teaching reading, get ready to ask a lot of questions. You might do well to request a second

Twisting test results

opinion from outside your district to advise you, as well, because the differing views of how to teach reading may reveal sharp disagreements. Inside staff who have had a hand in selecting instructional materials have a stake in defending their choices, of course.

The accuracy of your district's favored reading test may appear to be less exact when you relate it to the results of another test whose purpose is also to evaluate reading. Here is an example of two tests of reading skills given in the fall of 2019 to 435 second graders in a California district (see Figure 2.6). Each dot represents a student. The position of each dot on the field of this scatterplot corresponds to the student's scores on both tests.

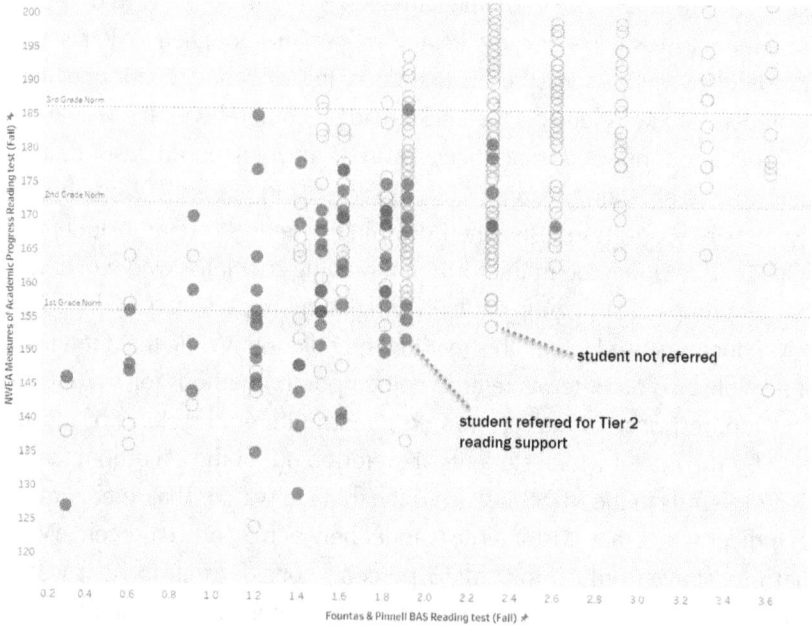

Find the link to a live version of this visualization at the following web page: https://www.k12measures.com/ch2/#fig2.6

Figure 2.6 Second graders' scores on two reading tests

Second graders' reading scores on two tests, given within weeks of each other in the fall of 2019. The degree to which teachers' evaluations of student reading agree and disagree with the results of a computer-administered interim assessment is clearly visible in the range of vertical spread at any point on the Fountas & Pinnell scale.

Source: K12 Measures. © School Wise Press

One test is bundled with a commercially successful curriculum, Fountas & Pinnell's Classroom program (F&P). It appears on the horizontal axis. According to the research center of *Education Week*, it enjoyed dominant market share in the U.S. market in 2019.[11] It adheres to the Balanced Literacy view of reading, and its curriculum for early elementary students includes illustrations on almost every page. The test also includes illustrations. The reading strategies encourage students to use visual cues to guess when they are struggling to sound out a word phonetically. The test is effectively an error report combined with a comprehension measure. You may hear it described as a running record. The teacher keeps score while a student reads a passage. The accuracy and speed with which a student reads a passage, combined with his ability to retell the story and demonstrate comprehension, constitutes the student's score. In this particular district, it is the test teachers trust the most and give most frequently.

The other test is the highly regarded Northwest Evaluation Association's Measures of Academic Progress (NWEA MAP) interim assessment of reading. Those scores appear on the vertical axis. The dotted horizontal lines indicate their national norms for first, second and third grades. The test is computer-based and is not timed, although most students complete it within 30–40 minutes. It measures a student's vocabulary and ability to identify key concepts, point of view and structure of both fictional and informational passages.

The results of the F&P test are arrayed on the horizontal axis. The numbers reflect a conversion of the test publisher's alphabetical designation of reading level to a numeric system that estimates the equivalent grade level. There are no published norm scale results for this assessment. In the middle range of the F&P test between 1.8 and 2.6 grade level equivalent scores are a lot of students whose teachers evaluated their reading skill to be very close to second-grade level using the F&P test. Yet if that were true, you'd expect these students to show roughly similar levels of mastery on the NWEA MAP reading test. Instead, what we see is *conflicting evidence* for many students in the zone around second-grade level. (The two tests show a closer degree of agreement for students at the lowest and highest ends of the scale.) Students in that middle range on the F&P test scored all over the place on the NWEA MAP reading, from first-grade to third-grade level. In fact, a teacher would have a very low likelihood of guessing the NWEA MAP reading score of her own students whom she recently scored close to second-grade level on the F&P test.

This example poses many questions. To what degree should multiple measures of the same skill agree? When evidence conflicts, what should you do? Is a test of reading that uses pictures as cues a reliable gauge of a student's ability to sound out letters and read words? When two test results disagree to a substantial degree, would you retest the student? If so, with which test? How certain of the evidence should you be before referring a student to the Tier 2 support team for extra help? If some teachers are evaluating students much more consistently with the NWEA MAP reading results than their colleagues, how might you spread their knowledge around?

Errors of interpretation

The best evidence from a test of the highest quality still must be interpreted. At this step of the process, a lot can (and does) go wrong. In fact, what psychometricians call "test validity" used to be considered an attribute of the test itself. But now, "validity" is officially considered a function of the quality of judgment of people who interpret it, according to the 2014 edition of the *Standards for Educational and Psychological Testing*. In fact, the topic is so important that it appears on the first page of the first chapter on validity which says:

> Validity refers to the degree to which evidence and theory support the interpretations of test scores for proposed uses of tests. Validity is, therefore, the most fundamental consideration in developing tests and evaluating tests. The process of validation involves accumulating relevant evidence to provide a sound scientific basis for the proposed score interpretations. It is the interpretations of test scores for proposed uses that are evaluated, not the test itself. When test scores are interpreted in more than one way (e.g., both to describe a test taker's current level of the attribute being measured and to make a prediction about a future outcome), each intended interpretation must be validated. Statements about validity should refer to particular interpretations for specified uses. It is incorrect to use the unqualified phrase "the validity of the test."[12]

In brief, it's the quality of human judgment applied to making sense of test results that makes it valid or invalid. As a result, we'll be paying extra attention throughout this book to this category of error.

California's misleading K–12 dashboard could lead to closure of the wrong schools

By David Osborne and Steve Rees, Published by EdSource, November 4, 2020

Students at Ánimo Ellen Ochoa Charter Middle School in East Los Angeles are learning at one-and-a-half to two times the pace of their grade-level peers, based on their state standardized (CAASPP) test scores for the last three years compared to the average for the state.

But the California Department of Education has labeled Ochoa a "low performer," based on how it ranks on various color-coded indicators on the California School Dashboard.

The department's report of school performance—the state's "dashboard"—is deeply flawed. For the 341 kids enrolled at Ochoa—96 percent of whom are socioeconomically disadvantaged, almost all of whom are Latinx and 24 percent of whom are still learning English—a flawed dashboard could lead to disaster. That's because the school district could close the school based on its ranking.

Ochoa is part of the highly respected Green Dot Public Schools, a Los Angeles nonprofit educational organization, which was recognized by the U.S. Department of Education as a high-quality charter school operator during the Obama administration.

But in high-poverty middle schools such as Ochoa, students often arrive several years behind grade level. Few of them are "proficient" in math or reading. Ochoa's students, while far behind, are making exceptional gains compared with students statewide. Yet the dashboard blends their test scores together with a year-to-year change measure that conceals both their high rate of growth and their low starting scores. These results only make sense when reported separately. They make no sense when blended together.

All but two states as of November 2020 have built measures of academic growth into their accountability reporting, designed to show whether students are catching up or falling further behind grade level. California and Kansas do not. The California State Board of Education only voted in 2021 to define a growth measure, and only by 2024 will that growth measure be calculated and published. As a result, California only measures year-to-year change. It takes a school full of kids and subtracts last year's students' test scores from this year's students' scores, as if kids in this year's class were more or less just like kids in last year's class. But for a middle school where kids in grades 6, 7 and 8 are tested, one grade level of kids departs and one arrives each year.

The dashboard also combines current test scores and change from last year's class to this year's class into one measure, another fatal logic error. These are two entirely different things.

Consider a middle school whose students were three years behind grade level, on average, last year. If this year they are only one year behind grade level, then that school would be performing spectacularly well. But its dashboard score for academics still would be orange or yellow—the equivalent of a D or C. If a school's status is low on any indicator but it has made huge improvements, the best it can earn is yellow.

When the State Board of Education considered its change measure at a July 2018 meeting, a group of 14 respected academic experts warned in a letter that, "The state's current 'change' model is unacceptable—it profoundly fails the validity test, and therefore it does not accurately represent schools' contribution to student achievement. Indeed, it is not clear what it represents at all."[13]

Later, in a paper for the "Getting Down to Facts" project, University of Southern California scholars Morgan Polikoff, Shira Korn and Russell McFall found the anticipated incorrect conclusions were indeed occurring as a result of the dashboard's flaws: current change measures are inaccurate in their identification most of the time.[14]

Fortunately, the California Department of Education has a group working on a new student growth measure. Unfortunately, the coronavirus pandemic forced cancellation of spring testing, which has put the 2020 dashboard on hold and delayed work on revamping the growth measure. The state should take the opportunity provided by this hiatus in dashboard reports to develop and put in place a credible measure of real growth and give it a prominent place of its own in the dashboard.

We have pointed to other problems, which you can explore further on your own (https://schoolwisepress.com/category/dashboard/). We support accountability for charter schools, but like all schools, charters deserve to be evaluated based on sound evidence. The California Department of Education has not yet produced it.

[Postscript: Ochoa won renewal of its charter due in part to their strong technical defense of their students' growth in test results, measured longitudinally for cohorts. The California State Board finally adopted a growth measure in spring 2021, but it will take effect only in 2024.]

Wrong vantage point

Test events produce data. Data is built into evidence, often designed to answer a particular question. Finally, people stand somewhere, view that evidence from an angle and reach a conclusion about its meaning. Well, it's possible to have the right evidence in hand, but to view it from an angle unsuited to answering your question. All evidence will be interpretable from almost any angle. But some angles are better than others. Not only must the angle be carefully chosen but also the altitude—your distance from the observations. For example, to answer questions about the growth of learning of schools full of students, you need a lot of altitude to rise above the detail of student-level data and see the patterns visible over multiple years.

Consider from what vantage point you need to stand to best view the evidence required to answer this question about math mastery of fourth graders: "Is the most current group of our state's fourth-graders scoring higher or lower in math than fourth-graders in 2015?" Your statewide assessment is well suited for this. It has probably been a stable test since 2015. It is scaled to record fluctuating levels of mastery. So, the vantage point to take to answer this question is the cross-sectional angle. You need to see the results of six years of fourth graders (allowing for one year of no tests during the pandemic).

What do we mean by the term "cross-sectional?" It means we're taking snapshots every year of different cohorts of fourth-grade students. Imagine you're standing on a riverbank taking photographs of students as they slowly flow by on inner tubes, kayaks and canoes. We take the 2021 snapshot of fourth graders, then the 2020 snapshot and so on, and then compare those snapshots from 2015 to 2021 (of course, taking the pandemic into account). The key to a cross-sectional vantage point is that we stand still as students move past us, and every so often, we take a picture of a bunch of *different kids at the same grade level*.

But suppose you wanted to see how much growth in math the students in your state have attained between grade 3 and grade 7 for the most recent three graduating class cohorts. This would require tracking those cohorts of kids over time, what is called a quasi-longitudinal view. The graduating Class of 2024 was in third grade in 2015 and seventh grade in 2019, and we'd have five annual test results in hand. For the classes of 2025 and 2026, we'd also have five test events in hand. We'd need three observers in our team, one for each graduating class. They'd need to be marathon runners, because they'd be running along the riverbank for five years, to keep up with each of the three graduating class cohorts.

It's called quasi-longitudinal because the students in each graduating class aren't exactly the same in successive years. Kids transfer into and out of each graduating class. This view is of the more or less the *same kids at successive grade levels*. If we had the ability to exclude those kids who transfer into and out of each cohort, we'd have a truly longitudinal view.

The world can look very different from these two vantage points. Be careful where you stand when answering questions that compare students over time. It is not uncommon for the cross-sectional and quasi-longitudinal views to lead to very different stories. In the next section, you'll find examples of both views and see what a difference this choice of vantage points can make.

Evidence not matched to the question itself

There are many variations on this type of error. The one I find to be the costliest and the most painful to watch as it is repeated year after year is the measurement of learning growth by comparing *entirely different groups of students to each other*. If your question is "How much growth in math knowledge and skill have our school's students gained, compared to the prior two years?" the usual answer follows the logic of an annual snapshot, the cross-sectional view (see Figure 2.7).

- Step #1: take the median scale scores of this year's third, fourth and fifth graders and sum them. (This assumes that only students in these three grade levels were tested.)
- Step #2: average those three median scale scores if the number of kids in each grade level is about the same. If not, you'll need to calculate a weighted average that accounts for the different number of kids at each grade level.
- Step #3: do the same with last year's third, fourth, and fifth graders.

- Step #4: repeat the process with the scores of the prior-prior-year's students. Now you have results over three years' time for the third, fourth and fifth graders.
- Step #5: compare the average scale score of this year's students from last year's and those of students in the year before that, and hope the current year's number is highest. If it is, you conclude this year's students have scored higher, and you state that *the school* has shown positive growth.

There's nothing wrong with this annual snapshot, as long as you remember that what you've done is take a *changing group of students* over time and averaged their test results, and then compared them. This view of the evidence of changing groups of students doesn't really answer the growth specific question we started with.

The problem is in the question. The question leads the analyst who is building the evidence from data to effectively put all the current year's

	2016	2017	2018	2019
3rd grade	2432	2402	2426	2430
4th grade	2438	2454	2464	2452
5th grade	2472	2498	2474	2486
Average of scores of grades 3, 4 and 5 (equal enrollment in all grades)	2447	2451	2455	2456

Figure 2.7 Cross-sectional view of math Smarter Balanced scores for students in a hypothetical K–5 elementary school district

Question: How did kids in our district do in math this year compared to prior years? Answer: about the same in 2019 as in 2018 and 2017 (comparing scale scores in gray), when imprecision and uncertainty are taken into account. This cross-sectional view of test results compares successive years of entirely different students' results.

students in one barrel and put all of last year's students in another barrel and the prior-prior year's students in a third barrel. Then seeing how these students' scores compared over the span of a year seems as simple as comparing the current year barrel from the prior years' barrels. If students were identical, this might be okay. But *students are not identical*. Treating them as if they were leads to this error.

If we restated the question more carefully, this error could be avoided. What if the question were: "How much growth in math skills have this year's fifth-graders attained, compared to their scores in fourth grade and third grade?" For comparison purposes, let's also see how that growth compares to the results for students making the same grade-level transitions in each of the prior few years. This approach would require tracking the same students over time. To summarize their results school-wide, you would follow a different logic (assuming your scale score intervals allow for cross-grade-level comparisons, something called "vertical equating" by psychometricians).

- Step 1: take all students who attended grades 3, 4, and 5 in your school, and completed fifth grade in 2019. Label this cohort Class of 2026. (They appear in light gray in Figure 2.8.)
- Step 2: do the same for those students who were fifth graders in 2018. Label this cohort the Class of 2025. (They appear in dark gray.)
- Step 3: calculate the average scale score gain for each of these two graduating class cohorts for the grade 3-to-4 transition, and again for the grade 4-to-5 transition.
- Step 4: if the enrollment of the two cohorts is about the same, and if you see moderate levels of student mobility, you may average the gain across years for each of those two cohorts, and then compare the difference. If their enrollments differ, you should calculate a weighted average.

In this approach, you are looking at *the same students over time*. The group you're analyzing (stat geeks may call them the "entity") is stable. The students in each cohort are the same, so you know whose results you're analyzing. This is a longitudinal approach, and it can be stretched to cover any number of years. It is best suited for answering questions about growth or progress. What a different math education these two cohorts of students have experienced. The kids in the Class of 2025 attained half the growth in

Figure 2.8 Quasi-longitudinal view of math Smarter Balanced scores for students in a hypothetical K–5 elementary school district

Question: How much growth in math did kids in each class cohort attain in our district over three years? Answer: they showed very different levels of growth. The students who were in fifth grade in 2019 (light gray) attained twice the growth of the students one year ahead of them (dark gray). Their scores were low in 2017 at the end of third grade. But they had an excellent fourth-grade experience, and their scores soared. This quasi-longitudinal view of test results compares the same students' results over three years.

math (42 scale score points from grades 3 to 5) than the kids in the Class of 2026 (84 scale score points).

Look how different this view of graduating class cohorts is from our first example, what we called the annual snapshot or cross-sectional view. The longitudinal view of graduating class cohorts compared three years of scores for more or less the same students. (Mobility, the transfer of kids into and out of the cohort, makes the cohort slightly different each year.) Students are stable. The curriculum is stable. The teachers change slightly year to year. What's being measured, then, is mostly their experience in math class from the end of grade 3 to the end of grade 5.

One precaution. You may be accustomed to using the "percent-meeting-standard" or "percent proficient" metric. If so, the arithmetic differs because you can't treat percentages like scale score integers. (Averaging percentages is a mistake. But averaging the number of kids who met standard is fine.) More importantly, the measure itself only describes those who have crossed a magic line. It is what stat geeks call a "threshold boundary" measure, and it only describes a single (and limited) attribute

Twisting test results

Entity	Metric	Vantage point	Duration	Context	Scoring method
Students (individual)	Scale score	Cross-sectional	1 year	School/district alone	Norm referenced
Subgroup	Percentage of students meeting standard	Quasi-longitudinal	2 years	Your district	Criterion referenced
Classroom		Longitudinal	3 years	Your county	
Grade level	Average/Median		4 years	Similar schools/districts	
School/district	Error margin		5 years +	Nearby schools/districts	
Graduating class cohort	Spread or standard deviation			Statewide average	

Figure 2.9 Six elements you should know about any assessment interpretation that claims to measure progress

If you can identify these attributes of an interpretation of a test that mentions growth or progress, you'll be less likely to misunderstand the claim.

of some students' scores. It decidedly *does not serve as a measure of all students' results* (see Figure 2.9).

☞ **Tip:** before you answer any questions about the meaning of test results, especially those involving change or growth, *slow down so you can identify the six elements that are part of every analysis.* Be mindful of your vantage point and evaluate the quality of the evidence before you answer. Every answer you give will require your choosing one variable in each of the following six categories: entity, metric, benchmark, method, time and context. Entity describes who or what is in the spotlight. Metric is the unit of measurement. Method is what we've called the vantage point, the angle from which you view the evidence. The benchmark is a function of the test's purpose and its scoring approach. Are students scored in comparison to each other, or is student mastery of standards being gauged? Time is the period over which growth is being measured. Context is a comparative framing of the evidence that enables you to put the results into a sentence that helps your audience understand the relative meaning of the results. Only after you understand the question you're trying to answer should you select the variables under each of these six categories to form your answer.

Excessive certainty

Beware of literal-minded assessment directors. An intolerance for ambiguity and adherence to dogma are sure warning signs that the wrong person is holding that job. Assessments *always produce fuzzy results*. The right person to assign the big job of interpreting test results is a person with a tolerance for ambiguity and an appreciation for assessments of high quality. The operational need by teachers to group students leads them to use tests as sorting machines. Sorting doesn't coexist with ambiguity easily. It causes friction and frayed nerve endings. But sorting is necessary, and it's best done with the ambiguity of test results in mind. When high-quality tests are able to classify students into performance levels (quartiles or quantiles) correctly just 80–85 percent of the time, you need people who can cope with uncertainty and who are ready to bring several forms of evidence to the table when making sorting decisions.

One of the deformations of the accountability era that resulted from excessively literal-minded administrators running curriculum and instruction was the focus on what they called "bubble kids." The notion was meant to describe students whose interim or benchmark test results put them close to a magic line (the line of "proficiency" or "meeting standard") that teachers wanted them to cross. This resulted in teachers paying less attention to students farther from the magic line, certainly an educational malpractice at worst and an unethical practice at best. But if teachers were more assessment literate, they'd have had a better grasp of the ambiguity of a student's score, especially on the SBAC or PARCC assessments. The imprecision of results on those tests was often large enough to span levels. So, true results would recur within that range of imprecision about 68 percent of the time. In other words, a "bubble kid" who scored a bit below the "meeting standard" line might have scored above the line if she took the test in the morning instead of the afternoon, or on a Thursday instead of a Wednesday.

The major test publishers include what they call classification error rates in their technical manuals. It is common to find a 25–30 percent classification error rate in the middle bands of a range of test scores—and that's for a standardized assessment with 45–65 questions. In truth, there were many kids scoring above those magic lines who might really be scoring in the lower band. Conversely, there were many kids scoring below the magic line who might really have true scores above the line, if the error margin were regarded seriously.

Misunderstanding the test's scale properties

What does a unit on a scale really mean? We know when we get on our bathroom scale that we're going to get an answer in pounds. When we measure the height of our children as they grow, we'll get an answer in inches or centimeters. But what is the value of a scale score unit on a math test?

Does the scale allow for cross-grade-level measures of growth? The test must have been designed intentionally to make that possible. It's an attribute of the test called "vertical equating" and without it, cross-grade-level comparisons remain off-limits.

Does the scale assign equal value to points in the earlier and later grade levels? Most tests don't. You can expect to see much higher scale score growth in the earlier grade levels than in high school, simply because younger kids gain mastery faster. And reading is a skill that most students have mastered by third grade. In reading, for most students there's not much gain to measure from grade 7 to grade 12. You should expect older students to show much smaller scale score gains in every subject than younger students, as a result.

How wide is the scale? Wider scales contain more units between the lowest and highest possible scale scores. In theory, that enables them to measure competency with greater precision. But in practice, measurement of learning is really *estimation*—and that's okay! There's a practical limit to what a unit on any scale means. For a clue to the limits of your district's tests, look at the standard error and confidence intervals in the technical manual.

What can be done to reduce inferential errors?

Many critics of testing have exploited embarrassing moments to recommend doing away with the big accountability tests given mostly in the spring. They argue that if tests contain design errors, or ambiguous test questions, or are inexact, or are too hard to interpret, or take up too much time, they should be abandoned altogether. Some test critics have pointed to major cheating scandals and blamed test-centric accountability systems for putting too much pressure on teachers and administrators. All those who wish to do away with testing altogether deserve a debate. We propose to give them one.

We favor improving the quality of assessments, the uses to which they are put and the quality of human judgment when interpreting results. Toward that end, we offer five changes to the ways that the education profession manages these measures of learning. They are, admittedly, blue-sky changes. None of them are easy. All of them return a bushel basket of benefits at relatively low cost. We are not the first to suggest these remedies. So, with no claim for originality, here are our recommendations in brief. You'll find these ideas detailed in fuller form in Chapter 7.

First, we'd like to see schools of education require that their courses of study for both teachers and leaders include quantitative measurement and assessment courses, grounded in the realities of life in schools: planning, program evaluation, instructional efficacy. Ellen B. Mandinach and Edith S. Gummer are two scholars whose books have documented the role that schools of education play in keeping their graduates in the dark about data and assessment fundamentals.[15] Popham's critical views of schools of education are reflected in his views of their graduates. "Put simply, most of today's educators know almost nothing about educational assessment."[16] Schools of education simply must stop sending data- and assessment-illiterate educators into the field.

Second, we'd like to see administrative credential programs require certification in data literacy and assessment literacy. Principals and district office leaders, like doctors, need to be able to speak the language of numbers, grasp the fundamentals of assessment, reason logically, think probabilistically and interpret the meaning of measures of learning aware of the inexact nature of the measurements they hold in their hands.

Third, we'd like to see state departments of education do much more to communicate clearly and fully the meaning of test results and disclose the "fuzzy factor" of imprecision and uncertainty. Why not also run help desks that are prepared to deliver answers to any principal or district administrator with a data or assessment question?

Fourth, we'd like to see districts ask their assessment directors to shoulder more of the responsibility for interpreting assessment results and take much of the burden off the shoulders of teachers. Assessment directors should be builders of evidence, providing decision support to others, combining evidence intelligently so students get the right kind of instruction at the right time in the right amount.

Fifth, we'd like to see assessment firms invest in higher-quality report designs and then defend these better-quality assessments against attack by the anti-testing crowd. If the test publishers formed a cooperative association and funded it to educate the voting public, opinion influencers and legislators, perhaps they'd enjoy greater acceptance by those they serve.

Closing thoughts on the mismeasurement of learning

John Hattie, in his book *Visible Learning*, calls teaching an "immature profession." Ironically, it may be the younger generation that helps the profession grow up. The younger leaders, principals and administrators who are at the start of their careers are steeped in the empirical intellectual tradition, welcome the appropriate use of technology and speak the language of numbers. They are prepared to recognize their data and assessment knowledge gaps. Many are moving on their own to close those gaps, and some are pressing their professional associations to do the same. This is heartening.

The medical profession, only 150 years ago, was filled with doctors whose education was rooted in pre-Socratic ideas. They treated patients with leeches and mercury, hoping to correct imbalances in the body's fluids. The science of medicine has advanced since then in what seems like a quantum leap. The statistical profession, for the past 100 years, had embraced an idea about the importance of "statistical significance" that was only overturned in March 2019. Now the journal of the American Statistical Association won't accept articles that include measures of statistical significance in their findings. Indeed, the advance of good ideas in other professions fuels my belief that the barriers to quantitative skills and assessment-savvy and empirical methods in the education management profession can be pushed out of the way, as well.

Links to extend your reading and interaction

The following link will carry you to additional resources, writing and dialogue about the topics discussed in this chapter. You'll also find live versions of the data visualizations in this chapter that are ready for your interaction.

We welcome your comments and continued exploration. You'll find all this on the chapter specific page on the book's website: https://www.k12measures.com/ch2

Questions to spark discussion

District leaders

1. What are the top five responsibilities of your assessment director? If you don't have an assessment director, think about the person responsible for assessment. Does that list include interpreting the meaning of test results for instructional leaders? If so, ask your assessment director what portion of her work year is spent doing that.

2. How does your district determine whether a student needs support gaining mastery of academic English? What is the quality of evidence used when you make that determination? Out of every 100 students you evaluate, how many do you think are identified as "English learners" who have the same level of mastery of English as your district's typical English-only students? Conversely, how many students who really need these supports do you believe you miss? Is that balance of false positives and false negatives one you're comfortable with?

3. Categorize the assessments your district is using in grades K–8, and list each of them in only one of the following four columns, based on their primary purpose: (1) identifying those students who are lagging the most or the most advanced; (2) diagnosing a skill or knowledge deficit specific enough that a teacher will be able to know what to do; (3) estimating grade-level mastery of subject matter or measuring academic growth of individual students; and (4) any other purpose. If you wanted to list one particular assessment in more than one of these categories, explain why. Now ask a colleague to do the same exercise, and compare your answers.

Principals and other site leaders

4. When a teacher assigns a student a grade at the end of the year that is out of line with the test results for that student, and the parents of that student request a meeting with you to discuss whether the grade was fair, what do you do to prepare? How much weight do you give to the test results? What questions do you ask the teacher?

5. When you're building your site plan for the year ahead, what evidence do you want to see to determine if you have one curricular strength or weakness? From what vantage point do you want to view it? How exactly do you determine relative strength or weakness? Where should you turn for additional evidence to corroborate your findings?

6. If you're an elementary school principal, do you know which of your early grade-level teachers is best at teaching reading? If you're a middle school principal, do you know which teacher is best at teaching math? How do you know this to be true? To what degree does this star teacher excel? How confident are you of these findings?

School board trustees

7. You are evaluating your superintendent, an annual event in your district of 1,200 students. In her prior review, she pledged to improve the teaching of reading. As evidence of success, she has shown an increase in the percentage of third, fourth and fifth graders who met state standards for English language arts. You're leading the review, and you don't think those results are sufficient to support the superintendent's claim of victory. You want to see more evidence, but what should you request?

8. Your unified school district has been scolded by your state's department of education for your students' math scores. They

fall in the lowest fifth of your state, based on the percentage of kids meeting or exceeding state standards. This has tarnished more than the reputation of your district. It has also tarnished your town's reputation, and the mayor has told you so. But you're well aware of the backstory. Kids are starting school with lagging math and reading skills. The math program relies heavily on real-world math problems, which require lots of reading. But most important, you see one-sixth of your students transfer out each year, to be replaced by kids who transfer in. So, your student turnover is quite high. Despite that, your students' rate of growth in math is strong. More than two-thirds of the kids are attaining more than the equivalent of a year's growth, measured in scale scores. You want the district to prepare a response you can share with local leaders and media. What is the evidence that would be the best counterargument to the state's accountability judgment?

9. You and your fellow board members want the district's leadership to take planning more seriously. You're especially interested in their bringing higher-quality evidence to the plan, especially when justifying their case for focusing resources on one or two areas needing improvement. To give the planning team a heads-up about your concerns, you're writing a memo that flags problems in prior plans and defining the attributes of higher quality evidence. When defining the evidence about student learning gains, what do you want to see? What are the attributes of higher-quality assessment evidence you want to see in the new plan?

Notes

1. Website of the National Center for Fair and Open Testing is www.fairtest.org.
2. W. James Popham, "Why Assessment Illiteracy Is Professional Suicide," *Educational Leadership* 62, no. 1 (September 2004): 82–3.
3. W. James Popham, "The Right Test for the Wrong Reason," *Phi Delta Kappan* 96, no. 1 (August 2014): 46–52.

4. American Educational Research Association et al., eds., *Standards for Educational and Psychological Testing* (Washington DC: American Educational Research Association, 2014).

5. Steven Rasmussen, "Smarter Balanced Tests—One Year Later, Same Shameful Tests," SR Education Consultants (blog), March 2015, http://mathedconsulting.com/2016/03/smarter-balanced-tests-one-year-later-same-shameful-tests/.

6. Steven Rasmussen, "The Smarter Balanced Common Core Mathematics Tests Are Fatally Flawed and Should Not Be Used: An In-Depth Critique of the Smarter Balanced Tests for Mathematics," SR Education Associates, March 2015, http://mathedconsulting.com/wp-content/uploads/2015/04/Common-Core-Tests-Fatally-Flawed.pdf.

7. Sally E. Shaywitz, "Dyslexia," *New England Journal of Medicine* 338, no. 5 (January 29, 1998): 307–12, https://doi.org/10.1056/NEJM199801293380507.

8. John Jacob Cannell, *How Public Educators Cheat on Standardized Tests* (Albuquerque: Friends of Education, 1989), https://files.eric.ed.gov/fulltext/ED314454.pdf.

9. *Standards for Educational and Psychological Testing.*

10. Rankin, *Standards for Reporting Data to Educators.*

11. Sarah Schwartz, "The Most Popular Reading Programs Aren't Backed by Science," *Education Week*, December 3, 2019, www.edweek.org/teaching-learning/the-most-popular-reading-programs-arent-backed-by-science/2019/12.

12. *Standards for Educational and Psychological Testing*, 11.

13. Morgan Polikoff and others, "Letter to the California State Board of Education," July 4, 2018, https://morganpolikoff.com/2018/07/04/letter-to-the-ca-state-board-of-education/.

14. Morgan Polikoff, Shira Korn, and Russell McFall, "In Need of Improvement? Assessing the California Dashboard after One Year," *Getting Down to Facts II*, Policy Analysis for California Education and Stanford University, September 2018, https://gettingdowntofacts.com/sites/default/files/2018-09/GDTFII_Report_Polikoff.pdf.

15. The resistance to change inside schools of education may be familiar to those inside higher education. But they are not as visible to those outside the castle gates. Three of their books are relevant to the barriers of progress inside schools of education. Ellen B. Mandinach and Edith S.

Gummer, *The Ethical Use of Data in Education: Promoting Responsible Policies and Practices* (New York: Teachers College Press, 2021). *Data Literacy for Educators: Making It Count in Teacher Preparation and Practice* (New York: Teachers College Press, 2016). Edited by them is this collection, *Data for Continuous Programmatic Improvement: Steps Colleges of Education Must Take to Become a Data Culture* (New York: Routledge, 2018).

16. Popham, *Unlearned Lessons*, 126.

References

American Educational Research Association et al., eds. *Standards for Educational and Psychological Testing*. Washington, DC: American Educational Research Association, 2014.

Cannell, John Jacob. *How Public Educators Cheat on Standardized Tests*. Albuquerque: Friends of Education, 1989. https://files.eric.ed.gov/fulltext/ED314454.pdf.

Hattie, John. *Visible Learning: A Synthesis of Over 800 Meta-Analyses Relating to Achievement*. New York: Routledge, 2009.

Mandinach, Ellen G., and Edith S. Gummer, eds. *Data for Continuous Programmatic Improvement: Steps Colleges of Education Must Take to Become a Data Culture*. New York: Routledge, 2018.

Mandinach, Ellen G., and Edith S. Gummer. *Data Literacy for Educators: Making It Count in Teacher Preparation and Practice*. New York: Teachers College Press, 2016.

Mandinach, Ellen G., and Edith S. Gummer. *The Ethical Use of Data in Education: Promoting Responsible Policies and Practices*. New York: Teachers College Press, 2021.

Popham, W. James. "The Right Test for the Wrong Reason." *Phi Delta Kappan* 96, no. 1 (August 30, 2014): 46–52.

Popham, W. James. "Why Assessment Illiteracy Is Professional Suicide." *Educational Leadership Magazine*, ASCD 62, no. 1 (September 2004): 82–3.

Rankin, Jenny. "Over-the-Counter Data's Impact on Educators' Data Analysis Accuracy." diss., Northcentral University, Arizona, 2013. https://pqdtopen.proquest.com/doc/1459258514.html?FMT=ABS.

Rankin, Jenny. "Remedying Educators' Data Analysis Errors with Over-the-Counter Data." *CCNews: Newsletter of the California Council on Teacher Education* 24, no. 4 (December 2013): 14–21. http://ccte.org/wp-content/pdfs-newsletters/ccte-news-2013-winter.pdf.

Rankin, Jenny. *Standards for Reporting Data to Educators*. New York: Routledge, 2016.

Rasmussen, Steven. "The Smarter Balanced Common Core Mathematics Tests Are Fatally Flawed and Should Not Be Used: An In-Depth Critique of the Smarter Balanced Tests for Mathematics." SR Education Associates, March 2015. http://mathedconsulting.com/wp-content/uploads/2015/04/Common-Core-Tests-Fatally-Flawed.pdf.

Rasmussen, Steven. "Smarter Balanced Tests—One Year Later, Same Shameful Tests." http://mathedconsulting.com/2016/03/smarter-balanced-tests-one-year-later-same-shameful-tests/.

Shaywitz, Sally E. "Dyslexia." *New England Journal of Medicine* 338, no. 5 (January 29, 1998): 307–12. https://doi.org/10.1056/NEJM199801293380507.

"SLDS Data Use Standards: Knowledge, Skills, and Professional Behaviors for Effective Data Use—Master Standards for School and District Leadership." Washington, DC: National Center for Education Statistics, U.S. Department of Education, 2016.

Wainer, Howard. *Uneducated Guesses: Using Evidence to Uncover Misguided Education Policies*. Princeton, NJ: Princeton University Press, 2011.

The hidden hazards of interpreting graduation rates

We'd like to find one aspect of a school's vital signs that is unambiguous, easy to count and likely to be interpreted correctly. I wish I could tell you that high school graduation rates fit these three criteria. But graduation rates are noisy, messy and filled with ambiguity. However, by becoming aware of where the noise in the signal is hiding, by seeing what's messy and ambiguous, you can become a smarter consumer of this vital sign. And if you're a district or school leader, you can boost your ability to see your students' progress more clearly and take steps to pave their many paths to graduation.

Numerators and denominators

The results you get when you're figuring out graduation and dropout rates is just a function of what goes up top in the numerator and what goes below in the denominator. Pay attention to who's counted in each. When you are asked about your graduation rate, you'd do well to back up and explain what goes into it before you explain what comes out of it.

Denominators

Let's start with denominators. Today, the U.S. Dept. of Education requires that all states use ninth-grade enrollment for a graduating class as the denominator. That makes the graduation rate a measure of a group of students who move more or less together toward graduation. This is also

Hazards of interpreting graduation rates

Table 3.1 Cumulative impact of 15 percent annual student turnover on a single graduating class cohort over four years

Composition of Class of 2020	9th grade	10th grade	11th grade	12th grade
Initial enrollment declining by 15 percent per year	300	255	217	184
New student enrollments (cumulative)	0	45	83	116
Total students enrolled	300	300	300	300
Percent of students remaining from initial enrollment	100%	85%	72%	61%

called a cohort. But note that it's not a perfectly static one. Students transfer out to other schools. Other students transfer in. Some students leave school altogether, what we call dropouts. This migration results in a less than perfect grad rate measure. That's why this measure of a group of graduating seniors, who are not exactly the same students as the group of ninth graders four years prior, is called by researchers a "quasi-longitudinal" measure. If they were exactly the same students, the measure could be called a truly "longitudinal" measure.

Let's take note of the impact of student mobility on a mid-size high school whose 2020 graduating class cohort started with 300 students in 2016–2017. If the attrition rate for this hypothetical Class of 2020 above is just 15 percent, and if newly arriving students arrive at exactly the same pace as students transfer out of the school, by the end of their senior year, only 61 percent of the students in that class will have started four years prior.

The higher your student mobility rate, the more your graduation rate is colored by the quality of education your incoming transfer students received elsewhere. One could argue that your students' graduation rate is most fully "owned" by your district for those students who have been with you for all 13 years. If that seems too dramatic, consider the high school view. If you are a high school principal, and half your graduating seniors have been with you for just two years, is it fair that your school receive all the credit (and all the blame) for their having graduated? Accountability can't be parsed into perfectly tidy portions. But as principal, you'd be wise to pay attention to the difference in outcomes of those students who have been enrolled continuously since ninth grade versus those who transferred in at eleventh grade. As superintendent, you could look at graduation outcomes for those who have been enrolled in your district since kindergarten, compared to those enrolled during the middle school years.

Districts serving a community based on an agricultural economy that depends on migrant labor see a very high student mobility rate. Schools serving communities that depend on large-scale employers in struggling industries may see layoffs and plant closures, causing many families to move away. Certainly, in the Great Recession of 2008, many blue-collar suburbs saw residents lose their jobs, lose their homes, pack up and move. Lots of migration out, combined with little migration in, results in a distortion of graduation rates.

Dropouts are not subtracted from the denominator of ninth-grade enrollment. Each student who was enrolled as a freshman whose family leaves your district requires tracing to see if the student reenrolled elsewhere. If the family moved within your state, that task should be traceable through your state's student longitudinal data system (SLDS), as long as the exiting student reenrolled in a public school. But if the student enrolled in a private school without telling you, or if the family moved out-of-state, you may never learn what happened. And that usually requires that your district assign that student an exit code that is treated as a dropout. Those are the rules of the game, as the U.S. Dept. of Education writes them. If your district is lucky enough to have a staff person in the front office with the skills of a private detective and the instincts of a bounty hunter, you'll find more of those students who left your district without notice. Your district's reward: fewer dropouts and an improved graduation rate.

You will need to adjust that ninth-grade cohort as students transfer in and out. Additions to the graduating class cohort result when students transfer in. For example, if a student enrolls in your district for the first time as a junior, you will add him to that graduating class cohort as a transfer-in. True, he will have been in school elsewhere for 11 years. Your district will educate him for another two years. But when he graduates, your high school and district get credit for that event. If your district is fully in control of a student's education, from kindergarten through high school, don't you believe you should "own" fully the organizational share of the outcome?

Hazards of interpreting graduation rates

Note that if your district includes a continuation high school (or a transfer school as they are known in New York), the question of when you transfer struggling students out of their comprehensive high into the continuation high will be reflected in the graduation rates of the last high school they attend. Control by site or district leaders of a student's assigned high school is a power that can be used well for the benefit of the student. But this power can also be misused to make a comprehensive high school's grad rate look too good. (Later in this chapter, you'll find observations on the unsuitability of traditional measures of graduation to continuation high schools.)

> ☞ **Tip:** take a look at the graduation and dropout rates of students who have been schooled in your district for eight years or more. See how that compares to students who have been continuously enrolled for fewer years. The Texas organization, Just-4-Kids, developed a method for comparing "stayers" and "leavers." It provided a valuable perspective on whether kids who were in your schools from kindergarten fared better or worse than those who were schooled, in part, elsewhere.

Numerators

Who's counted as a graduate, and who is not? Being clear about this is as important as being clear about the denominator—the base group or entity against which you're measuring those who graduate. It seems self-evident. Certainly, all states must count those who receive a diploma. But let's be thorough and consider who may not get a diploma. When we're taking stock of such an important measure, every change to the numerator matters. Let's look at three categories of *students who are excluded from the numerator*.

It took the U.S. Department of Education until the 2010–2011 school year to put a stake in the ground to define what a graduation rate would measure. They called it the "adjusted cohort graduation rate" and defined it as follows:

> The number of students who graduate in 4 years with a regular high school diploma divided by the number of students who form the adjusted cohort for

the graduating class. From the beginning of ninth grade (or the earliest high school grade), students who are entering that grade for the first time form a cohort that is "adjusted" by adding any students who subsequently transfer into the cohort and subtracting any students who subsequently transfer out, emigrate to another country, or die.[1]

First, what about students who want to take a fifth year to complete high school? Perhaps they were slower learners. Or perhaps they had job responsibilities to help their parents make ends meet. Or perhaps they were out with a serious illness for half of their senior year and needed an additional semester to make up the missing work. Or perhaps they were just a few units short of meeting the unit requirement. Or perhaps they needed a fifth year because they were unable to pass your state's end-of-course math exam, even though they earned a B grade in their coursework. Students like these should be counted in a five-year graduation rate. Indeed, most states have a way of doing just that.

Second, what about students who don't actually receive a diploma but instead opt to leave high school early without yet having earned the course credits that meet your state and district requirements? They might have checked out because they were overwhelmed by bullies at school. Or they might have gotten sick of school and grown bored being taught what they already know. Some students pursue a general equivalence diploma (GED), known in some states as a general education diploma, and it requires that students show what they know by taking either the GED exam from the GED Testing Service or the HiSET exam from the Educational Testing Service (ETS). States may have different rules that account for this early graduate differently. But the U.S. Department of Education rules on this are clear. They don't allow this student to be counted as a graduate even if he's earned a general equivalence diploma. Their regs are covered in a 32-page document they published in 2017: "Every Student Succeeds Act High School Graduation Rate Non-Regulatory Guidance."[2]

If a student graduates one year early from his own high school, completing the required courses and acquiring the number of units needed for graduation, this student remains in the numerator and denominator for his graduating class cohort. In effect, his graduation in three years is treated as if he graduated in four years.

Third, what about special education students, those whose learning disabilities make it impossible for them to take the courses required for graduation and pass them all? States have made provisions for this, most of them very particular. While states have provided varied pathways to a diploma for their special education students, the accountability rules in those states also differ widely. Some include special education students in the numerator. Some do not, defining their graduation rate for accountability purposes to describe only the general education program. But again, the U.S. Department of Education rules on this are uniform for all states. Even if a special education student meets the goals in her Individual Education Plan (IEP), that doesn't count as a graduation event in the school's statistics. But if a special education student with the most severe form of cognitive disabilities meets a state's requirement for an alternate diploma, that student is allowed to be counted as a graduate.

The student's point of view

Let's think about this from the student's point of view for a moment. What must a student do in your district and state to earn a diploma and be counted in that numerator? Again, the variation among districts and states is vast. Let's list the possible range of requirements.

Think of all the adult decision-makers whose judgment the student depends upon to make it to the graduation stage. *Teachers* decide what grades to assign a student. In some districts, this is within the strict limits of board policy. In other districts, it's left to teacher discretion, and at the high school level, some teachers relish the freedom to define their grading rubrics as they see fit. *Department heads* in some high schools decide whether to accept the middle school accomplishments on a freshman's transcript. In San Francisco, during the superintendency of Ramon Cortines, he discovered that one high school was requiring that incoming freshmen take algebra, even if they'd taken it and passed with flying colors in eighth grade. When he unearthed this particular principal's Lone Ranger approach, he firmly laid down the law and required every high school to accept middle school algebra as meeting the requirements.

The *district* has a lot of discretion in determining the criteria for graduation. The board can establish the minimum number of units required, as long as it's higher than the state requirement. In California, most districts require at least 210 units, a policy set by the school board. However, as of September 2021, the California Department of Education required only

130 units and the completion of 13 courses. A district's leadership can determine the minimal grade a student needs to earn in order to pass a course and also establish breadth requirements—courses a student must take in addition to the state required courses.

The *state* is the third party with the power to set the mark students must meet to earn a diploma. This can include minimum units required for graduation and specific courses to be taken. States will require that students clear some of these hurdles, but perhaps not all of them.

- Take a number of required courses and pass them;
- Attain a score on an end-of-course test in a key course or two high enough to clear a threshold of minimal competency;
- Take a number of elective courses, often meeting a breadth requirement, and earn a passing grade;
- Earn a number of units as a result of taking and passing those courses;
- Meet performance assessment standards (in some districts); and
- Pass a high school exit exam.

According to *Education Next*, 11 states still require that students pass a high school exit exam, applicable to the Class of 2020.[3] This minimum proficiency test was more fashionable between 2002 and 2014. In 2002, more than half the states required that high school students pass an exit exam to graduate. In those 11 states where they are still in place, these tests can be the sole reason why a student is unable to graduate.[4]

Consider the impact of this exit exam in California. From 2006 through 2016, the barrier blocking many California students from graduating was the requirement to pass the math portion of the California High School Exit Exam (CAHSEE). It required demonstrating mastery of eighth-grade algebra. But that course, Algebra I, which included factoring polynomial equations, had been a sticking point for many. Students who may have been good at basic algebra but not so good at the tougher content might have been unable to graduate. In fact, in California, in the last year the CAHSEE was administered (2015), only 386,369 out of 456,354 (85 percent) passed the math portion. Imagine the frustration for the students that year who weren't allowed to graduate. Their frustration led to much political friction, and eventually a bill to end the California exit exam became law in 2015.

What makes fair comparisons challenging

Variations in districts' graduation requirements

When teachers in different high schools in the same district use different grading standards, this will make the meaning of a diploma a little different in those schools. But when districts use their autonomy to set the bar for graduation higher—either by requiring more units or by requiring that students pass tougher courses—the meaning of a diploma begins to differ district to district. The higher a district sets the bar from the state's standard, the greater the difference in the diploma's meaning.

The graduation rate in too many states ignores the quality of student work and the rigor of courses taken, and only regards the quantity of units obtained in four years. Happily, some states like Indiana and New York have tiered diplomas. Indiana offers four tiers: the general diploma, the Core 40, the Core 40 with technical honors and the Core 40 with academic honors. The "40" refers to the number of academic units a student must earn.[5] New York offers three tiers: a Regents Diploma, a Regents Diploma with Honors, and a Regents Diploma with Advanced Designation. On top of that, they offer two subject specialty diplomas, the Regents Diploma with Advanced Designation with an annotation that denotes mastery in science, and another that marks mastery in math.

If the point of comparing graduation rates is to see how your district or school is doing at getting kids through four years of high school and earning a diploma, and if your state, like most, allows districts to establish their own graduation requirements, then you'll have to accept the fuzziness of the comparison. It's neither clean nor exact. It may be as much an expression of a district's standards as it is the persistence of its students and their mastery of course content.

This is not an argument for disregarding graduation rates. Rather, we're encouraging you to be street-smart about interpreting graduation rates with an eye to their unavoidable imprecision—what we call *fuzziness*. If you interpret differences in graduation rates using both street smarts and technical smarts, you'll be ahead of the game. This will spare you the embarrassment of boasting that your district's graduation rate is two percentage points above your county's average or offering public self-criticism when it's two percentage points below, when the meaning of that small difference may be highly questionable. The other benefit of being street-smart about interpreting this fuzzy graduation rate is knowing that if your district or high school has been scolded by your state accountability system because you are two percentage points shy of a threshold, you may have good reason to push back.

District dishonesty and academic fraud

For a small number of districts, there's an added factor that warrants attention: district dishonesty. District and school leaders can "cook the books" in a variety of ways, pushing students to graduate with a diploma in hand when they're far from capable of reading, writing or doing arithmetic anywhere close to grade level. Over the last 20 years, reporters have spotted many examples of unethical behavior. While bad actors are rare, systems whose rules produce bad events are all too common. Two tactics are worth mentioning so you can be alert to them: push-outs and false credit recovery.

Push-outs

In New York City in 2003, *"push-outs"* became a new term, jumping from the small world of education jargon into the general lexicon. It described a student who was encouraged to leave high school by a counselor, principal or teacher. Many of the students nudged out the door found their way to either another school or a General Education Diploma (GED). But others never returned to school. While they became an official dropout statistic, the human reality is that they were pushed out.

This news story from 2003, headlined "City to Track Why Students Leave School," from the *New York Times*, described the chancellor's response when the push-out problem led to a lawsuit filed by Advocates for Children on behalf of hundreds of students at one Brooklyn high school.

> This summer, in response to charges that New York City schools push out tens of thousands of students who have fallen behind their expected grade—and put them in bureaucratic categories where they will not be counted as dropouts—Chancellor Joel I. Klein acknowledged that there was a widespread problem that was a "tragedy" for many students and promised to fix it.

The day after The New York Times ran a lengthy article describing the problem, the chancellor sent a message to principals stating that he was committed to accurate reporting of the number of students who drop out or are discharged from the schools.

"It is a disservice to our students and ourselves to rely on shortcuts or play number games in order to make things look better than they really are," he wrote.[6]

Five years later, the group that brought the lawsuit, Advocates for Children of New York, continued to press New York City schools to support students, rather than push them out. Their understanding of more nuanced ways that principals fail to support struggling students led them to redefine "push-out," showing the varied forms that "push-outs" could take—from half-hearted counseling to providing few opportunities for make-up classes or tutoring.

School push-out: What is it?
By Advocates for Children of New York, February 2008

School push-out happens when students are illegally excluded from school. Students leave school for a variety of reasons. Some students leave school because they need to work full-time to help support their families. Others leave simply because they are moving, and their current school is too far away. In those situations, push-out has not occurred, as the school has done nothing to force the student to leave.

School push-out occurs when a student is encouraged or forced to leave school for reasons that are against the law. One example is when high school students in their late teens are told that they need to go to a General Educational Development (GED) program because they are too old and do not have enough credits to graduate from high school. School push-out can also occur when a school chooses to punish a student by repeatedly suspending him or her instead of attempting to address the problematic behavior, when a student is told she must leave the school because she is pregnant, or when a student is forbidden from returning to school because of a criminal record.

> Push-out is not limited to prohibiting a student from coming to school. Push-out also occurs when schools do not provide students with the academic supports they need. These supports could include special education services for students with disabilities, tutoring or services to pregnant and parenting students that will allow for them to participate fully in their school activities. When services are not provided, students may become discouraged by their situation and feel that their only option is to leave school. They are effectively pushed out of school because they are given no viable opportunity for an education.

Credit recovery

Three out of every four high schools run credit recovery programs to help students earn the credits they need to stay on track to graduate. About 6 percent of high school students take a course through credit recovery.[7] These programs often bring students to summer school. They can be held before or after school, too. When they're conducted properly, students get the good teachers they deserve, who know how to accelerate a student who hit the wall when she took a class she didn't pass. In fact, approaches for accelerating students have been developed that were very different from credit recovery. One approach, the Accelerated Schools Project, developed by Henry Levin, earned much praise in the late 1980s and 1990s for educating lagging students. Its approach—accelerating the pace of learning while improving the focus and liveliness of the classroom—was similar to the education of gifted-and-talented students. Its successes led to its adoption in almost 1,000 schools by 1996, just 10 years after its launch. Another scholar, Stanley Pogrow, developed a program named HOTS (Higher Order Thinking Skills), which was aimed at lagging students. He based his program on principles similar to Henry Levin's, and it grew to be adopted by about 2,400 schools and enjoyed by about 500,000 students. Compressing learning time can be done well. Other alternate approaches to graduation include performance-based assessment programs. For decades, diligent teachers have invented ways to legitimately help a struggling student earn a diploma.

But credit recovery has been misused in some districts to push a student at lightning speed through a fake shortcut to a phony passing

Hazards of interpreting graduation rates

grade in a course he previously failed or didn't take at all. A blog post in November 2019 by Catherine Gewertz in *Education Week* titled "Without Rules, Credit Recovery Is Just an Easy Ticket to Graduation" revealed the degree to which some school and district leaders have gone to get lagging students to graduate.[8] Compressing a semester's course into a single day of instruction, followed by an "open book" test at the end, is what research scholars are seeing all too often. Giving academic credit to a student who isn't given a teacher, or given the time necessary to master the subject matter, or a test to validate knowledge gained, is academic fraud.

One of the scholars whose work has brought critical attention to abuse of credit recovery is Nat Malkus, the deputy director of education policy at American Enterprise Institute (AEI). He and Amy Cummings wrote an opinion essay in *Education Week* in November 2018, titled "What We're Getting Wrong About Credit Recovery— Don't trust a school's graduation rate without checking its credit-recovery program."[9] His research paper followed a year later, "Practice Outpacing Policy?—Credit Recovery in American School Districts."

Malkus was not the first to document this fraudulent practice. *Washington Post* reporter Jay Mathews was writing about misuse of credit recovery in 2012. Scholar Russell Rumberger at UC Santa Barbara wrote about diploma falsification and credit recovery in his 2011 book, *Dropping Out: Why Students Drop Out of High School and What Can Be Done About It*.[10] Rumberger has been leading the California Dropout

> ☞ **Tip:** see if your district has a policy about credit recovery. Does it show regard for the quality of instruction? If it allows for online courses, what role does it require teachers to play? Who reviews and approves those online credit recovery courses? How available must teachers be to support students? What is required of teachers who are assigned to teach credit-recovery students? Do those requirements include subject matter expertise? Do students have an opportunity to ask questions and get answers quickly? Are periodic assessments given to the student to verify that she is learning during the course? Is there an assessment at the end of the course that can reasonably measure the student's mastery of the course content?

Research Project (CDRP) since he founded it in 2007. His own research and writing, and those of his colleagues at CDRP, have shed much light on dropouts.[11]

The growth of credit recovery offerings has been possible, in part, because many of the courses are available online. While online offerings, like all instructional materials, can range in quality from high to low, the online credit recovery field seems to tilt toward the lower-quality end of that spectrum. Nat Malkus found that misuse of online credit recovery programs was easy to spot. Those high schools that used online credit recovery courses 2.5 times more frequently than the national average were clear abusers, in his opinion.[12]

Fuzzy numbers require soft hands

Earlier we mentioned that graduation and dropout rate numbers are a bit fuzzy. Here's what I mean. Because they contain imprecision and uncertainty, you should handle them like a bar of soap in the shower. Hold them with soft hands. Squeeze too hard, and that bar of soap will slip from your hands. In making sense of data about human activity, soft hands will enable you to avoid two errors of judgment. First, you'll avoid making a mountain out of a molehill. That is, you'll avoid making a big deal out of a very small difference, perhaps a difference so small that it would disappear if one student had been assigned a different "exit code" by your district's attendance clerk. Second, you'll be more likely to see the mountains if you're not fussing with the molehills. The key here is in seeing the rate as integers that form both your numerator and denominator. This keeps the number of students visible at all times, what the stat-heads call the "n" size.

Finally, use your knowledge of the range of fuzziness in the numbers. If you have 15 students who left school without warning, whose location you were never able to determine, and you have to record them with an exit code that your state considers to be the equivalent of a dropout, why not back those numbers out *of your own calculations and* report them only internally? (This is not an evasion of your obligation to file your official dropout numbers with your state agency.) This adjusted view would only require that you remove the students whose outcome is unknown from both your numerator and denominator. The result would be an adjusted rate that describes the dropout and graduation rates of the students whose

Hazards of interpreting graduation rates

outcomes you definitely know. Alternately, you could estimate your unofficial dropout and graduation rates bracketing a range of possible outcomes. What if six of those 15 students were really dropouts, and nine left the state and reenrolled elsewhere? What might be the best and worst possible outcomes, and how would your graduation and dropout rates change in both circumstances?

Dropout rates: a vital sign that may point to many causes

Don't be too quick to infer that rising dropout rates reflect only disengaged students who are voting with their feet. Many factors might contribute to this trend. Administrators in the district office may have stopped investing a lot of time in tracing students who failed to reregister for school. Students during the pandemic of 2020–2021 and 2021–2022 school years may have dropped out of school to take care of sick family members. Or they may have left school to work to sustain their families due to a parent's illness or death. Some students remained enrolled in school, attending classes via videoconferencing tools, even though they had moved with their family out of state or out of the country altogether.

Changes in district policies can drive dropout rates, too. Consider a district that wants all its students to graduate with enough courses and high enough grades to qualify for admission to the state's four-year colleges. If the board comes to an agreement that this is *what all students should attain* and votes for a new policy that raises the bar for graduation, consider the consequences. Some students may decide a diploma is now unattainable and drop out of school. Others may try to clear that bar and not make it. The dropout rate may rise, as students who don't feel academically ambitious, or who don't care to go to college and would rather go to work or enter the military, vote with their feet.

Who is staying, and who is leaving? Might the ones who are leaving have good reason for doing so? One astute observer of American schools, Jay Mathews, wrote in the *Washington Post* that students who left high school have a lot to say and that those in charge would be wise to listen. Their reasons for leaving led Mathews in 1999 to write a book, *Class Struggle: What's Wrong (and Right) with America's Best Public High Schools.*[13] His advice to school leaders was simple. Just ask students why they're not happy in school and then do something to make them want to stay.

Reading and predicting graduation-related vital signs

Students rarely become dropouts in one fell swoop. They convey signals of disengagement along the way. Those signals are of two types: human voices and statistical artifacts of human activity. Both are valuable, but in different ways. Those human voices will provide you clues to why students are exiting. Counselors who are close to students, even while carrying caseloads of 500-plus students, should be your frontline listeners. Of course, you can also listen yourself. Go to students, and talk to them on their turf, one at a time. Or get a group together during lunch or after school and bring a trusted teacher along who knows them. Ask questions and listen with open ears.

Students rarely become dropouts all at once. If you look at the numbers closely, you'll see patterns. Talented analysts can help you look at individual student-level records over many years. Good database techs can write queries that help you extract these data, so you can deliver it to analysts who know how to look for the earliest clues that a student was disengaging from school. Most of them show signs of losing interest in school. Predictive modeling is what analysts can do to tease out those patterns in your district. If you can spot the early signs of a student's disengagement from school, the better your odds of helping that student reengage.

Predictive analytics are one way to identify those early signs. Although they aren't new to education management, education leaders have been slow to put the power of predictive analytics to work. Professional baseball teams have been at this since the 1990s, when Bill James codified his approach to better measurement of team performance and player skills. The Oakland A's manager, Billy Beane, applied Bill James's principles to the challenge of identifying talented players, a feat glorified by Michael Lewis in his book, *Moneyball*. It took a bit more than a decade for Bill James's methods to take root and then earn its place in a tradition-bound, old-school game where new talent was identified based on their instincts. But once it took root, it grew to become a dominant method that every team sought to apply.

Hazards of interpreting graduation rates

For an introduction to school-related uses of predictive analytics, start by reading "Schools Find Uses for Predictive Data Techniques," written by Sarah Sparks and published by *Education Week*.[14] For a look at predictive methods applied in action, I recommend a 2016 case study by two educators working with the Harvard Strategic Data Project: "Developing an Early Warning Indicator System in a High-Poverty Urban Context."[15] It reveals the story of how they traced signals of dropout indicators back to fourth grade for 3,478 students in Passaic, New Jersey. The lessons they learned about preventing future dropouts may be relevant to your district.

But there are other ways to squeeze meaning from the data in your hands. Simple trend analysis of daily or weekly events can sometimes reveal dramatic changes in a student's attendance, discipline record or grades. A cluster of smaller troubling signals may be an early warning of a student's trajectory away from school. The closer you can be to the moment warning signs emerge, the more likely a teacher or counselor can help a student head back on track.

Try examining the past few years of data looking at differences in the graduation and dropout rates for boys and girls, for instance. If your district shows boys dropping out of school at rates considerably higher than girls, you're in the mainstream. Is that actionable information? Sure. Just look at the way high schools work that attain equivalent graduation rates and attendance rates for boys and girls. Here's one example I can point you toward because I know its founders, Matt Wunder and Don Brann, and have visited one of their campuses, the DaVinci Science High School in Hawthorne and El Segundo, California. Students build things. They work in teams. Their academic work often takes the form of projects. This mode of active learning is one reason why their attendance rates have been in the high 90-percent range, and why 96 percent of the Class of 2019 graduated on time. By the way, the rate for boys and girls was identical. Other signs of success they share with pride: 98 percent of their graduates have completed the California college-prep curriculum, compared to 43 percent of students statewide; and 86 percent of DaVinci grads attended college right after high school, compared to 69 percent of students nationally.[16] They started this pair of charter high schools in 2009 to serve a blue-collar community on the edge of Los Angeles International Airport after leading an elementary district, Wiseburn ESD, to notable success. Their model was based, naturally, on a collaboration between the elementary district they had led and the new charter high schools they launched.

Continuation high schools have different vital signs

Why have continuation high schools (called transfer schools in New York) been so poorly served for so long by accountability systems? There's a lot of them, and their purpose is to educate those students who aren't prospering in comprehensive high schools. Since their role differs from that of comprehensive highs, why have so many states applied graduation and dropout rates to continuation high schools? They serve many students for only a portion of the school year. Many continuation high schools offer only grades 11 and 12. They often deliver educational opportunities of a different sort. Their leaders measure success differently than leaders of comprehensive high schools. Most important to note, many of the students they serve have been miseducated in the schools they previously attended. Other students may have parents whose lives have gone off track, and who have also seen their high school lives disrupted.

The trouble is that the data collected about students in continuation high schools aren't very relevant to the analytical project of estimating how well the schools they are enrolled in serve them. Both the relevant data and the measures of success that continuation high schools aim to reach are ill-defined. One watchful observer of high schools' vital signs, Russell Rumberger, director of the California Dropout Research Project at the University of California, Santa Barbara, had this to say.

> I think there are some genuinely good things going on in the alternative sector. I don't want to condemn the whole area. But we just don't know. . . . We don't really have any way to tell how much of it is done in a thoughtful manner and in how many cases it's really just a dumping process of "get them out of my school so my graduation rate goes up."[17]

Principals of continuation high schools have told me they have too little influence over the moment when a comprehensive high refers a student their way. Yet they are held responsible for getting all referred students to the finish line of graduation in four years. The timing of that referral is critical. If a student is referred after failing many classes, that student is likely to be, at best, somewhat demoralized and disengaged. At worst, that student may be angry and defiant. But if a student is referred earlier, and if the continuation high they're referred to is prepared to serve them well, then restoring that student's self-confidence and gaining knowledge and skills, along with class credit well earned, can certainly turn a student back on track to graduation.

The measures that should count for continuation highs should be individualized to each student, and only then rolled up into school level summaries. Among the factors that principals should gather are measures of the student's starting point of entry. Just as a doctor who is a general practitioner receives a new patient and runs a battery of tests after examining her, a principal should do the same on day one of each new student's arrival. The reason to take stock at the beginning of a student's arrival is to create a baseline from which you can plan that student's path and learn how far that student has progressed by the time he departs. This is admittedly a high mark to aim for, one that is simply not feasible given the limits of time and funding. With so many students arriving at different times in the school year, this establishment of a baseline is the only way to gauge what has resulted from your investment in that student.

For principals of continuation highs concerned about a fair evaluation of their team at the end of the year, it's time to champion your cause to the cabinet and to the board. When you propose some markers of success, you may find it helpful to consider some of the suggestions by Jorge Ruiz de Velasco and Daisy Gonzales in their 2017 report, "Accountability for Alternative Schools in California," published by Policy Analysis for California Education.[18] They suggest including indicators of school connectedness, as well as indicators of incremental progress en route to a regular diploma. They also suggest a one-year graduation rate for those who enroll as seniors.

Graduation rates: vital signs that can lead you in the right direction

You have an opportunity to put these numbers to work toward many constructive ends. But you can only do that if you see yourself as a builder of evidence. These numbers are the raw material. You are the builder. You have the best chance of realizing these opportunities if you:

- Pay attention to the quality of your building materials, and where data bricks aren't sound, create the reinforcement that is needed;
- Use soft hands in handling raw material that's fuzzy; and
- Remember that human activity created your raw materials, and be mindful of the changes you'd like to inspire that result in better raw materials in the future.

But you are building a body of evidence for a reason. It might be to persuade community leaders that your high school is doing better than it was five years ago at producing students who are ready to enter the work world or the world of college. Or it might be to challenge your high school principals to do better at keeping their freshmen and sophomores on track toward graduation. Or it might be to praise your counseling team for the work they've done. Or you might be striving to motivate your early elementary reading instructional teams to do a better job of helping struggling readers by showing them the human toll of weak reading skills on students in middle and high school.

The evidence you build needs to be presented as part of a story, and that story will contain an argument that includes evidence both hard and soft, statistical summaries and human stories. Don't expect the numbers

When grad rate problems land your high school in the accountability doghouse

Imagine that your high school's grad rate in 2019 was 72 percent. Obviously, your board isn't happy with this news. Although it's not so different from the 75 percent grad rate of the prior year, your state's accountability system has flagged your school as "red" because its graduation rate dropped below the official threshold of 75 percent. So now your staff is demoralized, and your town's leaders are troubled. What's the story? People want to know. Your graduation rate reflects a lot of human events. You need to make them clear.

Mobility

You know that your high school students in prior years have been graduating at rates between 75 and 85 percent for years. For a farming community, where families move more frequently, chasing agricultural and service jobs that aren't steady employment, you know that students who transfer into your high school in their junior or senior year are more likely not to graduate in four years.

No summer credit recovery

Your board passed a policy to discontinue credit recovery five years ago, when they discovered that it was being used in all the wrong ways. Students were being told they could cram a week of learning into two hours of work in the library. Books and teacher's aides, babysitting students in a "self-guided" learning program, had become the way that lagging students were treated to a summertime "fast path" to a diploma. Thankfully, your district has put an end to that, replacing it with an authentic credit recovery program with great teachers in charge.

No push-outs of marginal students

Your district has not been quick to transfer marginal students out of your comprehensive high school over to your continuation high. Your policy has been to keep them enrolled, and your people have worked hard to help them succeed. So where other high schools "push out" the students least likely to graduate, your high school has done the opposite—kept those kids enrolled and invested in their academic success.

Your people and your district's policies encouraged you to give them an extra year to graduate. As a result, your high school's five-year graduation rate is 83 percent, an entirely respectable number compared to other farming communities in your part of the state.

Unusual local circumstances

A large group of immigrant families moved to your town in 2013. The arrival of several dozen families from Chiapas, Mexico, brought a lot of students into your district who had been undereducated. Some were not able to read and write Spanish fluently. In addition, some of the families were indigenous

> Mixtec speakers. When their children arrived, many were adolescents, who soon ended up in your high school. Their path to graduation was clearly going to be a longer one. And there were enough of them that they pulled down your graduation rate.
>
> So how would you "visualize" this data story? Whatever your approach, you'd make clear that *students are not widgets*. They are humans, and their differences make your graduating class cohorts different, sometimes to a large degree. Your data story would need to account for all these factors, with *each cohort of students having a story of their own*.

alone to persuade. You'll need to make them part of a broader argument. The quality of your logic and the emotional impact of the human stories you share are every bit as important as the quality of your evidence.

Links to extend your reading and interaction

The following link will carry you to additional resources, writing and dialogue about the topics discussed in this chapter. You'll also find live versions of the data visualizations in this chapter that are ready for your interaction. We welcome your comments and continued exploration. You'll find all this on the chapter specific page on the book's website: https://www.k12measures.com/ch3

Questions to spark discussion

District leaders

1. Your board is driving you crazy with their concern about an apparent decline in the district's graduation rate. It's slipped from 92 percent to 87 percent, and they believe that to be terrible news. You're preparing a response for the next board meeting,

and you're aware you can't politically defend a decline. But you'd like to persuade board members that this apparent problem is not a large one. Your district's graduating classes are composed of about 300 seniors. So, this 5 percent decline is attributable to about 15 students. How would you put this issue in context? (Hint: consider those students taking five years to graduate.)

2. Your credit recovery program relies heavily on computer-delivered curriculum. It leads to happy students who complete those computer-based courses with passing grades, which lead to diplomas. That means happy parents and happy teachers. But you're wondering what students are really learning. How would you get a real-world answer to that question, one that isn't just a formal curriculum review?

Principals

3. You're in charge of the one comprehensive high school in your district. You are about to meet with your counterpart who is principal at the continuation high school. The topic is what is the ideal moment to recommend a struggling student transfer to the continuation high. What information do you want to have to build an evidence base for your opinion? What, in the end, is really the goal?

4. You are writing the site plan for your continuation high school. A few teachers and one parent are helping. The official measures by which your state agency judges your high school are ill-suited for the purpose your school serves. You have decided to create your own key indicators to measure your progress. What would you like to see as the top three elements?

School board trustees

5. Your board has been considering a new policy that would aim to get all high school students through a course of study that

qualifies them to apply to a four-year college. This idea has been tried in many districts and met with mixed results. The idea is controversial among the five board members and in the community at large. You are leading the board study team that's putting together a background briefing for the full board. What evidence would you like to include? What are your leading concerns about this college-ready-for-all approach? What evidence would be most relevant in documenting the risks this policy entails? What data do you need to build that evidence?

6. Your board is very committed to high graduation rates. But your district's grad rates have wandered between 87 percent and 92 percent for the past five years. Every year, the up-and-down fluctuation of your grad rate draws a great deal of attention from media and community leaders. You know that the fluctuations of several percentage points this way or that are of no consequence. But how can you best make that case without seeming to be dodging bad news in a year when grad rates dipped 2 percentage points?

Notes

1. "Public High School Graduation Rates," Institute for Education Science, National Center for Education Statistics, last modified May 2021, https://nces.ed.gov/programs/coe/indicator/coi.

2. "Every Student Succeeds Act High School Graduation Rate Non-Regulatory Guidance," U.S. Department of Education, January 2017, www2.ed.gov/policy/elsec/leg/essa/essagradrateguidance.pdf.

3. Matthew Larsen, "High-School Exit Exams Are Tough on Crime," *Education Next* 21, no. 3 (Summer 2021), www.educationnext.org/high-school-exit-exams-tough-on-crime-fewer-arrests-diplomas-require-test/.

4. Catherine Gewertz, "Which States Require an Exit Exam to Graduate?" *Education Week*, 2019, last modified 2019, www.edweek.org/teaching-learning/which-states-require-an-exam-to-graduate.

5. Indiana's graduation requirements are more fully explained on a different page on their state department of education website. https://www.in.gov/doe/students/graduation-pathways/diploma-requirements/.

6. Tamar Lewin, "City to Track Why Students Leave School," *New York Times*, September 15, 2003, www.nytimes.com/2003/09/15/nyregion/city-to-track-why-students-leave-school.html.

7. Nat Malkus, "Practice Outpacing Policy? Credit Recovery in American School Districts," American Enterprise Institute, November 21, 2019, www.aei.org/research-products/report/practice-outpacing-policy-credit-recovery-in-american-school-districts/.

8. Catherine Gewertz, "Without Rules, Credit Recovery Is Just an 'Easy Ticket to Graduation,' Report Says," *Education Week*, November 21, 2019, www.edweek.org/teaching-learning/without-rules-credit-recovery-is-just-an-easy-ticket-to-graduation-report-says/2019/11.

9. Nat Malkus and Amy Cummings, "What We're Getting Wrong About Credit Recovery," *Education Week*, November 26, 2018, www.edweek.org/technology/opinion-what-were-getting-wrong-about-credit-recovery/2018/11.

10. Russell W. Rumberger, *Dropping Out: Why Students Drop Out of High School and What Can Be Done About It* (Cambridge: Harvard University Press, 2011).

11. Leaders with an interest in helping more students graduate would be well guided by exploring the CDRP website, http://cdrpsb.org/.

12. Malkus and Cummings, "What We're Getting Wrong About Credit Recovery."

13. Jay Mathews, *Class Struggle: What's Wrong (and Right) with America's Best Public High Schools* (New York: Times Books, 1998).

14. Sarah Sparks, "Schools Find Uses for Predictive Data Techniques," *Education Week*, June 30, 2011, www.edweek.org/teaching-learning/schools-find-uses-for-predictive-data-techniques/2011/06.

15. Tara Chiatovich and Elizabeth Rivera Rodas, "Developing an Early Warning Indicator System in a High-Poverty Urban Context," Harvard Strategic Data Project Fellowship Capstone Report, 2016. https://hwpi.harvard.edu/files/sdp/files/sdp-fellowship-capstone-ewi-poverty-urban.pdf.

16. See the DaVinci High website, www.davincischools.org/impact/outcomes/.

17. Sarah Butrymowicz and The Hechinger Report, "Holding California's 'Continuation' Schools Accountable: An Investigation," *Education Week*, July 23, 2015, www.edweek.org/leadership/holding-californias-continuation-schools-accountable-an-investigation/2015/07.

18. Jorge Ruiz de Velasco and Daisy Gonzales, "Accountability for Alternative Schools in California," Policy Analysis for California Education, February 2017, https://gardnercenter.stanford.edu/sites/g/files/sbiybj11216/f/Accountability%20for%20Alternative%20Schools%20Policy%20Brief.pdf.

References

Chiatovich, Tara, and Elizabeth Rivera Rodas. "Developing an Early Warning Indicator System in a High-Poverty Urban Context." Harvard Strategic Data Project Fellowship Capstone Report, 2016.

Gewertz, Catherine. "Without Rules, Credit Recovery Is Just an 'Easy Ticket to Graduation,' Report Says." *Education Week*, November 21, 2019. www.edweek.org/teaching-learning/without-rules-credit-recovery-is-just-an-easy-ticket-to-graduation-report-says/2019/11.

Larsen, Matthew F. "High-School Exit Exams Are Tough on Crime." *Education Next* 20, no. 3 (Summer 2020). www.educationnext.org/high-school-exit-exams-tough-on-crime-fewer-arrests-diplomas-require-test/.

Malkus, Nat. "Practice Outpacing Policy? Credit Recovery in American School Districts." American Enterprise Institute, November 21, 2019. www.aei.org/research-products/report/practice-outpacing-policy-credit-recovery-in-american-school-districts/.

Mathews, Jay. *Class Struggle: What's Wrong (and Right) with America's Best Public High Schools*. New York: Times Books, 1999.

Ruiz de Velasco, Jorge, and Daisy Gonzales. "Accountability for Alternative Schools in California." Berkeley and Stanford, CA: Policy Analysis for California Education, February 2017. https://gardnercenter.stanford.edu/sites/g/files/sbiybj11216/f/Accountability%20for%20Alternative%20Schools%20Policy%20Brief.pdf.

Rumberger, Russell W. *Dropping Out: Why Students Drop Out of High School and What Can Be Done About It*. Cambridge: Harvard University Press, 2011.

Gaps mismeasured, misattributed and misunderstood

This chapter is about the measurement of differences and the ways that people understand and communicate those measurements. This admittedly modest aspect of the larger topic has received less attention than it deserves. Oddly, everyone says they're concerned about these gaps, but almost no one outside of the social sciences uses numbers to describe them. Consider that to be a warning sign.

Gap analysis is a hard-hat construction zone

When you're working to turn data into evidence to support an argument, consider yourself to be both an architect and a builder. In the construction field, they have a term for this: design-build. You are both designing how to assemble data, and you are building it into a work of well-structured evidence that will stand up to criticism and persuade people. Three factors make gap analysis a hazard zone. First, many people build their evidence with poor quality elements. The data they use don't mean what they think it means. They disregard imprecision and confuse noise with the signal they're seeking. Second, they don't allow for the possibility that someone who views their evidence from another vantage point might reach an entirely different conclusion. As builders, they've only viewed their creation from their own vantage point. Strong evidence gets that way after being viewed and critiqued from many angles. Third, the logic that links one observation to another may be flawed. Causality may be presumed, where only correlations exist. Bricks of data may have been connected by a faulty batch of mortar. Or those bricks may have been arrayed improperly. This is a hard-hat job.

For those who are viewers of gap analysis, it is also a risky proposition. You should regard evidence about gaps with care. Get some distance, bring your binoculars and examine the evidence from afar. Look at it from several angles. Then step closer and look for signs of skilled craftmanship. Just as a well-built house reveals the skill of the builder and architect, a poorly built structure will reveal its flaws if you look at it closely—corners that aren't true 90 degrees and doors that don't fit squarely in their frames.

In the examples that follow, we'll show you evidence that's flawed, and evidence that's well built. We'll share with you questions of varying quality, as well as evidence that at times doesn't really address the question at hand. Put on your skeptic's thinking cap. Toughen up your emotional armor. This is a conversation where moral and ethical issues—questions of fairness and equity—are front and center. Social justice questions and gap analyses are often intertwined. This makes a reasoned, logical approach to the measurement of gaps more important, even if it's more difficult.

Finally, a personal note is in order. My coauthor and I don't lack passion of our own on this topic. Our history of activism goes back to the sixties, and it includes civil rights work in California and New York. In fact, it is that commitment that makes us eager to untangle the snarled, gnarly arguments about gaps in achievement and opportunities to learn.

The blame game distorts gap analysis

Gap measures are often used—sometimes properly, sometimes improperly—as evidence of bias, both individual and systemic. The evidence of gaps has, for some, become a proof of inequality. The argument goes something like this. If academic talent is equally distributed among the population, why would some groups of students enjoy greater success than others? Here the conversation needs to go further but often doesn't. Kids come to school unequally prepared. Both home environment and parents shape readiness to learn. So, if the factors that cause differences in outcomes are a combination of home, heredity and schooling, to what degree do measures of gaps provide evidence about the influence of school alone? Can the influence of school alone be estimated?

If you are a site or district leader or a school board trustee, you have a big stake in finding the best possible answer to that question. In fact, the question that may matter most to you is this:

> Does being a student in our school or district lead to a widening of pre-existing differences between boys and girls or a narrowing of them?

Even better would be a discrete measure of the effect over time of your school or district on differences within stable groups of students (e.g., the graduating Class of 2028). The good news is that *this is measurable*. The bad news is that you need to have a talented social scientist at your side who has the skills to derive that answer. The methods used to tease out the effect of multiple factors that influence graduation rates or test scores, for instance, include technically complex methods. But when you've completed that difficult analysis, what can you do with that evidence? You can't change heredity.[1] Who might be color blind? Who has a hearing problem? Who has a neurological processing problem that will make learning to read a challenge? Only rarely can a school or district influence the home environment, for example, by encouraging parents to read to their kids. You are unlikely to learn from that analysis how to change schooling to moderate differences among students in their readiness to learn. All you may have in hand is an estimate of your district's relative contribution to the gap between boys and girls. Before starting on an analytic quest like that, you'd do well to clarify the question itself.

Schooling is just one influence shaping the gaps you're measuring

Let's back up and start, not with the measurement and the evidence, but with the question you're trying to answer. If your question is whether your district is contributing to unequal outcomes rather than lessening them, you need a clear measure of students' differences at the start of school. These human differences are vast, of course. Some of those differences can't even be seen. But others are observable, even in kindergartners. Do they know the letters of the alphabet? Do they know the names of colors? Can they distinguish similarities and differences among a group of five objects? Do they speak with ease, or do they struggle when speaking? Other differences, of course, are not observable.

Starting with this inventory of knowledge about each student's starting point, focusing on the observable factors that are most relevant to learning, you could take stock at periodic intervals of each student's progress across a variety of observable behaviors—like reading or writing, or plays-well-with-others. From this, you could gauge the differences among students as they grow older together. But with students in school about half the days of the year, you're able to take note of the learning opportunities you offer them only during those school days. But you're unable to note what learning opportunities they encounter at home, with friends, or enroute to and from school. You're also unable to note the degree to which each student is motivated to learn, admittedly a huge factor.

With these blind spots in mind, let's return to what we thought was a good question earlier:

> Does being a student in our school or district lead to a widening of pre-existing differences between boys and girls or a narrowing of them?

Let's see if our evidence from school gives us the ability to answer that question reasonably well. I am asking if you can tease out the effects that school has on a child, separate from the effects of home environment, heredity, friends and internal motivation. If so, you can reach a judgment about the influence of your school or district. A causal diagram should help make this question clearer. (The method and mathematics for doing this type of analysis is the work of Judea Pearl and Dana Mackenzie. Their book, *The Book of Why: The New Science of Cause and Effect*, explains fully this visual vocabulary.[2]) Each arrow in the diagram in Figure 4.1 indicates the influence of one factor on another. Pairs of arrows that point to-and-from a pair of factors (e.g., friends and child) indicate that each influences the other. Arrows that point in only one direction indicate influence in that one direction only.

A multicausal model of influences at work on kids in school

This diagram in Figure 4.1 shows the mix of four influences on a child and the effect of those factors on each other. It shows why it is extremely difficult to isolate the effect that's attributable to school alone. First, the influences are many. Second, some of these influences are interdependent

Gaps mismeasured

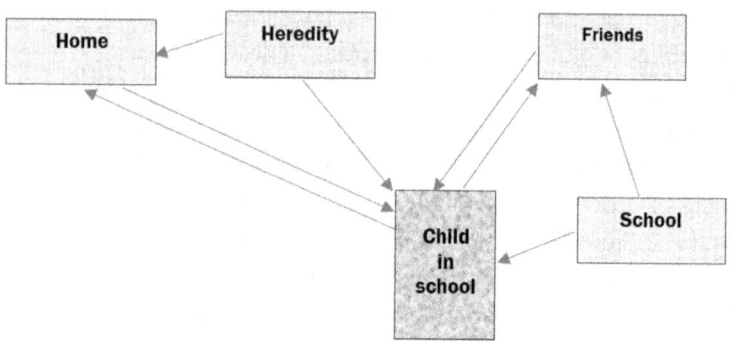

Figure 4.1 A multicausal model of influences at work on kids in school
A schematic showing the many influences at work on kids in school. Direction of arrows indicate the factor of influence (base of arrow) and its point of effect.

and reciprocal. They interact with each other. For example, note that friends are influenced by school, and at the same time, school influences these friends. In addition, the child is influenced by his friends. But at the same time, those friends are influenced by the child. Third, heredity and school extend their influence in two directions. This confounds our attempts to assign causality because heredity influences both the home environment and the child, and school influences both friends and the child.

Consider a child who's learning to read. The hereditary influence of parents on a struggling reader is direct. If a child has one parent with dyslexia, the child has a 40–60 percent probability of being dyslexic (Schumacher et al., 2007). But that parent, if he or she hasn't learned to read, or doesn't read to the child, or doesn't take the child to the library, has also created a home environment due in some part to heredity that also influences the child. In the end, with so many factors affecting a student's ability to read, the question as stated could best be answered with the help of analysts or social scientists. If you are brave enough to try this without skilled people at your side, you should at least seek an informed second opinion.

Before you begin your analysis, work on improving your question

The question becomes somewhat more answerable if it shifts to a particular subject in school where a child is unlikely to learn much about it outside of school. Math is the clearest example. So, let's restate our question so it pertains only to math.

> Does the experience of being a student learning math in our school or district lead to a widening of those differences between boys and girls or a narrowing of them?

Now we have a question where the paths of influence from friends are perhaps less powerful. Friends may have an attitude about math. But it is less likely to affect the child than their attitudes about reading, whether it's reading comics or going to the library. Doing math is a more private experience than reading. Also, the ability to do math is encouraged, fostered and developed almost solely in school. If a child has parents who do math at work, they rarely see it. If by chance they do see one of their parents doing math in the home environment, they would not be learning math by osmosis. When parents read to their children, they are expanding their knowledge of sounds and words and giving them practice making sense of stories. This rarely happens with math. For all these reasons, I'd say that attributing to school the primary causal influence of differences in students' math skills is a more reasonable proposition.

But one additional spin on the question makes it more answerable. Let's make it specific to one cohort of kids, the graduating Class of 2030.

> Were the math test scores of boy and girl students in the class of 2030 in our school or district closer together or farther apart in seventh grade than they were in third grade?

Now we've narrowed it to the same group of kids who form a graduating class cohort, and we've narrowed it down to the five years they were enrolled in your school or district, and also tested. Over that much time, the impact of math instruction should become more visible. Yet what does the answer to this question really mean in and of itself? Wouldn't it help if we could compare it to some other school or district? Let's restate the question as a comparison.

> Were the math test scores of boy and girl students in the class of 2030 in our school or district closer together or farther apart in seventh grade than they were in third grade, compared to the gap in scores of boys and girls in a handful of other schools or districts with highly similar students?

This is a question that earns four stars. Let's presume that the test data used are produced by a high-quality test, that students at the same grade level took the same test at about the same time of year and were taught the same curriculum and that it was a year untroubled by pandemics.

- Star one: it can be explained rather easily, in part because the least numerate person is likely to accept and understand a comparison of districts with highly similar students.
- Star two: it is limited to one cohort of kids who are more or less the same students over time. If you like, you could use your student information system to restrict this analysis to just those students who were continuously enrolled, giving you a cleaner look at your district's or school's influence.
- Star three: in spanning five years, it evens out instability that's more common in shorter-term measures of one or two years.
- Star four: you can extend this to eighth grade, and you can repeat it for other graduating class cohorts. You can also apply the method to other paired subgroups that are stable.

Exploratory and confirmatory approaches to building evidence

What we've done is build evidence to confirm a hunch or hypothesis. This is in contrast to an exploratory process, an entirely different approach that starts with a quest to discover a pattern that one hopes will lead to an actionable question. Keep these two methods in mind as you read this chapter. The exploratory approach is a more open inquiry. No one starts with a point to make or has an ax to grind. The exploratory approach is one where you should be ready to be surprised, ready to learn and open to discoveries. The confirmation process is one you will use to respond to critics or to make a point. But in building evidence to do so, you will be tempted to reach for the evidence that favors your case. Bias of self-interest is always at work. So, pick your evidence with care, and ask someone to poke holes in your argument. The best evidence is that which stands up to the toughest interrogation.

Most of us who have a point to prove or a position to defend go looking for evidence to support it. We've all done this. The more certain we are of our beliefs, the more likely we'll be to disregard evidence that contradicts our beliefs and to bend ambiguous evidence to better support our case. This is *confirmation bias* at work. It is a topic I urge you to explore, starting with a well-written encyclopedic entry in Wikipedia.[3]

In the face of the all-too-common desire to blame schools for every social ill, and in light of the passion that people bring to questions of gap measurement (and the sense of certainty that passionate people might bring to the discussion), I suggest you proceed with care. Here are the steps to follow, whether you're exploring or confirming.

- Clarify the question you're striving to answer.
- Find the data of highest quality that fits the question most closely.
- Build the evidence from those data with the care a master carpenter takes when building furniture from expensive wood. ("Measure twice, cut once" is the carpenter's advice.)
- Then express your evidence, both visually and in writing, so it matches the aptitude and attitude of your audience.

Let's apply those four steps to four hypothetical cases of gap analysis and apply our principles of inquiry, evidence and measurement to these real-world situations: disproportionate rates of suspension by ethnicity; gaps in test scores by ethnicity; gaps in opportunities to learn; and gender bias in grading.

Case #1: proving bias in discipline requires more than a tally of unequal suspensions

We've seen district after district look at evidence of student suspensions, comparing the rate at which students of different ethnic groups have been suspended, and then drawing conclusions. When the evidence is visible, in any district whose students are from several ethnic groups, it is all too common to see suspension rates for African American students exceed the suspension rates of students of any other ethnic group.

This raises a tough question. Is this indicative of harsher discipline meted out to those students by biased teachers and biased administrators? Or is it indicative of more rowdy kids who are African American getting in trouble? This led to painful consequences in the zero-tolerance era, when many districts took a stricter approach to discipline. The bad results of that stricter era thankfully evolved to a more student-sensitive approach and lower suspension rates for all. But the question of bias couldn't be answered by the evidence alone. Of course, determining fairness required a case-by-case review. And I can't help but wonder if many districts were ready to give this effort the time it deserved. Let's go through the analytical steps of this example.

Clarify the question

The real question is about fairness. Students have a way of cutting right to the heart of the matter. The high school kids I've known who were angry and hurt about the way teachers treated them consistently used two words: "fair" and "respect." The judicial system has a test for fairness, and it is "equal treatment under the law." Let's list the questions that get at equal treatment.

- Are different teachers enforcing the district's discipline policy equally? (consistency across teachers);
- Are those teachers applying those policies to different kids with an even hand? (consistency across kids by the same teacher);
- Are kids who break the same rule being suspended at the same rate? (consistency of suspension for the same violation of rules); and
- Are kids who break the same rule being suspended for the same number of days? (consistency of punishment measured in number of days).

These aren't the only questions. But they are questions for which factual evidence can be built from data that districts collect. If districts wished to answer tougher, more subjective questions (do teachers treat students with respect?), you could survey students, of course. In a high school, you could do that for every section, and by asking students in a high school with a six-section day to complete a short survey for each class, you'd have quite a treasure trove of qualitative evidence.

Find the data of highest quality that fit the question most closely

While the data for most of the previously mentioned questions are possible to assemble, they are not easy to create in full form. But it's feasible to create them in partial form. And that's the problem. You have recorded discipline events, sure enough. But you don't have evidence of a kid who acts up but is given a verbal reprimand by the teacher and not referred to the principal's office. Without knowledge of that *absence of discipline*, how can you evaluate fairness? Don't be satisfied simply counting what's easiest to count. If you're answering the question of fairness, do you want to count the *number of students suspended* or the *number of suspension events?* When some students are suspended repeatedly in the same school year, you will see those two rates differ. You might discover that 10 percent of the students you suspend account for 50 percent of the suspension events if they've been suspended time after time.

Evaluating the consistency of suspensions across teachers is also a challenge, but in this case it's possible. Most principals know all too well which teachers are the quickest to refer a kid to the office for suspension. Identifying the rate of referrals for suspension is not hard. It's no more difficult than analyzing the rate at which teachers are handing out grades of D and F. But to determine whether a teacher is biased against boys or Latino/Hispanic kids, you'd have to know the composition by gender and ethnicity of that teacher's sections. Again, the current era of student information systems makes that a relatively easy query. If a teacher is referring for suspension Latino/Hispanic kids at a rate that is roughly proportional to their presence in her classroom, that's one thing. If, however, a teacher is referring those Latino/Hispanic kids at 2.5 times the rate at which she is referring other kids, that's another matter. But it is still not evidence of bias.

Those kids referred to the office may, in fact, have broken the rules at 2.5 times the rate of others. So, what next?

Build the evidence from those data with care

Comparing the rate of referrals of this teacher to all others would provide a useful context for answering the question at hand. If fellow teachers, colleagues who are teaching the same kids, are also referring Latino/Hispanic kids at a rate two to three times higher than the rate at which they refer all other kids, that's parallel evidence. That is to say, if all teachers react at the same rate and in the same way to kids who are Latino/Hispanic who break school rules, then either those teachers are fair in their handing out disciplinary referrals, or they are all equally biased. This comparative approach to analysis does have a bias of its own, then. It rests on the assumption that the practices of the ensemble of teachers is a reasonable benchmark from which to identify the outliers—those who are inclined to discipline too much or too little, or who discipline one group of students more than another. When using this comparative method, it's best to always question the wisdom of relying on the reasonableness of the majority.

What evidence would be missing: the non-referred students whose behavior might have warranted a trip to the principal's office. If two students act up in the same disruptive way, and with the same fervor and effect, and one gets warned but the other gets referred to the principal's office, no record of the warned student's behavior exists. Only those who witnessed it will note the different outcomes. No evidence base is perfect, but be aware of what you're not able to see.

Let's build the evidence about the fairness of the judgment of the front office, an assistant principal who may not have the wisdom of Solomon, but whose job is to decide who gets suspended, and for how long. Building evidence here is easier. We have discrete events of referrals by teachers of students for discipline, a paper trail that records the rules broken and the circumstances, and more. In this hypothetical high school, one assistant principal makes the decision. A review of his decisions, then, should be fairly straightforward.

You could take a year or two of decisions, sorted by category of transgression, and look at the suspension decisions that resulted. You have three possible outcomes for each: no suspension, in-school suspension, out-of-school suspension. No less important, you have the duration of the suspension. Even if your school's disciplinarian isn't as fair as Solomon the Wise, you'd expect similar punishments for similar transgressions. Kids who mouthed off to their teacher or disobeyed should get treated similarly. Kids who got in a fistfight of similar seriousness and harm should get treated similarly. Kids who were bullying fellow students in similar ways should get treated the same way. If that front office discipline chief dished out harsher punishments to some of the kids who broke the same rules, and if those selected for harsher punishment were all girls, then the evidence would show that the discipline chief was biased against girls.

Show and tell your evidence effectively

You must match your evidence and your presentation to the audience. This may seem obvious, but it is often neglected. How many times have you been in the audience for a presentation that sailed over your head or under your feet? We've all witnessed these hit-or-miss presentations. What you can do to avoid the same error is simple: do your homework. Find out who you're presenting to, and aim directly at their level of interest, their education and their emotions.

Level of interest is easy to ascertain. If you're presenting to the school board, their members are interested in making good policies and gaining credibility with the public who votes them into office. They may also be on the defense if the board has been accused of expelling students unfairly. In all likelihood, their level of interest will be high, and their attention easy to gain in a public meeting. If you're meeting with principals, you'll have an audience that makes consequential decisions that affect students' lives. They'll want to be fair and learn enough to do the right thing. They'll want to be alert to early signs of bias in their own school.

Level of education may give you a clue to their tolerance for technical complexity. In addition, it's a clue to the language you use. Expressing quantitative evidence requires a certain precision, especially when presenting evidence that people often misunderstand. The rush-to-judgment of those who are seeking confirmation of their prior beliefs is one big risk you face in any presentation. So go slowly and provide rhetorical brakes that can

Gaps mismeasured

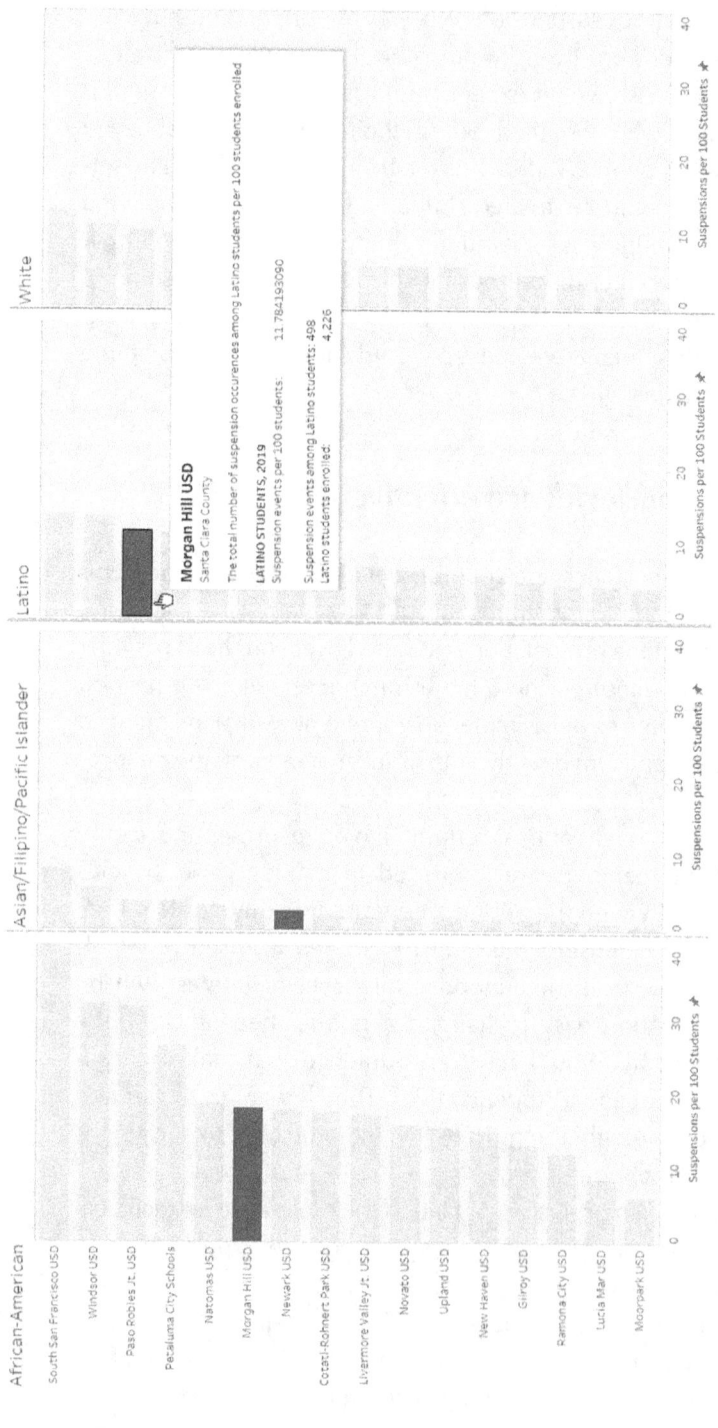

Figure 4.2 Suspension rates of students by ethnicity for 16 districts, 2019

The suspension event rate (rate-per-100 students) for students of four ethnic groups. It enables a school or district to see how their suspension rates compare to those in similar schools or districts. In addition, it reveals the disparity in suspension rates for students of those ethnicities.

You'll find a link to a live version of this visualization on the book's website at https://www.k12measures.com/ch4/#fig4.2

Source: K12 Measures. © School Wise Press

interrupt those who are going over the speed limit on the expressway of logical inferences. Use rhetorical questions to interrupt people who may be making illogical leaps. For example, when presenting evidence of disproportional suspension results, you can say, "Does this evidence alone point to bias in the way we handle student discipline? No, it doesn't. We need to know more before reaching that conclusion."

Adding comparative perspectives is certainly helpful. Comparing suspension rates of your school or district to others with highly similar students is one way to add a new vantage point to the analysis. Consider the analysis of suspension rates in Figure 4.2 created by the K12 Measures team of School Wise Press to help a client see how their suspension rates for students in each of four ethnic groups compared to those in highly similar districts.

Sixteen districts' suspension rates for students of four ethnic groups are represented in this leaderboard. Unlike a bar chart, where the same district's results appear in each row, in a leaderboard the results of districts are displayed in rank order. The district identity of any bar appears when you pass your mouse over it. In the "live" version of this, you could mouseover Novato USD and see its rank position in each of the four columns. The district for whom we did this work, Morgan Hill USD, appears as the darker bar. Each of those bars shows the suspension event rate per-100-students of students of each ethnic group. If you were in the cabinet of this district, this enables you to say, "I'm a little concerned about the suspension rate of our Latino students, because we were the district with the third highest suspension rate of Latino students of all 15 districts with students most similar to our own." This provides a new view of the relative frequency of suspensions, and it enables you to ask an actionable question next. "Which districts show lower suspension rates, especially of Latino students?" If you find any, you can call them and discuss how they attained those lower rates. Here's one example of a district within an hour's drive of Morgan Hill whose Latino suspension rate was half their own rate of about 12 per-100-students (see Figure 4.3).

Good evidence, expressed from a different vantage point, can also defuse hot arguments. The understandable passion people bring to the discussion of gaps, especially those that involve discipline, can easily turn a discussion into an argument. Sharing what you know and adding perspective as this visualization does can build the trust with your audience that's a precondition for all happy outcomes.

Gaps mismeasured

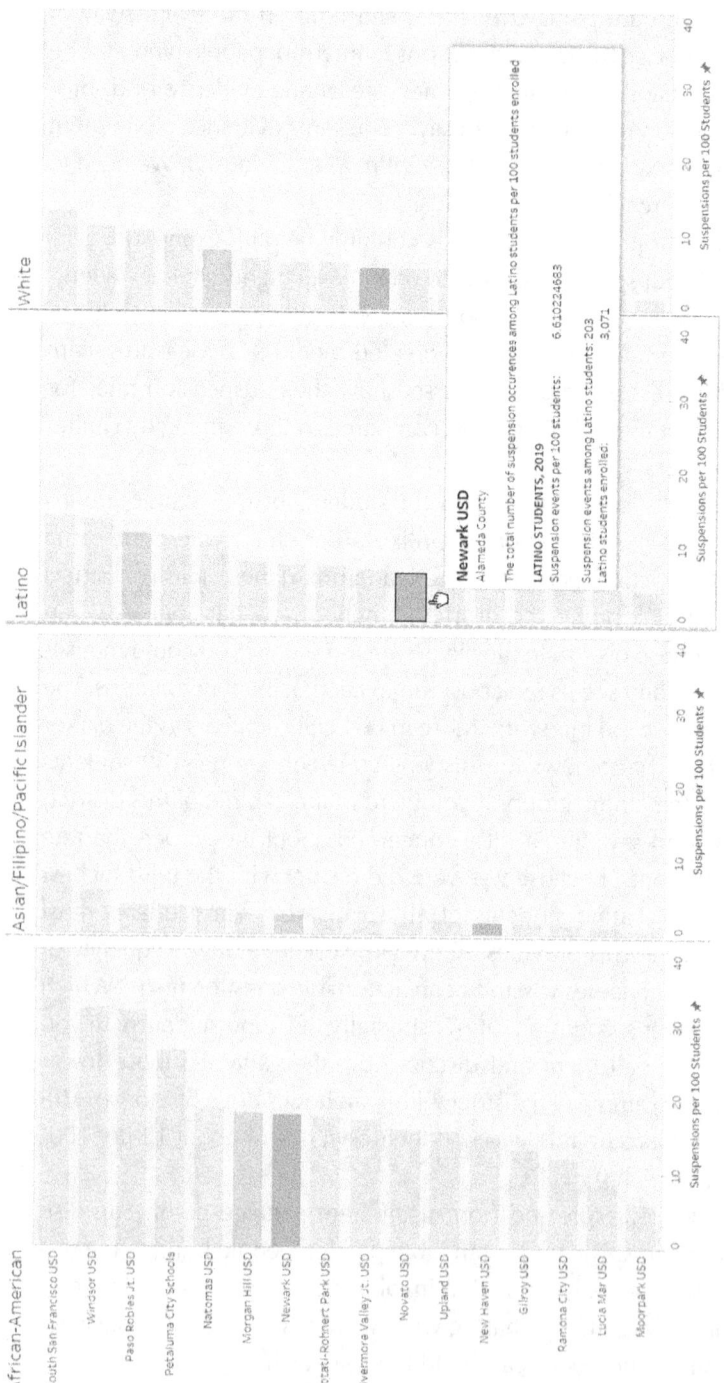

You'll find a link to a live version of this visualization on the book's website at https://www.k12measures.com/ch4/#fig4.3

Figure 4.3 Suspension rates of students by ethnicity for 16 districts, 2019
Newark's suspension rate for Latino/Hispanic students is half that of Morgan Hill's.
Source: K12 Measures. © School Wise Press

Case #2: measuring and explaining gaps in students' test scores

There's a lot of confusion to unravel in this twisted pile of yarn before we can get to the proper interpretation of gaps in students' test scores. Lots of that confusion begins with the question you bring to the table.

Clarify the question

The question you pose about gap measures sets your course. It defines the evidence you need. And when you get your evidence in hand, it leads to the limited range of actions you can take. So, form your questions with care. Lots of hours will be invested in answering your questions if you're a board member or cabinet-level leader and you ask staff to research your question. Making sure *you can act on the evidence* that's retrieved is a practical approach I favor. I confess that I'm biased toward practicality, empirical methods and a desire for action. This is why I'm troubled by how frequently I see districts' strategic plans and schools' site plans chasing questions that can't be acted upon. Let me share with you some examples.

> What is the gap in third-grade English language arts scores between students who received meal subsidies and those who didn't?

What's the action path once you know the answer? Do you hope to reduce the gap in test scores by giving all kids subsidized meals? Do you believe there's a direct cause-and-effect relationship? Or do you believe there's differences in the availability of books between these two groups? If it's the latter, perhaps you could try to hook parents into reading more themselves, or coming to school for night classes, or taking their kids to the library. But among the scores of district and site plans I've read, I've never seen an action recommended, based on the size of the gap measure, or its change in size over time.

> Is the gap in math scores on our statewide assessment in our middle school between White and Latino eighth-grade students larger or smaller than it was three years ago?

Gaps mismeasured

What's the action path once you know the answer? You've already reconciled yourself to comparing two completely different groups of students. If you were to look at the change in math scores for the same students as they progressed from grade 6 to grade 7 and grade 8, you'd have sounder evidence that reflects more clearly the effect of your school on those same kids over three years. But if you compare entirely different kids, you lose the clarity of estimating your school's effect. But for the sake of argument, let's say you did request an analysis of the same kids over time. Are you going to change their ethnic identity? Are you going to presume teachers are biased, and have them take an eight-hour professional development course in culturally responsive math instruction? Are you going to examine the textbooks to see if the book is of equal interest to students of any background? Are you going to meet with the math instructional team and discuss what ideas they have about motivating Latino students more, or revising their lesson plans to make them more relevant to students? Some actions are more promising than others, to be sure. But none of these are clearly leading candidates for success.

The current era's emphasis on identity leads site and district leaders to look perhaps too hard at the differences between groups of students, and *not hard enough on the barriers to learning that all students face*. If elementary school leaders were encouraged to examine whether they're teaching reading in ways that enable 90 percent of students to reach grade level, I suspect their site plans and district curriculum choices would look less at subgroup level differences and look more at how all students progress. If pandemic planning for return to school looked at why some students learned more through a laptop at home than through a classroom experience, I also suspect the answer would remove learning barriers for many students.

> How do the reading skills of our district's elementary school students compare to districts whose students are most like our own? And to what degree is that success enjoyed more or less equally by boys and girls, and different groups of students?

This is a great clarification because it puts the universal question about *all students* in front of the particular question about subgroups of those students by gender or ethnicity. It's also a great question because the answer is *actionable*. If you can identify other schools with kids very much like your own who are enjoying success where your students are lagging, you can call the site or district leaders and see how their approach to teaching reading differs from your own. That last step, compare-and-contrast with colleagues who are teaching students very similar to your own, is where your analytic investment will pay off.

Find the data of highest quality that fit the question most closely

That question requires, first, identifying schools whose kids are most like your own. The three factors that are likely to give you similarity of students in their readiness to learn are (1) parent level of education; (2) percentage of students receiving meal subsidies (a shortcut or proxy for household income); and (3) percentage of students whose first language is not English. This is bread-and-butter demographic data that all states collect.

The second type of data this question requires is a good measure of reading efficacy. You may have to rely on your state assessment for that. But that leads to two problems. The first problem is that the state assessments in most states begin at third grade. By that time, reading instruction has already occurred in kindergarten, first grade and second grade. The second problem is that the grade-level range of difficulty of those assessments stretches to about a grade below and above the grade level tested. (It may be greater than that in some grade levels and subjects.) That is the purpose of these state assessments—to estimate the degree to which students have mastered grade-level standards. So, if a fifth-grade student is reading at the third-grade level, her scale score could be close to the score of a student who is reading at the fourth-grade level. Both could land at the lowest obtainable scale score. That's quite a loss of information. You'll have evidence, but it will be most accurate for those students whose scores fall within a grade level of the grade level tested. When estimating gaps, you're very interested in capturing information about the lowest- and highest-scoring students. And that's exactly what you don't have when you rely on state assessments.[4]

Choose with care the test you'll use for this analysis. State assessments have the strong advantage of being given to all students in each state at the same time. You should have an easy time finding results from similar schools or districts. If, however, your district is using a reading-specific test, or a higher-quality interim assessment, one that includes assessment of early elementary grade-level reading skills, you are far better prepared to answer that question with higher-quality evidence. These assessments target reading skills and measure students more frequently. The more questions a student answers, the more likely the score will estimate that student's actual degree of mastery. Fifty questions asked three times a year results in 150 pieces of information. Compare that to a state assessment that presents 45–55 questions once a year. The interim assessment delivers three times the amount of information.

The second advantage of interim assessments is that their central purpose is to measure growth. They are not focused on the standards to the same degree that state assessments are. In addition, they are not designed to increase the spread among test-takers, as state assessments are. Because interim assessments now use computer-adaptive methods, they can deliver questions to students matched to their level of mastery, independent of their grade level. This should result in more accurate results.

The third advantage of reading-specific tests and interim assessments is that many firms offer versions of their tests for the youngest students—kindergartners and first and second graders. Is it possible to gauge the reading skills of students who are not yet reading? Yes. It may seem odd to test students in the earliest grade levels, but well-built tests can, indeed, estimate the emerging skills that lead to reading. Students' abilities to recognize letters, letter-sounds, similarities, differences and more can all be done intelligently. In addition, oral language fluency can be measured by teachers testing students one-by-one, or by using signal processing technology running on tablets, computers or smartphones. Interpretation of spontaneous, spoken language holds strong clues to a kindergartener's or first grader's readiness to read. When a student reads a written text out loud, advanced signal processing technology can interpret errors as accurately as teachers, and some technologies are equally accurate with students whose first language may be English, Spanish or Cantonese. Phonics skills can now be measured by more highly evolved computer-based assessments than were available five years ago.[5] The specific skills they measure are discrete enough to enable a teacher to use results as a guide to instruction.

The disadvantage of interim assessments is that the only way to compare results with similar schools or districts is when they also use the same interim assessment and agree to share results. Your testing firm should help you find those districts or schools. The top three firms each enjoy large enough market share that they could play matchmaker among their own clients. What they release are national norm tables. But those national norms may not be composed of students who closely resemble your own. If you were to find even one or two districts nearby whose students are similar to your own and who share the same interim assessment and agree to share results, you would be off to a good start.

Build the evidence

Let's presume you have in hand results from your state's assessment and that you're using those results to prepare a presentation to your board in a public meeting. Let's also presume that the assessment really tests reading. That is to say, we're presuming that your state's assessment looks at the complex of skills we call reading and dedicates enough questions to each of those skills so that the final scale score is a fair recap of what comprises reading. Just testing comprehension of written passages, for example, is not a full, multidimensional summary. It only looks at the result of reading. A more well-rounded assessment of reading of early elementary students would look at what makes comprehension possible: phonemic awareness, decoding skills, vocabulary.

You're going to be presenting results that show where your district stands, relative to the state average reading results, and to the results for districts serving similar students. You'll be working within the limits of the grade levels tested—grades 3, 4 and 5. You'll also be showing the difference in scores for boys and girls. What raw material do you need to build evidence to answer this question? For clarity's sake, let's repeat the question:

> How do the reading skills of our elementary school students compare to others that serve students most like our own? And to what degree is that success enjoyed more or less equally by boys and girls, and different groups of students?

Gaps mismeasured

Let's list what you'll need. Consider it a parts list for your construction effort.

- Span of time: minimum of three years of results, and the more, the merrier;
- Metrics: scale score (and if available, the standard error, a measure of imprecision, for your school or district);
- Benchmarks: state average scale score by grade level by year, and scale score for each similar district or school included in comparability set;
- Comparison set: at least a few schools or districts whose students are most like your own;
- Entity: for multiyear analysis, graduating class cohorts (so you'll be analyzing more or less the same kids over time) at the "all students" level and at the subgroup level for boys and girls; and
- Attributes of the entity: the factors most directly related to readiness to learn are parent education, the percent of students receiving subsidized meals and the percent of students who are identified as special ed students or emerging bilingual students (English learners). If you wish to see subgroup level results, of course, you'll need gender and ethnicity attributes.

Like a cook or carpenter, you'll need to be attentive to the quality of your raw materials. Some numbers are of higher quality than others. If you're analyzing the math achievement gap of boys and girls in your elementary schools and comparing it to the gap in schools serving similar students, you will have to be mindful of *partial information*. Only some grade levels are tested, only some standards are tested and standards that are tested are given different numbers of test items. You will also need to be mindful of *the degree of imprecision* in your test results. That imprecision is a function of many things, especially the number of students tested, the number of test items answered. When you try to estimate the size of gaps between two groups of students, you are reckoning with imprecision from both. Psychometricians are used to making sense of imprecise evidence. But the rest of us are less accustomed to that approach. And many state departments of education reveal that imprecision—sometimes called the standard error of measurement—only in the technical manuals. Rarely will district leaders, principals or teachers ever see a hint that the test numbers are imprecise, inexact. But the size of that imprecision is known. And yes, the size of that imprecision matters. It enables you to estimate the size of gaps, allowing for the imprecision.

To show what can be done with the right materials in the hands of analysts in command of the right tools, let's take a look at the way that the National Center for Education Statistics expresses the gap measures on the National Assessment of Educational Progress.

Show and tell your evidence effectively

The National Assessment of Educational Progress (NAEP) has been the nation's report card for a long time. It was first given in 1969 to a large sample of students in grades 4, 8 and 12 in every state, enabling us to see what students in those three grade levels know and can do. Under the steady hand of the leadership of the National Center for Education Statistics (NCES), it has won enough funding from Congress to allow it to be administered every two years in four subject areas: mathematics, reading, science and writing. Starting in 2001, with the passage of the No Child Left Behind law, any state that received federal funding for Title I had to give the NAEP test in reading and math to a portion of its students. This provided for full participation in a test that was quite stable over many years.

Keep in mind it is designed to answer questions about the changing levels of academic mastery of students in the same grade level (or age) over time. A typical question that can be answered well by NAEP evidence is "How have the reading or math skills of eighth-graders changed from 2007 to 2019?" Note that the NAEP has remained a fairly stable and steady instrument since 2001, when they began testing math and reading in all states every two years.

Because of this stability, the analysts at the National Center for Education Statistics (NCES) have been able to analyze many trends, including gap measures. Figure 4.4 offers one example, showing the math scores of eighth-grade students who identify as white and Latino/Hispanic, from 1990 through 2019. This big view makes the longer patterns clear. The difference in the two groups' scale scores has been steady from 2009 through 2019.

The reason these forms of representation are sound is that they meet the test for showing level of achievement and relative gaps of achievement

Gaps mismeasured

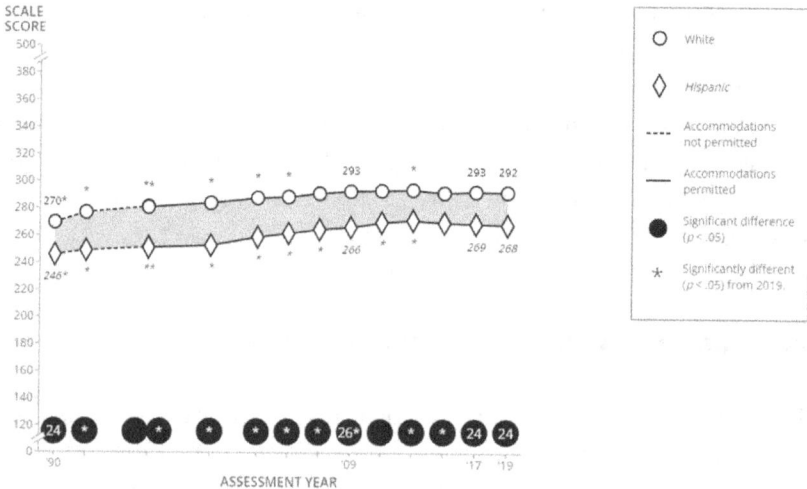

Figure 4.4 Scores of white and Latino/Hispanic eighth-grade students on the National Assessment of Educational Progress from 1990 to 2019
This shows the scores of white and Latino/Hispanic eighth-grade students on the math portion of NAEP from 1990 to 2019.
Source: National Assessment of Educational Progress

at the same time. You can put what you see into words, and if you do so clearly while displaying these visualizations, your audience should be able to nod in agreement—or perhaps disagree—but with the same evidence in front of everyone. Showing 29 years of scores also avoids games that can be played by those who select a starting point for a trend only because it favors their argument.

However, one of the limits of taking a single grade level and viewing its students' score differences year by year is that you are missing the opportunity to view the size of the gap change over time for the *same group of students* (a truly longitudinal view), or next best, *the same graduating class cohort* (a quasi-longitudinal view). If you were to look at the results for the same students over time, the pattern would enable you to answer a different question: "Is the math achievement gap growing, shrinking or remaining constant as our students advance grade level by grade level through our school or district?" This observation leads to a cautionary tip. Choose your words carefully when summarizing this evidence. Opportunities for misunderstanding diminish as the clarity of your words rise.

Case #3: measuring gaps in opportunities to learn

Why isn't there more discussion about creation and distribution of opportunities to learn, those very factors that are entirely in the hands of leadership? In our view, this is where education leaders and board members have the greatest freedom to act, and the greatest responsibility to do so. Opportunities to learn are what schools are expected to create. Indeed, opportunities to learn are the reason schools exist.

When district leaders recruit teachers, and when high school principals design master schedules, they have their hands on the controls. The results are not dependent upon student effort or parent involvement. Students, parents, teachers and voters are right to expect that those opportunities are of high quality and are distributed fairly. The measurement of opportunities to learn, and the variation in student use of those opportunities, should simply be one part of every district's disclosure report to its public. Your state may impose accountability reports on your district and schools. But if you are a board member or district leader, you are free to add to those reports what you consider to be important and to express it as you see fit.

School assignment policies

In too many communities, segregated housing patterns result in segregated schools. Housing patterns aren't the fault of district school boards or administrators. But accepting segregated housing patterns as if they were "natural" boundaries is a surrender to biased practices. Many districts in the U.S. have created approaches to enrollment that deliberately cross segregated housing lines. It's not easy. It's certain to spark pushback. School board meetings won't be boring if you take this step.

I don't want to discuss the question of how to draw attendance boundaries to minimize de facto segregated housing patterns. Although it is a part of a district's ability to create equal access to high-quality opportunities to learn, I wanted to mention it because it is a big part of a district's DNA. How a district shares access to its schools is as basic as it gets.

Rather, I want to discuss what you do with teachers and courses that may differ across school sites. In addition, I want to suggest that giving parents a choice of school sites within your district enables you to free parents of feeling trapped by boundary lines you drew. Rather than defend the district assigning students to schools, why not let the students and their parents choose their schools?

Why are school assignment policies so related to the equal sharing of opportunities to learn? Like it or not, schools earn reputations in every district. One middle school gets a reputation as a better school, another as a rougher one. One high school gets a reputation as a college-bound high, and another as a skill-building campus that prepares students for work. These reputations may be untrue, contain a kernel of truth or be largely true. But whatever their degree of truthfulness, those leading and governing districts have in hand the ability to measure how their middle or high schools differ. In this era of public mistrust of government, you can build stronger bonds of trust with your public if you share what you know about the variation across schools of teachers and course offerings, about differing kinds of support for lagging students and leading students. These result in opportunities to learn that must differ.

Teacher assignment across school sites

You have information about teachers, site by site. They are at the heart of variation among sites in opportunities to learn. While you may not control who works where, if your district is bound by labor agreements that let teachers choose schools based on seniority, you know the consequences. The sharing of your knowledge of attributes of teachers is one small step to creating opportunities to learn, because you're opening up all resources in your districts to what parents and students believe suits them best.

Those attributes that you know well that you might share with your public include:

- Years of experience teaching;
- Years worked in your district;
- Years continuously on staff at current school;
- Gender;
- Level of education attained;
- Credential held and year obtained; and
- Subject area specialization.

Some of these facts may already be in your school accountability report cards. But you might consider making the data more understandable in comparative form, site by site. You could provide this as an informational flyer to parents of students already enrolled, close to the end of the school year, as you encourage them to reenroll next year.

I looked toward the health sector for models that districts might follow. By stroke of good luck, I found that Kaiser Permanente, a large health maintenance organization in Northern California, where I was a member for 30-plus years, made available a flyer about each doctor in their system. Doctors themselves wrote a short personal statement, and Kaiser added relevant facts about those doctors from their records. This appeared in examination rooms, waiting rooms, and on Kaiser's website. It's a way to get acquainted, and it helped patients new and old feel more connected to their doctors.

The master schedule's key role

The evidence of equitable distribution of opportunities to learn is encoded in the master schedule. Your high school's enrollment, your funding and your ability to compete for teachers all are limiting factors, of course. However, I encourage you to take a fresh look at your high school's master schedule with the following equity-related questions in mind: Are the resources equally available to students in all programs, and are those resources of equivalent quality?

Who teaches whom? If your most junior math teachers are assigned to teach your developmental math courses, and your most senior math teachers assigned to teach the most rigorous math courses, have you created opportunities to learn of roughly equal quality at both ends of the spectrum? Are your long-term English learners assigned to teachers who have the right credentials to help them gain mastery of academic English, and finally get reclassified as fluent English proficient?

Do you have enough seats available in enough sections of college-bound courses so that all students who want to take that course will face no barriers to enrolling? Or do you have a thin inventory of high-demand classes, which turns registration into a student-versus-student roller derby competition? It's not fair to students to make them fight for access to a course that's key to their futures and unnecessarily in short supply.

Have you assigned teachers to work out-of-field of their subject area authorizations? In some states, this is not allowed. In other states, it's acceptable only with a board's granting a waiver. But whatever the laws in your state, assigning a teacher to lead a course in which she lacks subject-matter expertise and a formal subject-area authorization is often bad move. It often marks a lower quality opportunity to learn.

How well matched are the courses to the interests of its students? If 90 percent of your sections are dedicated to college-level course work, and 50 percent of your graduating seniors have chosen a path to the workforce or the military, then your master schedule constrains the opportunities to learn that your students care most about. Have you balanced demand for courses to the supply you've created? Work force prep courses and multiple pathways toward work-related professions would be a needed addition for that school. The question for those leading or governing districts is how actively you listen to students when they tell you what future they're aiming for, and the extent to which you direct your budget and staff to meet their desires.

Case #4: building evidence to detect gender bias in teachers' grading practices

Most district leaders and school board members declare their commitment to equitable practices. Yet this concern rarely leads to measurement of those things adults in charge are clearly responsible for: teacher bias in awarding grades; the assignment of high school teachers to particular subjects and students; and the unequal investment in creating educational opportunities for students pursuing a career or college path. The first of these—teacher bias in grading—is the focus of this case.

These are the adult decisions where the line of causation is straight and clear. That makes it decidedly different than examining differences in test scores, which are the result of a vast combination of factors and for which teachers and administrators have only a partial responsibility.

To be sure, a measurement project to detect teacher bias would be a political hot potato. It would take courage for both the district leaders and the school board trustees to take a stand like this. In some districts, it could lead to friction with their teachers union. It might require putting equitable treatment of students higher on the priority list than teacher job rights, especially if a teacher with seniority turns out to have displayed biased grading policies. Would a discipline action be required? Might that lead to a grievance hearing? Would students request a retroactive adjustment of their grades? Any boost to a college-bound student's grade-point average could help that student gain admission to the college of his choice. Teacher bias in grading could be a make-or-break factor in a student's gaining admission to the college of her choice, making it a potential harm with high-stakes for any student.

Methods of building evidence of bias in grading

The method here is that you start with someone's assertion. Let's say, for instance, that your district's parent advisory committee has accused your district of gender bias favoring girls in teacher-assigned grades in middle school. You are the assistant superintendent of curriculum and instruction, and your superintendent has asked you to look into the accusation. You turn to your assessment director and ask how she would determine the degree to which that charge might be true.

Your district already has in its hands the knowledge of each student's teachers, subject by subject, section by section. It possesses the knowledge of grades assigned by those teachers to each student. It possesses the history of each student's courses, and grades earned, as well as test scores for some subjects. If a teacher is particularly strict in grading all students, giving more Ds and Fs and fewer As and Bs than other teachers, that's one thing. But if a teacher assigns primarily boys the lower grades, that might reveal bias. But don't be too hasty to reach that conclusion. All over the United States, girls outscore boys in English language arts, in some places to a large degree.[6] So, if one teacher assigns girls higher grades than boys, that teacher is hardly out of the ordinary. But if that teacher assigns all girl students over two years' time higher grades than boy students, this consistency would support the theory that the teacher's judgment is biased.

How might you discover a pattern of bias? How do you estimate the amount of bias? Can you also gauge how confident you are in your findings? There are several approaches worth trying. You could compare the frequency with which other teachers in the same school assign lower grades to boys than to girls, and then compare each of the teachers who favor girls over boys to the median difference between boys and girls. The farther out from the median you go, the greater the difference. If that difference is noticeably larger for the five teachers in your high school who graded boys more harshly, you have evidence that's worth exploring further.

A deeper look at those students taught by those five teachers would be a prudent next step. Look at the grades of those students—boys and girls—in the other classes they take. Run two simple tests. The first test would be to compare the grades of each student in the class taught by the teachers you suspect of gender bias to the grades they earn in other classes. If some of the boys' grades are lowest in the class taught by the teacher you suspect of bias, that may be due to natural variation of students' academic skills. But if a large proportion of the boys' grades are lowest in the class taught by those you suspect may be biased, then you are seeing additional evidence of possible bias. If you were to run the same test on girls' grades and compare the proportion of girls with lowest scores in that suspected teacher's class to the proportion of boys with lowest scores, you'd have yet another piece of evidence that estimates the size of the bias.

You might also compare the students' grades in the prior years to the grades earned in the same subject taught by the teachers you suspect to be biased. This historical comparison of consistency in math grades over time is handy, because you would expect a student who has earned a grade of B in math in grades 6 and 7 would also be capable of earning a B in grade 8. The more students you can pull into this analysis, the firmer your conclusion, because variation in any single student's results is not surprising. But a decline of a full point in grades assigned to 50 out of 70 boys in math would indicate a troubling pattern.

Finally, you could also look at the association of interim assessment results against teacher-assigned grades. True, grades don't solely reflect a student's mastery of a subject. Many teachers include other factors into the grades they assign: class participation, attendance, homework and more. But if in eighth grade, a bunch of boys' interim assessment results are higher than the grades they've been assigned by five of your teachers, then you've got evidence of a problem.

Customary methods of visualizing gaps

Let's contrast two approaches to visual evidence about gaps. The first approach is common but flawed. It lacks context, ignores imprecision and invites misunderstandings. It just delivers the numbers. The second approach is not simple because it delivers rich context, reveals imprecision and paves the road to real understanding. The good news is that this second approach is already built. It is free. It is yours for the asking, and we'll show you how to use it.

The customary representation of gaps in test scores

The common ways of expressing differences in test scores deserve more attention than they've received. While most contain some technical errors, most of which are visible and vary in importance from the trivial to the large, all contain logical assumptions that are not visible on the surface. It is the logical consequences that are perhaps more damaging, especially if they are not made explicit.

Washoe County School District, Nevada

This visual representation of the 2019 Smarter Balanced English/language arts test results of the students in grades 3–8 is all too common (see Figure 4.5).[7] This is intended to speak for itself, like many tables of descriptive statistics. But the message is not self-evident. Before calling out its technical flaws that make the intended message harder to see, I want to underscore its unstated premise. The premise is that students' test scores vary by ethnicity *primarily because of their school experience*. In pursuit of better insight into the origins of these differences in test scores, we need far better evidence than this to understand the degree to which many factors in combination have led to these gaps.

This bar chart's technical flaws are many. The chart's title lacks a reference to grade levels represented, leaving the less informed reader to assume that it describes all students in the district. The vertical axis lacks a legend. Despite a legend for colors, we have no clue what those levels represent. The results appear as a 100 percent stacked-bar view, with the lowest level scores at the bottom. This makes it easiest to compare the student subgroup based on their level 4 (lowest) score band. But to compare them based on the highest two levels (1 and 2), we have to print the bar chart and turn it upside down, or stand on our head. We also have no idea

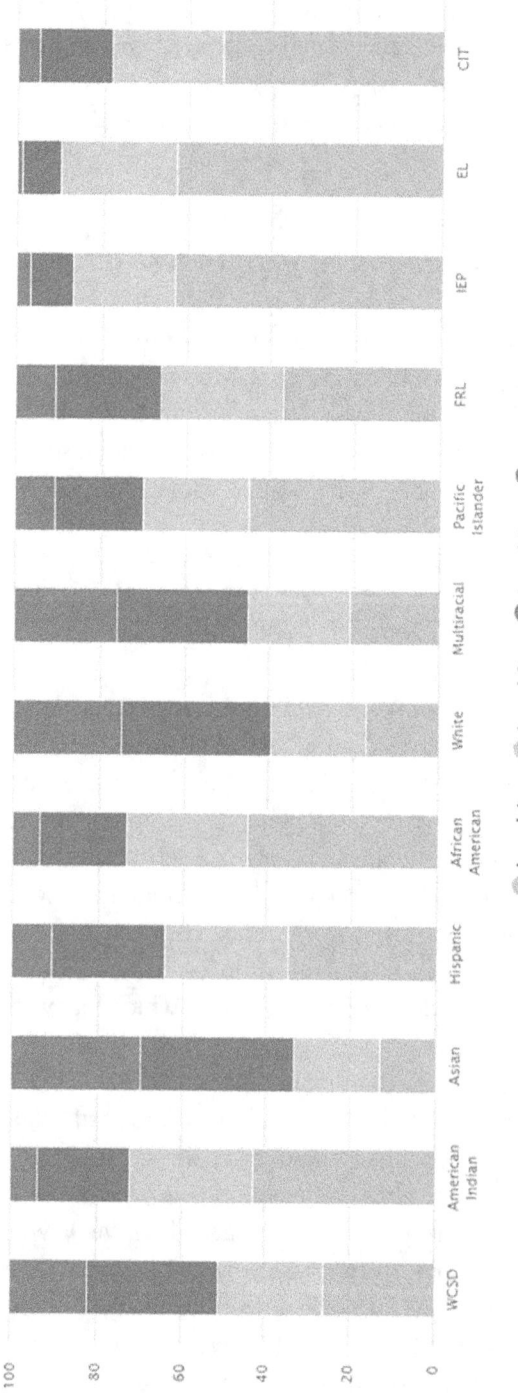

Figure 4.5 Student subgroup results by score level on Smarter Balanced English language arts test (2019), Washoe County, Nevada School District

The 2019 Smarter Balanced test results in English/language arts for all subgroups, shown by score level. This stacked-bar display urges readers to compare proportion of students who scored lowest.

Source: Washoe County, Nevada School District

of the number of students represented in each subgroup, nor do we know the number in each segment. This would enable us to disregard subgroup findings for very small numbers of students. We are denied knowledge of the category assignment error, which is published in the technical manual to the Smarter Balanced assessment.

We are not surprised to see the English learner students in the column second from the right have such a large proportion of students' scores in the level 1 (lowest) band. They are not yet considered to be fluent readers and writers of academic English. We are also not surprised to see students with individual education plans (those in the column third from the right) have the largest proportion of students scoring in the level 1 band. They have a learning disability. But what do these results mean? Without a context and without benchmarks, how is anyone to answer that question?

National Assessment of Educational Progress and the hazard of comparing states' results

The National Assessment of Education Progress (NAEP) is known as the nation's report card, and it has also sparked a hot national debate. One of those debates is whether it should be used as evidence to compare how states' educational systems are faring. It wasn't until 1988 that Congress authorized trials of state-level reporting. Those trials occurred in 1990, 1992 and 1994. Only in 1996 did NAEP release the first posttrial results that could be interpreted at the state level. To persuade some states to participate that had been reluctant through the trial period, Congress, when it passed the No Child Left Behind legislation in 2001, told states that if they wanted to get Title I money, they had to participate in NAEP.

But is that a sufficient common ground to enable the NAEP to allow for a comparison of how well states are educating their students? Or can the NAEP results enable a person to reach conclusions about the quality of schools in their state, compared to others? Well, if each state had students of a similar background, the answer would be "yes." With parents of similar education and household income, and with parents who have equivalent abilities to read, write and speak English, that comparison would be okay. But that's far from the reality. When reporters compare state-level results every two years when the NAEP data are released, what are they reporting?

They are reporting about *who* took the NAEP, and *how they scored* on math and English language arts. The attributes of the 9-year-olds, 13-year-olds and 17-year-olds (equivalent to students in grades 4, 8 and 12) vary greatly from state to state. Just consider the differences in the proportion of students who in the fall of 2018 were English learners in Texas (18.7 percent), Minnesota (8.5 percent) and Ohio (3.4 percent).[8] That human factor will have a considerable effect on students' NAEP results. Combining their human differences together with their scores, state by state, results in quite a messy mix when you try to compare states' results. What you get is a mix of both.

More discrete comparisons are possible. You could compare the results of your state's Hispanic/Latino identified students to students of the same ethnicity in another state. Yet this reveals another question. Is similarity based on ethnicity alone sufficient to establish a reasonable basis for comparison? What if students' economic well-being (as expressed through the proxy measure of whether a student is eligible for free or reduced-price meals) is also different in the states you select for comparison? What if parents' level of education also differs in a way that corresponds to ethnicity, too. You'd then have two confounding factors wrapped up in your analysis of students of the same ethnicity across states. The comparison you make should simply be one you do with eyes wide open. That means, you should *not attribute score differences to ethnicity alone simply because that was the single attribute you used to cluster them.*

Many more trip wires await the unwary who wander into the minefield that is NAEP. Morgan Polikoff has written a handy summary of these hazards in a blog post titled, "Friends don't let friends misuse NAEP data."[9] His essay provides ample warnings of what he terms "misNAEPery," and a few examples of misuse of NAEP results by presidential candidates and even a secretary of education. An article in *Education Week*, "When Bad Things Happen to Good NAEP Data," offers more sobering examples of mistaken conclusions by people in high places who should know better.[10] Tom Loveless, a former Brookings expert, added an important examination of what "proficiency" means in NAEP's reports.[11] One thing it decidedly does *not* mean is "grade level" achievement. He also reveals a rather heated debate about the validity of NAEP's achievement levels, citing a report from the National Academy of Sciences that called the NAEP achievement levels "fundamentally flawed."

Exemplary models of gap measurement: Stanford Educational Opportunity Project

A talented team at Stanford, led by Sean Reardon, who is professor of poverty and inequality at their Graduate School of Education, came together in 2009 to form the Center for Education Policy Analysis (CEPA). Unlike many centers of scholarship, which aim to influence other scholars and policy-makers, Sean Reardon and his colleagues at CEPA also aimed to inform practitioners. Out of this group, Sean Reardon led the formation of the Stanford Education Data Archive (SEDA). They started work building a research asset that all scholars could use, a 10-year compilation of students' test results, together with data about the schools and districts these students attended. They stirred this pot of data soup together with Census Bureau data about the communities served by these schools and districts and invited hundreds of researchers to use it wisely. The results included dozens of research papers about inequality, a few of which caught the attention of the *New York Times'* reporting teams who reported on some of the more interesting papers.

In 2019, the Stanford Educational Opportunity Project debuted their Educational Opportunity Explorer. This advanced the power of their storytelling considerably by adding to test scores two additional measures: test score trends and the learning rate. The learning rate is their measure of growth in students' scores, and they've done so over 10 years' time starting with the period from 2009 to 2018. The visual representations include a map, a dynamic scatterplot and a report you can generate and download, without cost. It is indeed a gift to those who care about educational opportunity. Want to filter results by geography? Limit your results to one state? Examine gaps by gender, ethnicity or socioeconomic status? Want to compare results across a set of districts or schools? It's all there.

Their statistical methods for creating a common denominator for all states' test results required some heavy lifting. In brief, they used the National Assessment of Educational Progress to equate each state's test, using only the results of students in third grade through eighth grade. Scale scores of tests were converted into an equivalent of grade level, which they defined as the average result nationally each year. While psychometricians resist using the term "grade level" at all, Sean Reardon's SEDA team favored using the vocabulary the rest of us speak. The compromise was a wise choice. If you care to examine their methods, you'll find their documentation to be clear to a non-statistician.[12]

We have used their Educational Opportunity Explorer to tell three different stories, each of them a tale of two districts. All look at the difference in results between Latino/Hispanic and white students' test scores. The three pairs offer comparative views while telling three different gap stories. These are cautionary tales, designed to alert you to the power of context, the power of comparative measures and the hazards that await those who ignore the nuances. Case A offers two districts with small test score gaps, but with big differences in the level of their students' test scores. Case B presents two districts with big differences in both their socioeconomic profiles and test score gaps. Case C examines districts in two college towns and raises the question of whether test scores or learning rates should be what your gap analysis measures.

Case A: small test score gaps but substantial difference in levels of test scores

Here is a tale of two districts that both show no test score gap and very little difference in district free-or-reduced-price lunch or community socioeconomic factors. The districts are Bloomfield, Indiana, and Warren Consolidated School District, Michigan. Where they do differ is in the level of achievement their students' test scores imply. Here's how they appear on the Stanford Educational Opportunity Explorer (see Figure 4.6). In this representation, the socioeconomic status of the district's community is on the horizontal axis, and average test scores are on the vertical axis. (Scores in math and English language arts were merged by the Stanford team for the purpose of reducing imprecision in the results.) Bloomfield appears above the national average line for test scores (horizontal line), and Warren Consolidated Schools appears below the line. Because both districts sit nearly equidistant from the vertical center line that marks the national average for family's socioeconomic status, we know the communities both districts serve are similar in this respect.

Gaps mismeasured

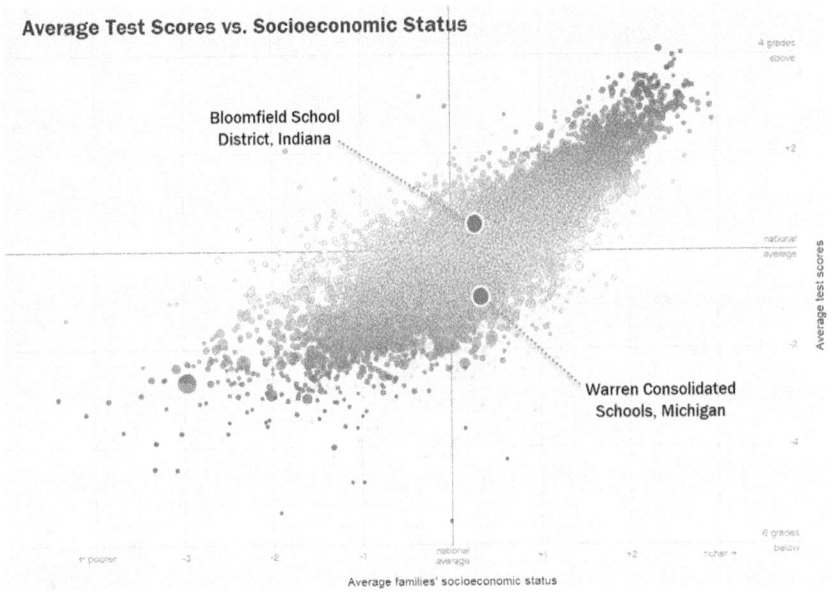

To explore this image interactively, go to https://tinyurl.com/ytc5w5b2 on the Stanford Educational Opportunity Explorer's website, or explore it on the book's website at https://www.k12measures.com/ch4/#Fig4.6.

Figure 4.6 Average test scores vs. socioeconomic status in Bloomfield School District, Indiana, and Warren Consolidated Schools, Michigan

The average test scores from 2009 to 2018 for students of Warren Consolidated Schools were well below that of the scores for students in Bloomfield School District. Note that the two districts had equivalent family socioeconomic status just slightly higher than the national average.

Source: © Sean F. Reardon and The Educational Opportunity Project at Stanford University

But in the next step, we can see the average test scores of both white and Hispanic students at the same time for both districts. Hispanic students' scores are represented on the vertical axis and white students' scores on the horizontal axis (see Figure 4.7). The Warren Consolidated Schools' Hispanic students' scores were -0.82 grade levels below the national average, and white students' scores were almost equally below (-0.69 grade levels). In Bloomfield School District, Hispanic students' average scores were +0.5 grade levels above, and white students' scores

Gaps mismeasured

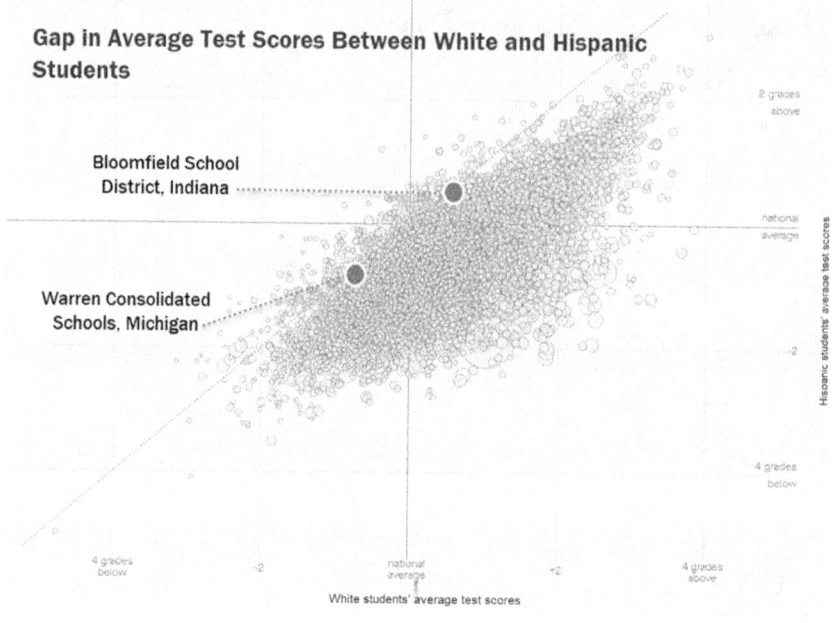

To explore this image interactively, go to https://tinyurl.com/mr2ss487 on the Stanford Educational Opportunity Explorer's website, or explore it on the book's website at https://www.k12measures.com/ch4/#Fig4.7.

Figure 4.7 Gap in average test scores between white and Hispanic students in Bloomfield School District, Indiana, and Warren Consolidated Schools, Michigan

While students' scores in the two districts are far apart, within both districts there is a negligible gap in scores between white and Hispanic students. That's why both districts appear on the diagonal line.

Source: © Sean F. Reardon and The Educational Opportunity Project at Stanford University

+0.6 grade levels above the national average. This is why both districts fall on the diagonal line that defines the points where both subgroups' scores are the same. In effect, both districts have no test score gap for their Hispanic and white students over this 10-year period. But in Bloomfield, those scores were above the national average for both Hispanic and white students. In Warren Consolidated Schools, those scores were below the national average.

To complete this analysis, we need evidence of a more specific nature about the socioeconomic differences separating the Hispanic and white students themselves. After all, if we have a measure of differences in test results, shouldn't we be equally attentive to differences in those contextual factors that also tend to affect academic accomplishment? The Stanford team has put their talents to work and has created the evidence that enables us to see this, as well. In this scatterplot, we're looking at gaps of both kinds. The vertical axis displays the gap in average test scores between Hispanic and white students. The horizontal axis displays the gap in the free-and-reduced-price meals rate between Hispanic and white students. This is an economic measure different from the community socioeconomic measure. Both districts fall right at the intersection of the two "zero gap" lines (see Figure 4.8). Warren Consolidated shows a tiny 0.13 grade-level difference in their Hispanic and white students' average test scores. Bloomfield shows an equally tiny 0.10 grade level gap. So we can say that in both districts, their students' negligible test score gap is equivalent to their negligible meal subsidy gap.

Note that most, but not all, of the districts that appear here (the 10,000 larger districts in the U.S.) fall to the right of the vertical "no gap" line describing district free-and-reduced-price lunch rate. Those to the left of the vertical center line are those where the proportion of Hispanic students getting meal subsidies is smaller than the proportion of white students getting meal subsidies. And most of the districts are also above the horizontal "no gap" line that describes test score differences between Hispanic and white students. This is a dramatic display of the entanglement of economics and ethnicity. You may choose to pay attention to one factor, but you'll always get a big dose of the other.

The lesson to be learned from this comparison is that there are many ways that students of different ethnic groups can end up with equivalent test scores. When the socioeconomic factors are equal, the equivalence of test results is welcome news, but it's not the only news worth noting.

Gaps mismeasured

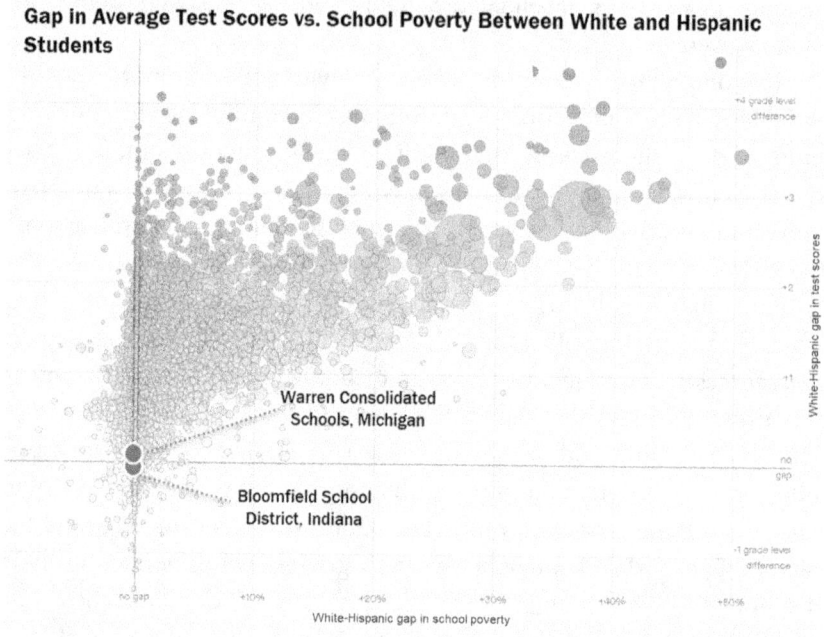

To explore this image interactively, go to https://tinyurl.com/mr2ss487 on the Stanford Educational Opportunity Explorer's website, or explore it on the book's website at https://www.k12measures.com/ch4/#Fig4.8.

Figure 4.8 Gap in average test scores vs. school poverty between white and Hispanic students in Bloomfield School District, Indiana, and Warren Consolidated Schools, Michigan

This view plots the white–Hispanic test score gap against the white–Hispanic meal subsidy gap. The purpose is to see the degree to which those two measures of difference are similar in size. For these two districts, both gap measures are close to zero.

Source: © Sean F. Reardon and The Educational Opportunity Project at Stanford University

Case B: big difference in socioeconomic profiles, and big difference in test score gaps

Here's a tale of two districts that are on opposite sides of the tracks. Aldine ISD in Texas is pretty far to the left of the national average socioeconomic scale (-1.07 standard deviations below). Rosemount-Apple Valley-Eagan,

Minnesota, is pretty far to the right of the national average (+1.46 standard deviations above). What's interesting about this pair of districts is that their students' average test scores parallel their communities' socioeconomic well-being. Aldine ISD's student's average scores from 2009 to 2018 were about -0.74 of a grade level below the national average. Rosemount-Apple Valley-Eagan's students' average scores, on the other hand, were about +1.42 grade levels above the national average (see Figure 4.9).

Now let's examine the average test scores of both white and Hispanic students at the same time for both districts (see Figure 4.10). Hispanic students'

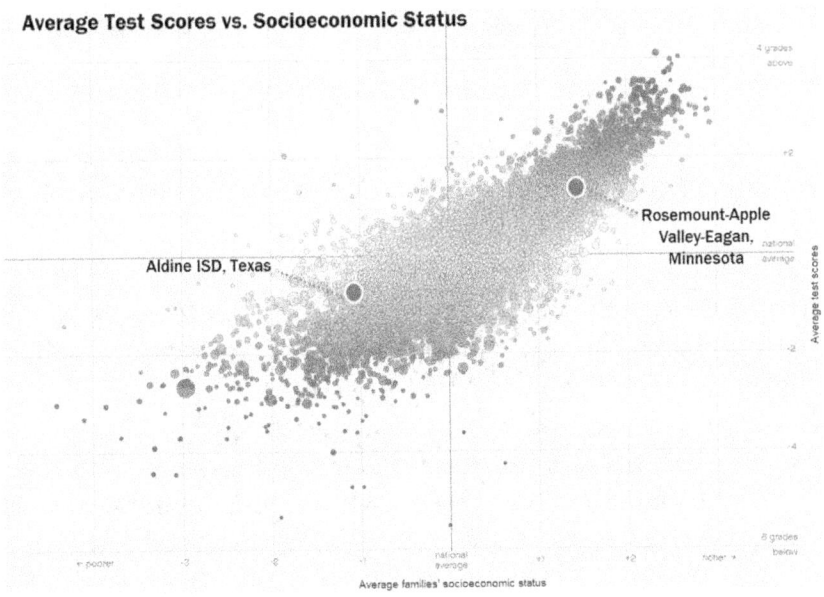

To explore this image interactively, go to https://bit.ly/30Xs3d2 the Stanford Educational Opportunity Explorer's website, or explore it on the book's website at https://www.k12measures.com/ch4/#Fig4.9.

Figure 4.9 Average students' test scores vs. socioeconomic status in Aldine, Texas, and Rosemount-Apple Valley-Eagan, Minnesota

The average test scores from 2009 to 2018 for students of Aldine ISD were well below that of the scores for students in the Rosemount-Apple Valley-Eagan District. But also note that the two districts served families that were vastly different in education and income.

Source: © Sean F. Reardon and The Educational Opportunity Project at Stanford University

Gaps mismeasured

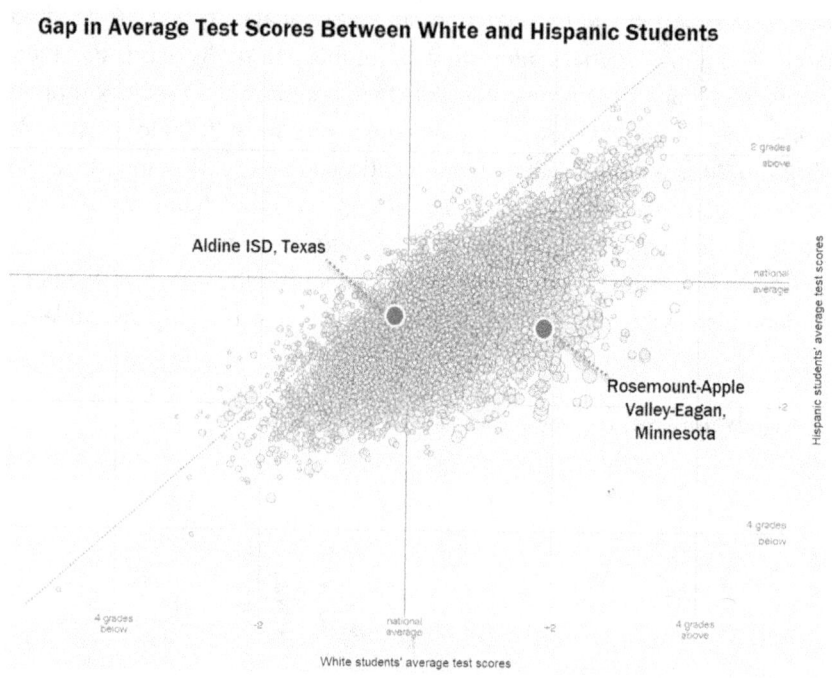

To explore this image interactively, go to https://tinyurl.com/3bb8sz5u on the Stanford Educational Opportunity Explorer's website, or explore it on the book's website at https://www.k12measures.com/ch4/#Fig4.10.

Figure 4.10 Gap in average test scores between white and Hispanic students in Aldine, Texas, and Rosemount-Apple Valley-Eagan, Minnesota

The test scores of white and Hispanic students in Aldine ISD are a small distance apart (.41 grade levels). That explains their proximity to that diagonal "zero gap" line. But the gap separating white and Hispanic students in Rosemount-Apple Valley-Eagan is quite large (2.63 grade levels), which is why they are so far from the diagonal "zero gap" line.

Source: © Sean F. Reardon and The Educational Opportunity Project at Stanford University

scores are represented on the vertical axis, and white students' scores on the horizontal axis. The Hispanic students' scores in Aldine ISD were the equivalent of -0.59 grade levels below the national average, and white students' scores were a bit less below (-0.18 grade level), a difference of .41 grade levels. In Rosemount-Apple Valley-Eagan, Hispanic students' average scores were -0.74 grade levels below the national average, and white students' scores +1.89 grade levels above the national average on average over the period from 2009 through

2018. The gap separating these two subgroups is the sum of those two numbers: the equivalent of 2.63 grade levels. Aldine ISD falls close to that diagonal "zero gap" line, while Rosemount-Apple Valley-Eagan district falls far to the right. In geometric terms, comparing the Hispanic–white test score gaps, we just compare the distance of each district from the "zero gap" diagonal line.

Here's the third step of this analysis: gap measures of student specific economic and test score factors (see Figure 4.11). This is a measure of just

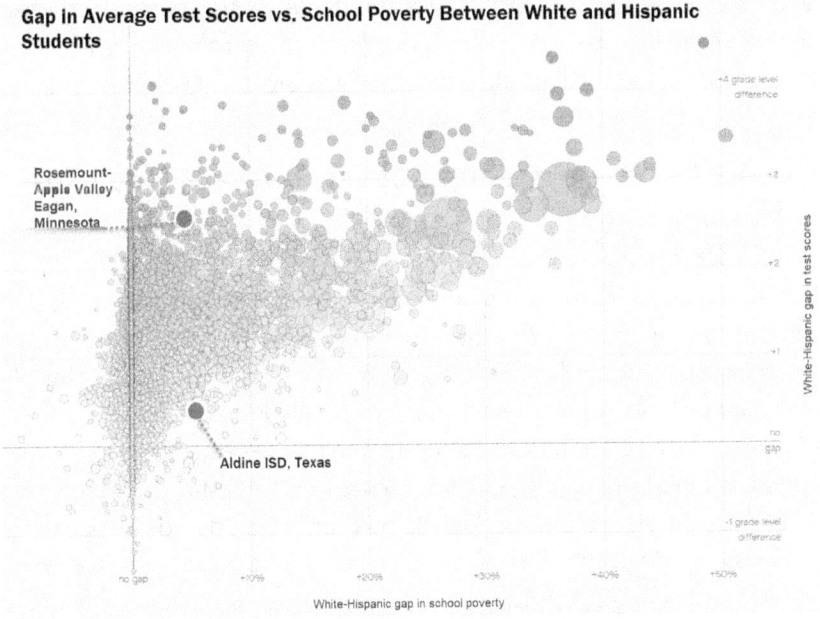

To explore this image interactively, go to https://tinyurl.com/3bb8sz5u on the Stanford Educational Opportunity Explorer's website, or explore it on the book's website at https://www.k12measures.com/ch4/#Fig4.11.

Figure 4.11 Gap in average test scores vs. gap in school poverty between white and Hispanic students in Aldine, Texas, and Rosemount-Apple Valley-Eagan, Minnesota

This view plots the white–Hispanic test score gap against the white–Hispanic meal subsidy gap. The purpose is to see the degree to which those two measures of difference are similar in size. For these two districts, the meal subsidy gap between white and Hispanic students is small and nearly identical (4–5 percent). Yet the white–Hispanic test score gap within these two districts is vastly different.

Source: © Sean F. Reardon and The Educational Opportunity Project at Stanford University

Gaps mismeasured

differences. It is stronger because the socioeconomic differences describe the Hispanic and white students themselves. The vertical axis displays the gap in average test scores between Hispanic and white students. It's about 0.41 grade levels in Aldine ISD, Texas, and the equivalent of about 2.63 grade levels in the Rosemount-Apple Valley-Eagan district. While we've seen this in the prior scatterplot, we haven't seen it expressed together with economic gaps. The horizontal axis displays that gap in the free-and-reduced-price meals rate between Hispanic and white students, and as you can see, it's a fairly small gap in both districts: about 4–5 percent for both districts. This leaves us wondering why two districts where the free-and-reduced-price meals gap separating Hispanic and white students is so small would see such a large gap in test scores.

Case C: test score gaps may be less relevant than gaps in learning rates

Two suburban mid-size communities, each of which is home to sizable colleges, are quite similar in their socioeconomic profiles, based mainly on levels of household income and education. They are geographically separated by 2,800 miles: the Charlottesville City Public School District in Virginia and Chico Unified in California. The question that these two rather similar school districts pose is fundamental to the question you are trying to answer. Do test scores themselves hold the meaning you're pursuing? Or does *the rate at which students learn provide stronger evidence* when building estimates of gaps?

The two districts hug the vertical center line, showing a very similar socioeconomic profile in their communities (see Figure 4.12). Their students' average test scores sit just above and below the horizontal line defining the national average. Charlottesville's students' average scores were +0.37 grade levels above that line, and Chico's students' average scores were -0.58 grade levels below the line. The distance between them, then, is equivalent to about one grade level (0.95).

But now, let's look at the learning rate over the period 2009–2018. Learning rate is just an estimate of how much students learn in one year in school. To derive this, the Stanford team calculated grade-to-grade improvements in performance within each graduating class cohort. Their view is that learning rates are the single best measure of what schools and districts add to what students bring to school.[13]

Gaps mismeasured

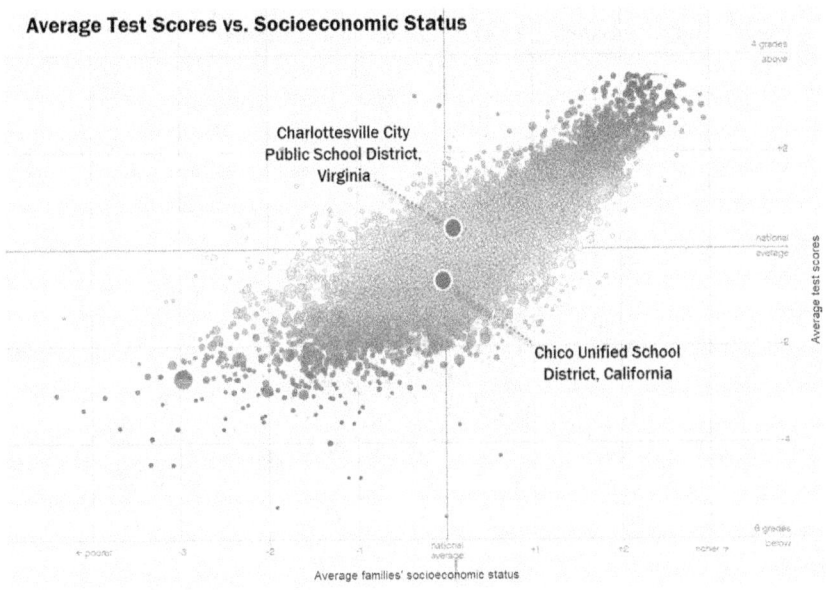

To explore this image interactively, go to https://tinyurl.com/2sft4k9k on the Stanford Educational Opportunity Explorer's website, or explore it on the book's website at https://www.k12measures.com/ch4/#Fig4.12.

Figure 4.12 Average students' test scores vs. socioeconomic status in Charlottesville City Public School District, Virginia, and Chico Unified School District, California

The average test scores from 2009 to 2018 for students of Chico USD were the equivalent of about one grade level below that of the scores for students in the Charlottesville Public Schools. Note that the two districts served families that were quite similar in their socioeconomic attributes.

Source: © Sean F. Reardon and The Educational Opportunity Project at Stanford University

The two districts have *switched positions*. Now Chico is above the national average, and Charlottesville below, and the difference between the two is much larger than their difference in test scores (see Figure 4.13). Chico's students over those 10 years learned at a rate that was about 24 percent higher than the national average learning rate. Charlottesville's students learned at a rate about 20 percent lower. In other words, by these estimates, students in Chico gained the equivalent of about five years of achievement in four years' time.

Gaps mismeasured

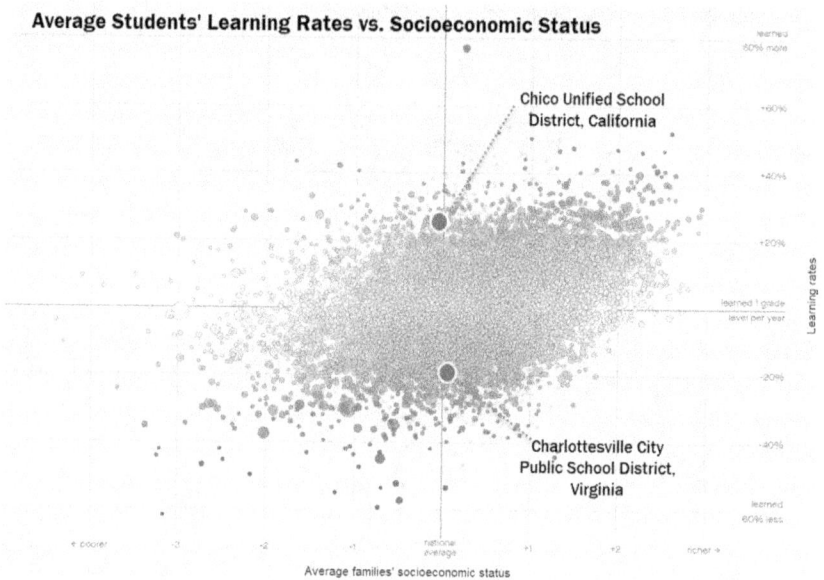

To explore this image interactively, go to https://tinyurl.com/yt32y7hs on the Stanford Educational Opportunity Explorer's website, or explore it on the book's website at https://www.k12measures.com/ch4/#Fig4.13

Figure 4.13 Average students' learning rates vs. socioeconomic status in Charlottesville City Public School District, Virginia, and Chico Unified School District, California

The learning rates of students in these two districts reveal that Chico USD students learned at a rate about 24 percent higher than the national average, while students in Charlottesville Public Schools learned at a rate about 20 percent below the national average.

Source: © Sean F. Reardon and The Educational Opportunity Project at Stanford University

Now let's look at the difference in test scores and learning rates for students who identify as Hispanic and those who identify as white. The contrast between these two views is stunning. First, the gap in test results finds the two districts to be pretty far to the right side of the "zero gap" diagonal line. But their students' results by ethnicity are quite different. In Charlottesville, Hispanic students' results, on average over this 10-year period, were very close to the national average (-0.28 grade levels below). Their white students' results, on the other hand, were far to the right of the vertical center line (+2.35 grade levels above). Chico's story is the converse, with the scores of white students sitting right on top of the vertical center line indicating the national average (-0.02 grade levels below). But their Hispanic students' test scores were well below the national average (-1.76 grade levels below).

Two factors are noteworthy when comparing the test score gap in Figure 4.14 with the learning rate gap in Figure 4.15. First, rather substantial gaps in students' test scores in Figure 4.14 (expressed in the distance of both districts from the diagonal "zero gap" line) is in contrast to the identical learning rates of Hispanic and white students in Figure 4.15 (with both landing right on the "zero gap" line). This means that on average, both white and Hispanic students *learned at about the same rate*. Chico's Hispanic students learned at a rate about 22 percent higher than the national average, and white students at a rate about 24 percent higher. In other words, whatever magic was at work in Chico over those years between 2009 and 2018, students of both ethnicities enjoyed its benefits to the same degree.

The second factor is that the two districts have very different learning rates. Hispanic students in Charlottesville learned at a rate about 15 percent below the national average, and white students at a rate about 14 percent below. That's a considerable deficit. You'll see a lot more districts up and to the right of Charlottesville along that diagonal "zero gap" line than down and to the left. Chico, on the other hand, sits quite far from the mass of districts in the middle, with relatively few districts displaying higher learning rates along that diagonal line.

Which gap would you rather be talking about? If you follow the crowd and discuss test score gaps, you're discussing an outcome that includes the differences kids bring to school on their first day in kindergarten. In other words, you're discussing the kids' differences as well as the differences in what happened to them in school. If, however, you examine the gap in learning rates, you're narrowing down what you're really measuring to emphasize the influence of the school or district on student learning. By looking at learning rates, have you been able to exclude every influence other than school? Of course not. But you've been able to control for those things in life that influenced kids before they started school. This enables you to see with much greater clarity the effect of your school and district on the kids who have enrolled. In the end, for those who share responsibility for leading, managing and governing schools, for those who are teaching, isn't that the measure you're seeking?

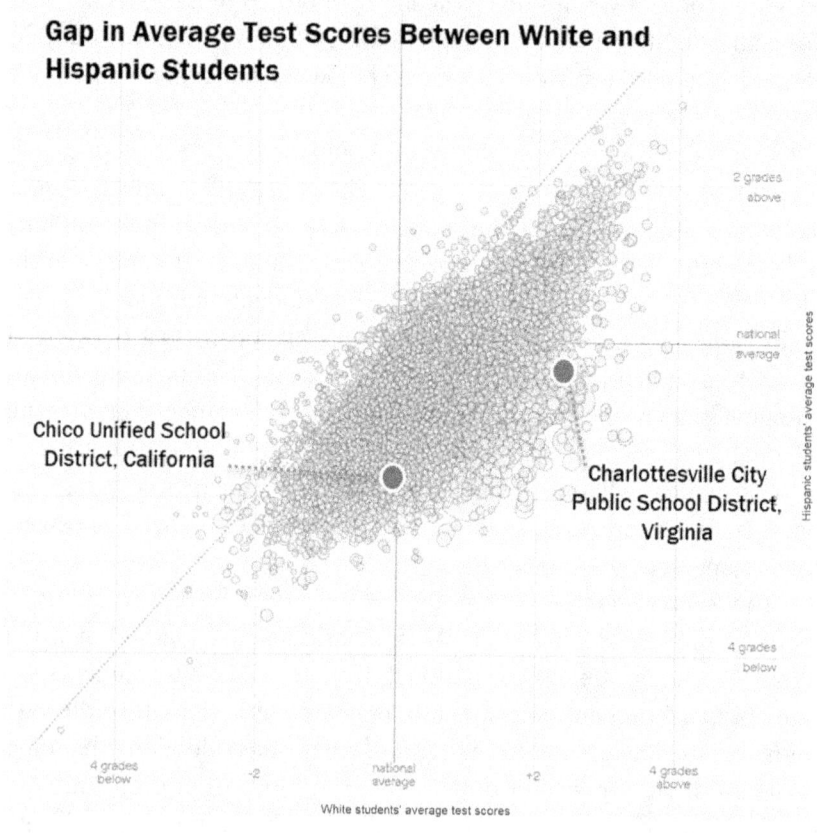

To explore this image interactively, go to https://tinyurl.com/mrtyhpza on the Stanford Educational Opportunity Explorer's website, or explore it on the book's website at https://www.k12measures.com/ch4/#Fig4.14

Figure 4.14 Gap in average test scores between white and Hispanic students in Charlottesville City Public School District, Virginia, and Chico Unified School District, California

The white–Hispanic test score gap in both districts is large. In Charlottesville, white students' scores were the equivalent of 2.35 grade levels ahead of the national average. But their Hispanic students' scores were 0.28 grade levels below the national average. Chico USD's pattern was the reverse. White students' scores were right at the national average, and Hispanic students' scores 1.76 grade levels below.

Source: © Sean F. Reardon and The Educational Opportunity Project at Stanford University

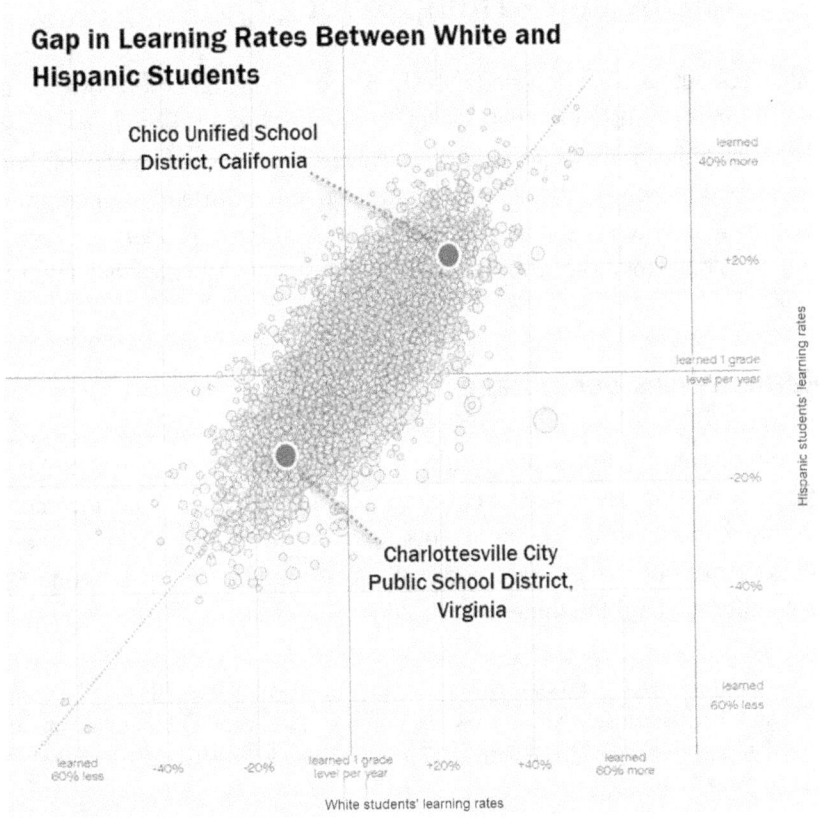

To explore this image interactively, go to https://tinyurl.com/43xhczmu on the Stanford Educational Opportunity Explorer's website, or explore it on the book's website at https://www.k12measures.com/ch4/#Fig4.15.

Figure 4.15 Gap in learning rates between white and Hispanic students in Charlottesville City Public School District, Virginia, and Chico Unified School District, California

There is no effective gap in learning rates between white and Hispanic students in these two districts. That is, white and Hispanic students are learning at about the same rate in Chico USD. The same is true in Charlottesville. What differs are the actual rates at which students learn in the two districts. In Chico USD, both white and Hispanic students are learning at a rate about 20 percent higher than the national average. In Charlottesville City Public School District, both white and Hispanic students are learning at a rate about 14–15 percent lower than the national average.

Source: © Sean F. Reardon and The Educational Opportunity Project at Stanford University

Gaps mismeasured

Talking and writing about gaps

Talking about gaps can tongue-tie the best of us. The good news, however, is that the art of expressing quantitative relations with words has been refined over the years. In 2015, the highly esteemed University of Chicago Press published the second edition of a book that's contributed to the cause of clear communication about numbers. It is *The Chicago Guide to Writing about Numbers*,[14] and it is a bible for those who speak and write using the language of numbers.

Ratios versus percentages

When discussing test score results, I favor using ratios to explain the differences. This also makes it easier to explain both level of achievement and the gap that separates them. Let's take an example of a school where 36 percent of boys met or exceeded the state standard in math, while 54 percent of girls did the same. You could say,

> About 36 percent of our boys and about 54 percent of our girls met the math standard. Because we have the same number of boys and girls enrolled, about 1.5 times as many girls met that achievement mark as did boys.

If you are discussing those test results, using a scale score metric, you have a different challenge because scale scores are abstract. Unlike the easier idea of "percent meeting standard" scale scores hold no self-evident meaning. This leaves us to explain the scale score difference in points, and then, if possible, interpret that difference into terms your audience might better understand. Again, presume you're the principal, reporting your results at a school board meeting. And let's consider the test results to be from your state assessment.

> Our eighth-grade students' English language arts results this year were as we expected, consistent with their seventh-grade results. They attained a median scale score of 2580. When we compared results of boys and girls, here's what we found. Girls attained a median scale score of 2590, and boys 2570. This gap difference of 20 scale score points is modest in size, and similar to what we observe in the state as a whole.

The last sentence gives your audience an external frame of reference—a gap measure comparing boys and girls statewide—that enables them to reach a judgment. Is their school's gender gap bigger or smaller than that of the state? If so, is it big enough to worry about? You've told them that you're not worried about the difference.

A similar semantic trap with percentage of increase or decrease awaits us all. Because so many people have a weak grasp of math, I suggest you avoid measuring gains or declines in percentages. Instead, when feasible, try to use integers or fractions rather than percentages in those moments. For example, a decline from 30 percent to 20 percent of third graders scoring "below standard" in reading is a reduction of one-third. That's a big deal, and more likely to be understood correctly than if you called it a 10 percentage point decline.

Percentage points versus percent

When discussing the percent of students who score at or above a threshold like "meeting standard," or when discussing graduation rates, you will be expressing numbers in the form of percentages. Be careful here. *Percentage points*, when used to express differences in graduation rates, are absolute measures. If the graduation rate of a high school were 80 percent, but girls graduated at a 90 percent rate, and boys at a 70 percent rate, you could correctly call this a 20-percentage point gap. But you could also say that girls graduated at 1.29 times the rate of boys (90 minus 70, divided by 70). Similarly, you could say that girls graduated at a rate 29 *percent* higher than that of boys. The words that distinguish these two—percentage points and percent—may seem like semantic hairsplitting. But it matters. "Percent" implies a relative unit of measure. "Percentage point" implies an absolute unit of measure.

The challenge of discussing gap measures

Gap questions are among the most challenging for those governing or leading schools or districts. Whether you're an educator or a parent, an advocate or a taxpayer, you'll find that passions will run high. This makes the quality of your evidence and reasoning all the more important. Almost everyone has data in hand when they talk about gaps. But not everyone is able to build coherent, persuasive stories from those data. For models, you might look to the work of the late Hans Rosling, a Swedish economist and data-explainer whose videos and data visualizations on the website of Gapminder, the organization he and his wife, Anna, created.[15] His TED talks are legendary, and one he delivered in Berlin in 2014, "How not to be ignorant about the world," has garnered over six million views in seven years.[16]

When taking stock of achievement gaps—outcome measures like graduation rates or test results—ask yourself these questions before you go public with your evidence:

- Do you really know the nature of the measurement itself? If it's test results, what was the test's purpose? For instance, are you inferring a gap in mastery of reading skills of third graders, with a test or set of tests that's designed to do just that? Or are you using an English/language arts test that was designed to do something broader?
- Are you aware of the imprecision in your measurements? When working with test results, are you making visible the imprecision so your audience has the benefit of seeing it?
- Are you using the right method for comparing the results of two groups of students? If social scientists often disagree on the best statistical method to use, don't be too hasty when you choose your own method.
- Have you selected the right metric, especially when measuring learning? Should you use learning rate rather than test scores to make your point?
- Are you showing level of results and the gap separating whatever groups you've chosen? This is essential if you are to create a context that enables you and your audience to draw reasonable conclusions.

When taking stock of gaps in opportunities to learn, the data you need are likely to sit in your administrative records. Facts about teachers, teacher assignments, courses offered, student demand for those courses, screening tests used and more are all readily available. All that's needed is a clear agreement about what factors are most important to your school or district.

With that clear definition in hand, you should be able to build evidence that begins to describe your district's track record in creating equitable opportunities to learn.

Some human qualities may help you remain well grounded in the heat of debates. A bit of caution and humility should help keep in check the impulse to assign causality too quickly. Your open ears, combined with your well-tuned b.s. detector, should help you detect logical fallacies advanced by colleagues, critics and community leaders. A critical eye for the quality of evidence is essential. And empathy for people who may object to your district's policies or practices will go a long way toward moving your discussions away from the heat of friction and toward the light of illumination.

Links to extend your reading and interaction

The following link will carry you to additional resources, writing and dialogue about the topics discussed in this chapter. You'll also find live versions of the data visualizations in this chapter that are ready for your interaction. We welcome your comments and continued exploration. You'll find all this on the chapter specific page on the book's website: https://www.k12measures.com/ch4

Questions to spark discussion

District leaders

1. Your district's English learner parent advisory board wants to know why the gap in graduation rates between English-only students and English learner students is the highest in your county. What evidence would you want to assemble to answer this question?

Gaps mismeasured

2. The gap in math scores on your state assessment between your white and Latino/Hispanic eighth-grade students has grown larger each year over the last five years preceding the pandemic. Now a local advocacy group has asked to meet with you to discuss it privately. This has bothered you, too, so you welcome the opportunity to figure out the contributing factors. To prepare for this meeting, what do you ask your curriculum assistant superintendent to do? What questions do you ask of your assessment director? What do you ask your high school math department chair to bring to the table?

Principals

3. You are writing your high school's site plan, and the district leadership has asked you to pay attention to equitable learning opportunities. You've never really looked at the experience of teachers assigned to teach developmental courses against the experience of those assigned to teach the more rigorous courses. As you walk through this comparison, you are reminded that your district's collective bargaining contract lets teachers request the courses they prefer to teach, based on seniority. What do you write in your site plan about this problem of teacher job rights producing an inequitable distribution of teacher talent? What do you tell your staff to do to reverse this pattern?

4. A group of PTA parents are meeting with you to discuss their concern that some female teachers are grading girls more favorably, and boys more harshly. Your middle school has a grading policy in place, and it defines how much of a grade can be based on attendance and behavior, how much on participation and how much on mastery of subject matter. Given the clarity of this policy, how might you examine the evidence of teacher-assigned grades to see if there's evidence of gender bias?

School board trustees

5. You have been the president of this school board for three years, and you are tired of hearing empty promises about equity. You are committed to doing something new, different and substantial. You've called for a study session and want to propose an equity audit. Your focus is on those things the adults in the district are responsible for: creating equitable access to high quality educational opportunities. What are the top three elements you'd want to include in that audit? And how would you go about reviewing them?

6. Your community is divided about what resources should be invested in your most challenged students and schools. Advocates and organizations are demanding higher funding for low-performing schools. You are facing a budget shortfall and want to explore the possibility of reallocating funding from existing programs to new programs. Who should be invited to participate in a budget review and possibly present to the board? How will you develop the questions for staff and what data will you ask for?

Notes

1. A 2014 study by David Figlio and others noted that babies' birth weights are a surprisingly strong predictor of how those babies will prosper in school. Across all ethnic groups and socio-economic groups, the pattern was persistent. Their study was based on analysis of records of three-fourths of all children born in Florida between 1992 and 2002. The study's authors matched birth records with school records, which were housed in a state-wide data system. The evidence sparked debate among doctors of the benefit of full-term pregnancies. The study, "The Effects of Poor Neonatal Health on Children's' Cognitive Development," was

published in the December 2014 issue of the *American Economic Review*. https://doi.org/10.1257/aer.104.12.3921.

2. Judea Pearl and Dana Mackenzie, *The Book of Why: The New Science of Cause and Effect* (New York: Basic Books, 2018).

3. "Confirmation Bias," Wikipedia entry, accessed December 15, 2021, https://en.wikipedia.org/wiki/Confirmation_bias#Science_and_scientific_research.

4. A parallel problem of underestimated gaps may also be due to the meal subsidy metric itself. Susan Dynarski—professor of public policy, education and economics at the University of Michigan and faculty research associate at the National Bureau of Economic Research—believes that socioeconomic gaps are larger than they appear. Her essay in the *New York Times* of August 12, 2016, titled "Why American Schools Are Even More Unequal Than We Thought" argues that the customary measure of economic disadvantage, the free-and-reduced-price meal subsidy, masks the magnitude of the learning gap. How long a student qualifies for meal subsidies has a close relation to the level of household income in that student's family. Her study revealed that students who qualify for meal subsidies every year is about one-third larger than the gap that is typically reported. She notes from her Michigan study that about 50 percent of the students were receiving meal subsidies, but just 14 percent of all students received meal subsidies every year they'd been in school. www.nytimes.com/2016/08/14/upshot/why-american-schools-are-even-more-unequal-than-we-thought.html.

5. Signal processing technology in the hands of linguists and neuroscientists has made it possible to interpret speech more accurately, quicker and at lower cost than ever before. Some scientific teams have now applied this to the riddle of measuring the oral fluency of young students who are emerging readers. The state of the art of this research is explained in this 19-minute video recording of a presentation delivered by Jared Bernstein (Analytic Measures and Stanford University) to the Behavioral Measures of Language conference held in Venice, Italy, in 2020. The paper, "Automated Measures of Spoken Language for Monitoring and Diagnosis," while aimed at fellow scientists, is entirely understandable to

nonscientists. The other authors of this paper are Jian Cheng (Analytic Measures, California), Terje B. Holmlund (UiT The Arctic University of Norway), Elizabeth Rosenfeld (Analytic Measures, California) and Dominic Massaro (University of California, Santa Cruz). https://vimeo.com/422675697.

6. A study published by the Stanford Education Archive (CEPA working paper 18–13) documented gender gaps in math and English language arts. The authors of the paper—Sean Reardon, Erin Fahle, Demetra Kalogrides, Anne Podolsky and Rosalia Zárate—titled "Gender Achievement Gaps in U.S. School Districts" documented that girls in grades 3 through 8 outscored boys nationally in English language arts by roughly 0.23 standard deviations. Their study covered about 10,000 school districts from the 2008 to 2009 through the 2014–2015 school years. The paper is available from https://cepa.stanford.edu/content/gender-achievement-gaps-us-school-districts.

7. "2018–19 Smarter Balanced Results," Washoe County, Nevada, School District website, www.wcsddata.net/data-topics/smarterbalanced/2018-2019/.

8. "English Language Learners in Public Schools," by the National Center for Education Statistics, last modified May 2021, https://nces.ed.gov/programs/coe/indicator/cgf.

9. Morgan Polikoff, "Friends Don't Let Friends Misuse NAEP Data" (blog), On Education Research (website), October 6, 2015, https://morganpolikoff.com/2015/10/06/friends-dont-let-friends-misuse-naep-data/.

10. Stephen Sawchuck, "When Bad Things Happen to Good NAEP Data," *Education Week*, July 4, 2013, www.edweek.org/ew/articles/2013/07/24/37naep.h32.html.

11. Tom Loveless, "The Brown Center Chalkboard: The NAEP Proficiency Myth" (blog), Brookings (website), June 13, 2016, www.brookings.edu/blog/brown-center-chalkboard/2016/06/13/the-naep-proficiency-myth/.

12. Documentation of the methods used by the Stanford Educational Opportunity Project is accessible from their website, https://edopportunity.org/methods/.

13. This explanation on the website of the Stanford Educational Opportunities Project explains the dramatic difference between viewing learning rates and test scores. The case in point contrasts the relative affluent suburban district of Anne Arundel Public Schools in Maryland with the Chicago Public Schools. When looking at test scores in the two districts, students in Anne Arundel are 1.37 grade levels above the national average, and Chicago students about 1.45 grade levels below. But when viewing students' learning rates, students in the Chicago Public School district shine, attaining about six years of growth in five years' time. The opposite is the case in Anne Arundel. https://edopportunity.org/discoveries/affluent-schools-are-not-always-best/.

14. Jane E. Miller, *The Chicago Guide to Writing about Numbers*, 2nd edition (Chicago: University of Chicago Press, April 2015), https://press.uchicago.edu/ucp/books/book/chicago/C/bo19910133.html.

15. Gapminder's website can be found here: https://gapminder.org.

16. Hans and Ola Rosling, "How Not to Be Ignorant about the World," a speech filmed at TEDSalon in Berlin, June 2014. TED video (18:56 minutes), www.ted.com/talks/hans_and_ola_rosling_how_not_to_be_ignorant_about_the_world.

Resources

Epstein, David, and ProPublica. "When Evidence Says No, But Doctor Says Yes." *Atlantic*, February 22, 2017.

Fahle, Erin, and Sean F. Reardon. "How Much Do Test Scores Vary among School Districts? New Estimates Using Population Data, 2009–2015." *Educational Researcher* 47, no. 4 (2018). https://doi.org/10.3102/0013189X18759524.

Figlio, David, Jonathan Guryan, Krzysztof Karbownik, and Jeffrey Roth. "The Effects of Poor Neonatal Health on Children's Cognitive Development." *American Economic Review* 104, no. 12 (December 2014): 3921–55. https://doi.org/10.1257/aer.104.12.3921.

Hattie, John. *Visible Learning: A Synthesis of Over 800 Meta-analyses Relating to Achievement.* New York: Routledge, 2009.

Miller, Jane E. *The Chicago Guide to Writing about Numbers*. 2nd edition. Chicago: University of Chicago Press, 2015.

National Institute of Medicine. *National Priorities for Comparative Effectiveness Research*. Washington, DC: National Academies Press, 2009. https://doi.org/10.17226/12648.

Pearl, Judea, and Dana Mackenzie. *The Book of Why: The New Science of Cause and Effect*. New York: Basic Books, 2018.

Pogrow, Stanley. *Authentic Quantitative Analysis for Education Leadership Decision-Making and EdD Dissertations: A Practical, Intuitive and Intelligible Approach*. 2nd edition. Tecumseh, MI: International Council of Professors of Educational Leadership, 2017.

Pogrow, Stanley. "How Effect Size (Practical Significance) Misleads Clinical Practice: The Case for Switching to Practical Benefit to Assess Applied Research Findings." *The American Statistician* (March 2019). https://doi.org/10.1080/00031305.2018.1549101.

Reardon, Sean F. "The Economic Achievement Gap in the US, 1960–2020: Reconciling Recent Empirical Findings." Stanford Center for Education Policy Analysis Working Paper 21–09. November 2021. https://cepa.stanford.edu/sites/default/files/wp21-09-v112021.pdf.

Reardon, Sean F. "Educational Opportunity in Early and Middle Childhood: Using Full Population Administrative Data to Study Variation by Place and Age." *The Russell Sage Foundation Journal of the Social Science* 5, no. 2 (2019): 40–68. https://doi.org/10.7758/RSF.2019.5.2.03.

Reardon, Sean F., Erin Fahle, Demetra Kalogrides, Anne Podolsky, and Rosalia Zárate. "Gender Achievement Gaps in U.S. School Districts." Project of the Stanford Education Data Archive, 2018. https://cepa.stanford.edu/content/gender-achievement-gaps-us-school-districts.

Reardon, Sean F., Demetra Kalogrides, and Kenneth Shores. "The Geography of Racial/Ethnic Test Score Gaps." *The American Journal of Sociology* 124, no. 4 (2019). www.journals.uchicago.edu/doi/abs/10.1086/700678.

Rich, Motoko, Amanda Cox, and Matthew Bloch. "Money, Race and Success: How Your School District Compares." *New York Times*, April 29, 2016. www.nytimes.com/interactive/2016/04/29/upshot/money-race-and-success-how-your-school-district-compares.html.

Schumacher, Johannes, Per Hoffmann, Christine Schmäl, Gerd Schulte-Körne, and Markus M Nöthen. "Genetics of Dyslexia: The Evolving Landscape." *Journal of Medical Genetics* 44, no. 5 (2007): 289–297. doi:10.1136/jmg.2006.046516.

Wasserstein, Ronald L., Allen L. Schirm, and Nicole A. Lazar. "Moving to a World Beyond '$p<0.05$'." *The American Statistician* (March 2019). https://doi.org/10.1080/00031305.2019.1583913.

Logic errors when identifying and evaluating English learners

The mismeasurement of students who are considered by districts to be English learners is all-too-common, highly consequential, and in some cases, illegal.[1] Three factors collide. First, there's the *semantic confusion*. After all, we're always learning English. What is the line that distinguishes the degree of English fluency of a 6-year-old from a family that speaks English only, from a 6-year-old whose family speaks Spanish and occasional English? Second, there's the *logic problem* of trying to define the attributes of a group of people whose members change over time. Today's English learner may very well be reclassified next year as English fluent. Third, there's the *measurement problem* itself. How, exactly, do you assess kindergartners' four dimensions of fluency—reading, writing, speaking and understanding—reasonably accurately, and then combine those four factors into one number that's well suited for a decision that has huge consequences for the student, and expensive consequences for the district?

In the interest of untangling the mess that's been made of this, we will proceed with care, in light of the harm that has resulted from misidentifying students at the start of this process; creating high hurdles for them to clear to exit English learner status; misclassifying some English learners as students with disabilities or special education students; and denying English learner students access to the core curricula and college-prep electives.

Let's begin to untangle the semantic and logical confusion by pretending we're a visiting delegation of Vulcans from the Starship Enterprise. Vulcans are high in logical thinking and low in emotional intelligence. To understand what makes an English learner different from other students, we have to ask the Earthlings some naïve, fundamental questions.

DOI: 10.4324/9781003272915-6

Logic errors when identifying English learners

- Aren't all 5- and 6-year-old students learning English? Why do you only call some of them English learners?
- Why are some students who have partial mastery of two languages called multilingual, and others called English learners?
- How do you know when they have learned English?
- How long might a quick learner take to become English fluent? How about a slower learner?
- When students are unable to write, how can you evaluate their thinking or determine if they've learned a lesson?

We Vulcan visitors have by now discovered that academic English is an entirely different flavor of English than that which is written in text messages or spoken on the playground. We've also learned that *the key to school is reading* and that the language of instruction is English. So those who can't read English or those who can't decode English words can't get to the knowledge and skills they're supposed to attain. We can now unravel this riddle, viewing the strange, illogical habits of earthlings from the Vulcan's point of view.

Who are English learners, really?

The younger students dubbed English learners are really learning two languages at the same time. Some advocates, as a result, favor a different term: emerging bilingual students. But formally, in most states, English learners are students who meet two criteria. First, they are children of parents who fill in a form declaring that a language other than English is spoken at home. The form, called a Home Language Survey, usually contains two to six questions. States differ in the rules they tell districts to apply when interpreting parents' answers to those questions. When this parent questionnaire contains any single answer of "yes," that student then proceeds to the second step: a test. If they score below a cutoff score on that English language proficiency test, then that student is considered an English learner.

Students are tested when they first enter school to see if they can understand and speak English at a level that is considered roughly equivalent to other students at their grade level. If they enter at grade 2 or higher, their writing skills are also likely to be tested. This test is intended to sort students into two groups—those who are confirmed to be so far from grade-level English fluency that they are, indeed, English learners, and those who are not. Parents are then informed of the results of this test and given the right to accept or decline the test's findings. Once a child has been identified by this test as an English learner, and a parent has accepted the test's results, then the child's status as an English learner is official.

If you are imagining English learners as immigrants, you're only imagining 28 percent of them. The remaining 72 percent were born in the U.S. These are national figures from the 2016 American Community Survey, a program of the U.S. Census Bureau. According to their data, about one out of every seven students in urban schools is an English learner. But in rural schools, about one out of every 25 students is an English learner. While two-thirds of English learners are in the elementary grade levels (K–5), one-third are in grades 6 through 12. In sheer numbers, there were five million English learner students in the U.S. in 2017, about 10 percent of all students.[2,3]

The Home Language Survey form

Let's examine the form that parents complete when they register their child for school. The Illinois's language survey asks just two questions: "Is a language other than English spoken in your home?" and "Does your child speak a language other than English?" If the family is a three-generation family, for example, and the child's grandmother speaks the language of the "old country"—be it Tagalog, Spanish, Mixtec, Farsi, Vietnamese, Hmong or Russian—then the child is considered to possibly be an English learner. If the child speaks and understands English as well as his peers but can also understand the Tagalog spoken by his grandmother, this form would lead to the child's being given a test of English fluency. Several logic flaws are apparent here. The attribute of the family is assumed to accrue to the child. The possibility that the child is bilingual is disregarded. The parent is not asked the child's favored spoken language.

The questions on most states' forms don't ask the parents' estimate of their children's abilities to read or write in their first language. Nor do they ask the parent about their own degree of comfort reading or writing English. This form only asks questions about the languages spoken at home.

Logic errors when identifying English learners

This is in distinct contrast to what the Census Bureau asks in its American Community Survey questionnaire:

- "Does this person speak a language other than English at home?"
- "What is this language?"
- "How well does this person speak English?" (very well, well, not well, not well at all)

The rules used by states to interpret this Home Language Survey vary. Some, like Illinois, ask only two questions. Others, like Nevada and Colorado, ask five questions. But in every state I reviewed, a "yes" answer to *any one question* leads to the student going to the next stage: taking a test.

- In California, if the parent answers *any of the four questions* with a language other than English, the district is required to test the child's mastery of English.
- Texas asks only two questions: "What language is spoken in the child's home most of the time?" "What language does the child speak most of the time?" If a language other than English is offered as an answer to *either* of these two questions, the child must take a test.
- Florida asks three questions: "Is a language other than English used in the home?" "Did the student have a first language other than English?" "Does the student most frequently speak a language other than English?" If the parent answers "yes" to *any* of these three, the student must be assessed by the district to determine if he is really an English learner as Florida defines it.
- New Mexico asks six questions, and one of them asks the parent whether their child understands when someone speaks in a language other than English. Another asks if the child translates the family's language of choice into English. If the parent answers *any* of these questions with a "yes," the child must be tested.

Whatever questions state departments of education tell their districts to ask parents, the questions are about both the family and the child. Also, in all states, if a parent answers *any* question indicating that *someone* in the family speaks a language other than English, the child is suspected of being an English learner (not bilingual) and required to take a test. Consider this scenario. A family in your district comes to your district office to register their 5-year-old daughter for kindergarten. You ask the mother to complete your state's Home Language Survey. The mother, noting that her parents live with them and they speak Spanish primarily, answers "yes" to the question on the form about a language other than English spoken in the home. However, the mother, who is a software engineer and speaks three languages fluently, dutifully informs the district employee that her home is a trilingual home and that her daughter speaks and understands both English and Spanish. However, the district employee finds no place for this information on the form. As a result, the child has to take an English language fluency test and face the risk of being incorrectly classified as an English learner.

The tests used to confirm EL identification

The tests vary considerably, state by state. Some tests are screeners. Some of them were created for the sole purpose of confirming that a student might be an English language learner and in need of support services. These screeners tend to be shorter and have the benefit of being focused on doing one thing really well. So, if they're given correctly and interpreted properly, they should provide the most accurate results. One example in this category is the WIDA screener, from the World-Class Instructional Design and Assessment Consortium (WIDA). Forty states are now part of the WIDA consortium, which is led by the University of Wisconsin.

Other tests are multipurpose tests and may be used to (1) identify English learners; (2) determine when those EL students have attained sufficient mastery of English that they can be reclassified as fluent; and (3) measure the incremental progress of EL students along the way. No test can do all things equally well, despite the claims of their publishers. All tests do some things better than others. The 10 states outside the WIDA consortium are using seven different assessments. Texas, California, Oregon and Ohio have their own tests. McGraw-Hill created the LAS-LINKS test, the Language Assessment Scales. Pearson created the SELP, the Stanford English Language Proficiency Test. These tests are used by a handful of states.

But what they have in common is that they all measure the four dimensions of English fluency: reading, writing, speaking and understanding. They also share a common weakness. There is no national agreement on what constitutes that clear line when a student has attained English language fluency. It is up to the states to define this and to press their districts to accept that definition. With the four dimensions of fluency to measure and a rubric that establishes the line of mastery for each, they all depend upon clear standards and consistent interpretation of results. You can appreciate the delicate balance and exceptional skill required in this juggling act. With such high stakes riding on each interpretation for every student—at their first enrollment, at each grade level and at the end stage where each student hopes to demonstrate mastery of each of these four dimensions—it's critical to get it right. A student's educational life is at a fork in the road, both on entry into the English learner category, and at the exit point.

How often are these test results wrong, and to what degree?

It's worth asking how frequently these tests return an incorrect result. It might be a score that underestimates the student's actual English language skills, resulting in a false positive. Or it can be a score that overestimates the student's actual English language skills, resulting in a false negative, the failure to identify a student who needs support. The California English Language Development Test (CELDT) was a test that some scholars believed to be unusually imprecise. Katie Stokes-Guinan and Claude Goldenberg, both at Stanford, published a paper in 2011 titled, "Use With Caution: What CELDT Results Can and Cannot Tell Us."[4] Based on the results of a study done by the assessment firm CTB/McGraw-Hill in 2005, they wrote that "up to 30 percent of students might be incorrectly classified by the CELDT [as English learners]." This classification error rate is higher than the generally acceptable classification error rate found in statewide summative assessments of about 20 percent. Their report, which was based on the 2003–2004 edition of the CELDT, continues:

> When a student is administered the CELDT for the first time (i.e., initial classification), the CELDT score is typically the only criterion used to make the decision. This fact means that an inappropriately high CELDT score will prevent a student who may need language supports from being identified as an EL, and an inappropriately low CELDT score will result in a student's receiving an unwarranted EL designation.[5]

The imprecision of the CELDT was greater when used to measure progress or a student's readiness to be reclassified as fluent in English, and it had different consequences. The same scholars noted that when CTB/McGraw-Hill gave 1,384 students a different test of English fluency that had been in the field for much longer, and then also gave them the CELDT, the two tests classified students in the same proficiency category *only 40 percent of the time*. (Note that this California test was retired in 2019 and replaced by the English Language Proficiency Assessments for California.)

Evidence that the CELDT was likely to overidentify students as English learners emerged from this startling study conducted by the California Department of Education (CDE) in 2011, "A Comparison Study of Kindergarten and Grade 1 English-Fluent Students and English Learners on the 2010–11 Edition of the CELDT."[6] In this study, a group of about 1,690 English learners (kindergartners and first graders) identified from a pool of 10,025 students, and 2,500 who had only spoken English in monolingual, English-speaking homes were given the CELDT. The students were drawn from 100 schools. *Seventy-four percent of the English-only kindergarten students* scored below the threshold for English proficiency set by the CDE. If those students' parents had indicated on the Home Language Survey that they spoke a language other than English at home, their children would have been classified as English language learners. This experiment of the CDE's, revealing that *74 percent of students who were raised in English-only homes and spoke English* would have been classified as ELs, should have caused higher-ups to put on the brakes and regroup. But no corrective action was taken.

Katie Stokes-Guinan and Claude Goldenberg did not intend to single out the CELDT for criticism. They wrote, "The issues we have discussed pertaining to the CELDT also apply to other measures of English language proficiency used by educators in other states." Their paper should encourage you to ask how imprecise your state's test of ELs might be when determining who is really an English learner? To what degree is your state's test under- or overidentifying them? Does your state's version of the Home Language Survey and your state's method of interpreting its results send too many students, too few or just the right number to take this test? When your district shoulders the responsibility for a decision as important as this—consequential for the student and for the district—you should be alert to how much risk you're facing. The possibility of misclassifying a student initially, or in misjudging their exit point from the EL supports, is measurable.

Logic errors when identifying English learners

> ☞ **Tip:** most important is knowing what you can do to minimize the harm to students by lowering the risk of mistaken classification. If you know where the errors in judgment are most likely to occur, you can create risk-reducing validation steps of many kinds:
>
> - Retesting students who are close to exiting EL status but can't quite clear one hurdle;
> - Rebalancing the way your district scores the four different dimensions of English fluency;
> - Revising your Home Language Survey to add more age-appropriate questions about the child's first language proficiency, and her ease in speaking and understanding English;
> - Interviewing parents whose survey responses indicate a student might benefit from EL support services to gather more exact information about the student's English skills; and
> - Making sure you're not setting a standard of English fluency that's higher for English learners than it is for students from English-only homes.

When do English learner students get to exit EL status?

When I asked a California district administrator how hard it was for his district's students to reach the exit point where they would stop being English learners and be reclassified as fluent in English, he told me, "It's like a roach motel. Easy to enter. But you don't really leave." We both shook our heads. This unpleasant figure of speech is not the only one I've heard. Others include: "ESL Lifers," "Forever LEP" and "The 6 Plussers." In truth, it is all too easy to be identified as an English learner student, and all too hard to reach the point of reclassification as English proficient. What makes it hard is that in most states, there are many criteria to satisfy to exit EL status, and all of them need to be met. Indeed, this problem of under-identification of students ready to exit EL status was the subject of the California State Auditor in 2005. Their audit of eight districts looked at a sample of 180 ELs and discovered that *62 percent were not reclassified, despite having met their district's criteria.*

The problem of under-identification of EL students ready to exit EL status was the focus of a study by Peggy Estrada from the University of California at Santa Cruz and Haiwen Wang from SRI International, which compared how two California school districts helped or hindered their English learner students on their paths to English fluency. Their final report was published in the *American Education Research Journal* in April 2018[7] and involved 78,627 students in two districts, studied over three years in one district, and two years in the other. It was a study in contrasts, with one district setting higher hurdles for EL students to clear than the other.

Students in grades 3 through 9 in both districts were the subject of the study in year one. The same cohort of students was the subject of study in years two and three. The reclassification rate in the first year of the study in the stricter district (11 percent) was nearly half the rate of the more tolerant district (19 percent). In the second year of the study, the stricter district's reclassification rate (8 percent) was almost one-third the rate of the other district (22 percent).

I attended the roundtable discussion at the 2018 American Education Research Association (AERA) annual conference where Peggy Estrada led a discussion of their findings and was impressed by their care in documenting the mechanisms by which a district actually held back English learner students who were ready to enter the mainstream program. The authors pointed to the combination of factors that made exiting EL status so difficult for so many students in the district with the tougher criteria.

- Use of up to four criteria to determine English fluency, all of which had to be satisfied;
- Allowing teacher opinion of students' English fluency to override test results;
- Including curriculum embedded assessment results, in addition to CELDT and California Standards Test results when determining English fluency;
- Ambiguous criteria for reclassification;
- Sloppy data management; and
- Weak administrative effort to obtain parents' consent to reclassify their kids.

Logic errors when identifying English learners

The rate at which students in each district met each of the criteria, both separately and in combination, reveal the painful consequences of overly strict multiple criteria.[8] The consequences of threading the needle of meeting all requirements was compounded in one district by allowing teachers to overrule students' test results. This discretion resulted in 1 to 3 percent of students who met all criteria being denied reclassification status. Estrada and Wang's study makes the case that giving teachers the power to veto student reclassification is neither fair nor wise.

Your state, no doubt, has its own approach to reclassification. Texas requires that only two criteria must be met by EL students—pass either a TELPAS or LAS Links assessment and get an approval from a teacher. Illinois has an even simpler process, requiring that EL students pass the WIDA ACCESS for ELLs 2.0. Nevada shares Illinois's approach. New York has a one-step program that relies on its own test, the New York State English as a Second Language Achievement Test (NYSESLAT). The range of approaches is evident if you skim the summary that the Education Commission of the States has prepared.[9] Although the summary reflects the state of policies as of 2014, the range of approaches among the states remains wide in 2020. As you examine your state's approach, remember that the fewer hoops to jump through, the clearer the path to exiting EL status.

How long does it take for English learners to make it to English fluency?

Since the standard for English fluency is vague, the measure of how long it takes to reach this fuzzy state is equally vague. Some states say five years. Others say six or seven. The most cited paper on this question, written by a team of scholars led by Kenji Hakuta, found that oral proficiency takes from three to five years, while academic English takes four to seven years to master.[10] The paper is based on studies of two California districts and two Canadian districts. Because the two California districts included 27,000 students, 10,400 of whom were English learners, the study's authors were able to look at student results across parent education levels, as well. Their paper helped calm the political and policy debates considerably.

What is troubling, however, is that the paper's call for states to invest in longitudinal data was, for the most part, not heeded. Most states continued to view English learner progress, not of cohorts on a longitudinal basis, but of students by grade level on a snapshot basis, viewing all kids enrolled in a particular grade level, school or district, year by year. This made it quite difficult (or impossible) for state accountability systems to answer sensible questions like this:

> How long, on average, does it take for a Spanish-speaking student who starts school in kindergarten to attain fluency in academic English in our district, compared to the state average?

Ten years later, a study by Laurie Olson with Californians Together looked at questions like this, pointing to a large portion of students who had not yet gained command of academic English after six years.[11] She called them long-term English learners, and in her review of 175,734 middle and high school students, discovered that 59 percent of ELs were in this long-term category. In one-third of the 40 districts in her study, more than 75 percent of their English learners were, in fact, long-term—meaning they had been classified as EL for six years or longer. Their report advised districts to look at English learner data differently, in particular, to analyze English learner achievement data by length of time in United States schools and by English proficiency levels, and analyze data longitudinally for the same students over time. She and her organization made the report a wake-up call. Indeed, the report did wake up many. But the persistence of the problem of school districts creating long-term English learners warranted a follow-up report 10 years later.[12]

Making the right decision may require bending the rules

By Chris Moggia, Director of Digital Learning and Assessment, PUC Schools, Los Angeles, California

California schools are required by law to ask parents to submit a Home Language Survey when students first enroll in a school. In one of my elementary schools, the fifth sibling of a particular family entered kindergarten and the parents dutifully submitted their Home Language Survey indicating that a language other than English was spoken at home. Normally, this would trigger the need to administer a test—the English Language Proficiency Assessments

175

Logic errors when identifying English learners

for California (ELPAC)—to determine the student's level of English proficiency. The results of this test then classify the student as either an "English Learner" (EL) or as an "Initially Fluent, English Proficient" student (IFEP).

However, the site leadership, having an eight-year relationship with this family, also knew that the father was a native English speaker and that all four siblings were fluent English speakers. The district was aware that the mother also spoke Spanish with her children. The mother subsequently submitted a written note that said, in effect, "We want our daughter to have the same instructional program as her brothers and sisters." Our school leadership interpreted this to mean she wanted a traditional curriculum and did not want her daughter placed in bilingual education or English language development classes. So, we identified her as "English only" in our state reporting system. She finished her kinder year on track with our school.

Next year, the family withdrew their daughter and enrolled her in a different school district for first and second grades. The mother, noting that her daughter was not making sufficient academic progress, removed the student from the other district and returned her to our school for her third-grade term.

We then received notice that the previous district had reviewed her Home Language Survey and deemed the student to be a "TBD," language status to be determined, arguing that we should have given her the Initial ELPAC test. So, three years after we determined the student was "English only," we were compelled to administer a test that we knew to be unnecessary.

The story's happy ending is that, in the end, the girl did not have to take the ELPAC. It took us several months of back-and-forth emails and phone calls to the California Department of Education to reach that decision. But if we'd failed, and did have to administer that test to her, and if she'd not passed, imagine the problem we'd have been stuck with. State regulations would have required we treat her as an English learner, in conflict with the instructions given to us by her parents and our fuller knowledge of her multilingual home life.

Mismeasuring the progress of English learners

Ever-English learners don't disappear

For over two decades, every state has had to measure how English learners are doing—their graduation rates, their test scores, their discipline rates and more. These measurements end up in school and district accountability reports, and in plans those districts submit showing what they'll do in return for getting Title III dollars from the U.S. Department of Education to support the education of English learners. The problem with this is that states only account for English learners until they're reclassified. Students who have been ELs but have now become English fluent, and are therefore reclassified, suddenly *disappear from the data about English learners.*

This is so deeply illogical that it deserves a name: the "transient entity" error. Consider the other categories of students that get compared to each other or analyzed over time—students of different genders or ethnicities. Those categories can be viewed over time, or compared to each other, because the members of those categories don't change. Gender and ethnic identity are, for the most part, permanent attributes, allowing for rare exceptions. But other attributes change over time. A student's free-or-reduced-price meal status changes as his family's household income changes. A student's special education status may change as the severity of his learning disability changes. Certainly, a student's limited proficiency with academic English changes intentionally. Treating the students who are considered EL in one year, but not another, as a subgroup of students like boys and girls, and then trying to compare them to others, or track them over time, is going to lead to flawed evidence and mistaken conclusions. The most disheartening false conclusion is that English learners as a group start behind and fall further behind each year.

For instance, if you want to evaluate the rate at which English-learner students graduate from high school, wouldn't you want to include in the denominator all students who had ever been classified as English learners? If you did that, you'd be answering what is likely to be your *real* question: "What portion of the graduating class of 2020 *who have ever been classified as ELs* graduated on time?" If, on the other hand, you used status-quo definitions of English learners to calculate a graduation rate, you'd only learn what portion of the students in the graduating Class of 2019 still classified as ELs in their senior year graduated on time.

An answer to the "transient entity" problem: ever-ELs

But we can do better. Indeed, if we were to look at students who have at any time been classified as English learners, including those who later are reclassified as English proficient, we can solve the transient entity problem.

This approach requires creating a group called "ever-ELs," students who have at any time been tagged as English learners. This is not hard to imagine. If we were discussing a taxonomy of insects, we'd simply be arguing that the caterpillar is not an order of its own, but rather a stage of development of Lepidoptera, butterflies. Perhaps modernizing the classification system of the school world would be a good start.

When you do that, this new ever-EL group gets credit for the higher graduation rates and higher test scores of reclassified English learners who attained English fluency. In fact, it's not unusual to see those reclassified English learners scoring higher on state tests than their English-only counterparts. Not only are they bilingual. Their test results are often among the highest of all language-related subgroups. Shouldn't these successes be attributed to the whole group that was, at any time, dubbed English learners? Shouldn't the beauty of the butterfly be credited to the caterpillar?

In California, the leaders of the department of education took this request to their federal counterparts and asked if they could create the "ever-EL" group and include their results in their accountability reports. The feds replied with thumbs-down. This form of bureaucratic intransigence is an unfortunate factor in the mismeasurement of these students' vital signs. The good news is that, like all human decisions, it can be reversed. States can report it both ways, if they wish, complying with federal regs and advancing their own view of how to account for the educational accomplishments of English learners. A little initiative and gumption by state and district leaders could result in this "both/and" solution.

The "transient entity" error also results in masking the academic progress made by students who are reclassified. A study of NAEP data from 2003 to 2015 by two scholars, Michael J. Kieffer and Karen D. Thompson, discovered that multilingual students' (primarily composed of ever-ELs) scores increased a lot more than their monolingual peers. The gain of multilingual fourth-grade students was nearly twice the size in both reading and math. For eighth graders who were multilingual, their gain in reading was more than three times that of their monolingual peers in reading, and more than twice as much in math.[13]

Mismeasuring reclassification rates annually

Habits are hard to give up, and habits of mind are no exception. One habit that leads to frequent misunderstandings is the taking of annual snapshots of the status of students in schools and then comparing one year's snapshot group to the snapshot taken in the prior year. Although students move into and out of schools at quite a pace, we treat them as if they're more or less the same, interchangeable parts, like widgets. Most of the time, we want to know how much progress has occurred. So we look for evidence of improvement over the years. And to do that, *we need to track the same kids*. The longer we track them, the more confident we can be in our conclusions because the natural volatility of short-term aberrations are averaged out.

The annual reporting of reclassification rates is, in effect, a series of snapshots that reveal too little. Since the process of becoming fluent in English takes many years, why not track it over many years, and do so for the same group of students. If you're in a district, you can create this multiyear view of the same, exact students back to when each student enrolled. If you're in a state agency, your student longitudinal data system enables you to do the same. With this longer view, you will learn how long it takes for students to acquire English fluency, and if your student data set is robust, how long it takes for students who enter at kindergarten, at third grade, or at sixth grade. If you capture the first language of students, you'll also know the average time it takes for speakers of Vietnamese, Spanish, Hmong and Farsi to reach the mark of English fluency. You'll also be able to see the extent to which each grade-level team contributes to the English fluency of EL students in each graduating class cohort.

Visualizing the pace of reclassification of English learners

The question of pace of progress toward mastery of academic English is a thorny question. It entails debates about which method is best suited to advance English learners to fluency. Students who are pushed too soon out of the nest of supportive services may not prosper in the regular classroom. And students who are retained in the nest too long become academically segregated. By late middle school, they may be denied electives and access to a more rigorous curriculum. Within the same district, it's common to find conflicting views among educators about the best pace to pursue toward reclassification of English learners. However, wouldn't it help those educators to evaluate their policies and practices if they could see the consequences? By comparing any district to those with highly similar students in similar communities and looking at the *pace of reclassification of English learners over time for graduating class cohorts*, at least the empirical evidence would be in front of everyone for discussion.

Let's look first at one district, Napa Valley USD in California. It's a district I know well, because the team I lead, the K12 Measures group, has been providing analytic support to the Napa County Office of Education for four years. On their request, we built the evidence they needed to answer questions of importance to district planning teams. We did so using quasi-longitudinal data, in effect accepting the natural changes in the composition of a graduating class cohort due to student mobility. While students transfer into and out of schools and districts, and while the rate of student mobility varies place to place and over time, it's far better to have quasi-longitudinal data than none at all. Using these data, which are publicly available from the California Department of Education, we created an ever-EL group by stitching together the two subgroups of English learners and those students who have been reclassified. Then rather than look at changes year to year over all students enrolled, we look at one graduating class cohort at a time. In Figure 5.1, we have identified for the ever-EL students in the graduating Class of 2024 the percentage of them that have attained English proficiency and been reclassified.

Figure 5.1 depicts the year-by-year percentage of students in the Class of 2024 who were at any time considered to be English learners who have attained English fluency. Over these five years, this cohort of students progressed from grade 3 through grade 7.

Napa Valley USD is a big district, with 1,200 to 1,500 students in each grade. Seventh grade included about 1,300 kids in 2018–2019, about 603 of them either English learners or reclassified as English proficient. The bubble chart in Figure 5.1 shows, for the graduating Class of 2024, the percentage of English-learner students who have become fluent in English and were reclassified. It is cumulative, with increasingly higher proportions of ELs reclassified each year. This visualization shows five years of progress for about 670 ever-EL students who moved together from third grade in 2015 through seventh grade in 2019. It appears to be fairly linear, with only the seventh-grade pace flattening out.

Logic errors when identifying English learners

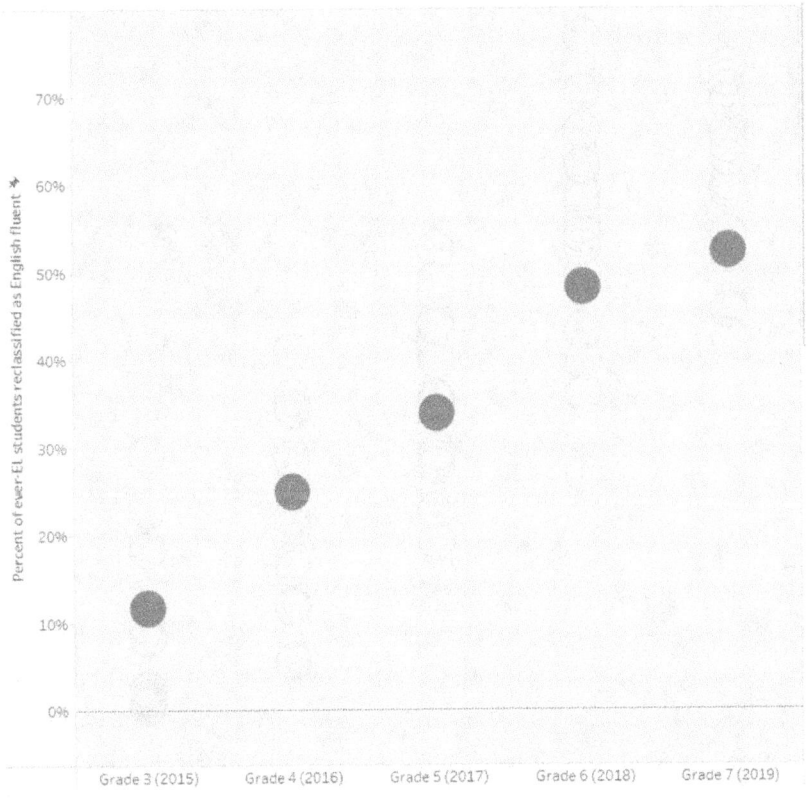

You'll find a link to a live version of this visualization at the following web page: https://www.k12measures.com/ch5/#fig5.1

Figure 5.1 EL students making progress toward proficiency, Class of 2024 over five years: Napa Valley USD alone

Source: K12 Measures. © School Wise Press

You can see that this group of ever-EL students finished third grade with about 12 percent of their English learners reclassified as fluent. By the time they finished seventh grade, about 52 percent were fluent. Okay. But is that the right pace? Is that faster or slower than other districts with students like theirs? To answer that, we identified 15 districts whose students were very similar based on attributes that have the biggest effect on student learning: parent education, household income (subsidized meal status) and English fluency. These districts were also serving the same grade levels with similar enrollment.

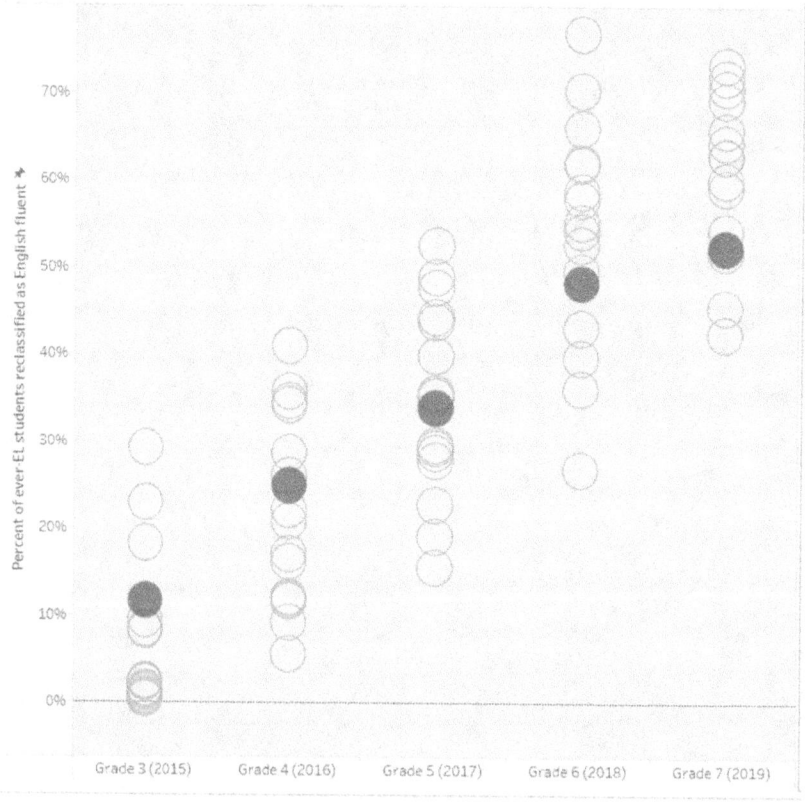

You'll find a link to a live version of this visualization at the following web page: https://www.k12measures.com/ch5/#fig5.2

Figure 5.2 EL students making progress toward proficiency, Class of 2024 over five years: Napa Valley USD and 15 similar districts
Source: K12 Measures. © School Wise Press

Figure 5.2 compares the client district to 15 districts with highly similar students, showing over five years the percentage of students in the Class of 2024 who were at any time considered English learners who have attained English fluency.

Now let's look at the results for Napa Valley USD, framed in a context of 15 similar districts. Suddenly, a different conversation is possible. The ghosted dots stacked above and below the orange dot are those 15 districts. In a live environment (available from the previously mentioned link), you could pass your mouse over any of those similar districts and compare its

Logic errors when identifying English learners

reclassification pattern with Napa Valley USD's. But we now see that in fourth and fifth grades, the pace of reclassification was in the middle of the pack of similar districts. But by seventh grade, it was third from the bottom. One of these similar districts was within an hour's drive of Napa Valley USD. That district, Fairfield-Suisun USD, makes for an interesting comparison. (It appears in Figure 5.3.)

English learner students in third grade in both districts start at about the same level. About 10–12 percent have been reclassified by the end of that year. In fourth grade, Fairfield-Suisun USD doesn't reclassify anyone. But by the end of fifth grade, they've reclassified almost half (48 percent)

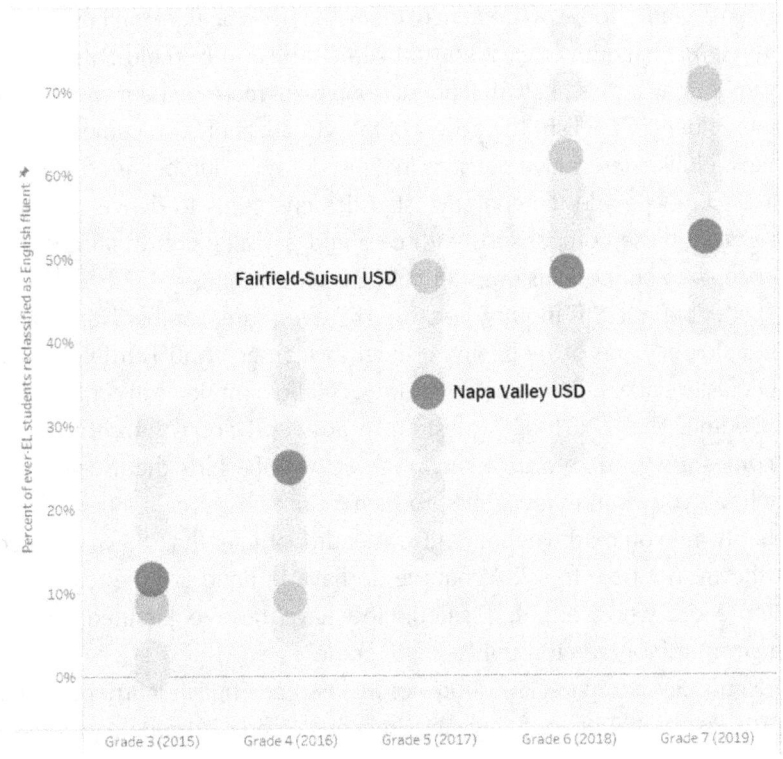

You'll find a link to a live version of this visualization at the following web page: https://www.k12measures.com/ch5/#fig5.3

Figure 5.3 EL students making progress toward proficiency, Class of 2024 over five years: Napa Valley USD and Fairfield-Suisun USD

Source: K12 Measures. © School Wise Press

of their 539 English learner students. They continue in grades 6 and 7 to advance more students to English fluency. By the end of seventh grade, 71 percent of the English learner students in this graduating Class of 2024 have been reclassified. That's 1.5 times the proportion attained in Napa Valley USD. What questions might this pose if this were your district?

Figure 5.3 compares Napa Valley USD to just one district nearby whose students were very similar, showing over five years the percentage of students in the Class of 2024 who were at any time considered to be English learners who have attained English fluency.

What makes this so powerful is that it tells a story. The story is about 670 students in Napa Valley USD's graduating Class of 2024, who when they started school together were all considered to be English learners. By the end of seventh grade, about 50 percent of them had become fluent in English and been reclassified. However, if they'd been enrolled in Fairfield-Suisun USD just an hour away, it's likely that about 20 percent more of them would have become fluent in English. The power of this visualization also comes from its context. Unlike descriptive statistics that just deliver a number as an attribute of a group of people, comparative statistics enable us to derive meaning. If we make those comparisons with care and pay attention to fairness and balance, then our conclusions will hold greater meaning.

Let's continue this inquiry, because we're not sure whether Napa Valley USD's slower pace of reclassifying English learners (and Fairfield-Suisun USD's faster pace) led to better outcomes. A little humility is in order before proceeding. That is a tough question to answer. I don't think that better outcomes are reducible to a single factor. Ask the kids themselves, and they'll tell you what matters most to them about being reclassified. They'd probably tell you readily whether it was earlier or later than they preferred. But they're not here to ask. What we do have in hand are the test results for those kids who were reclassified. How have these reclassified students done from third grade through seventh grade?

Figure 5.4 compares the scores of reclassified English learner students in the Class of 2024 over five years' time, from grade 3 through grade 7, to those of reclassified English learner students in 15 highly similar districts. The test was California's version of the Smarter Balanced test, and both English language arts (left panel) and math (right panel) are presented.

Here's the answer. Keep in mind that the reclassified Napa Valley USD students included in this category grew in numbers as more of them met the criteria for reclassification to fluent, English proficient. Let me describe

Logic errors when identifying English learners

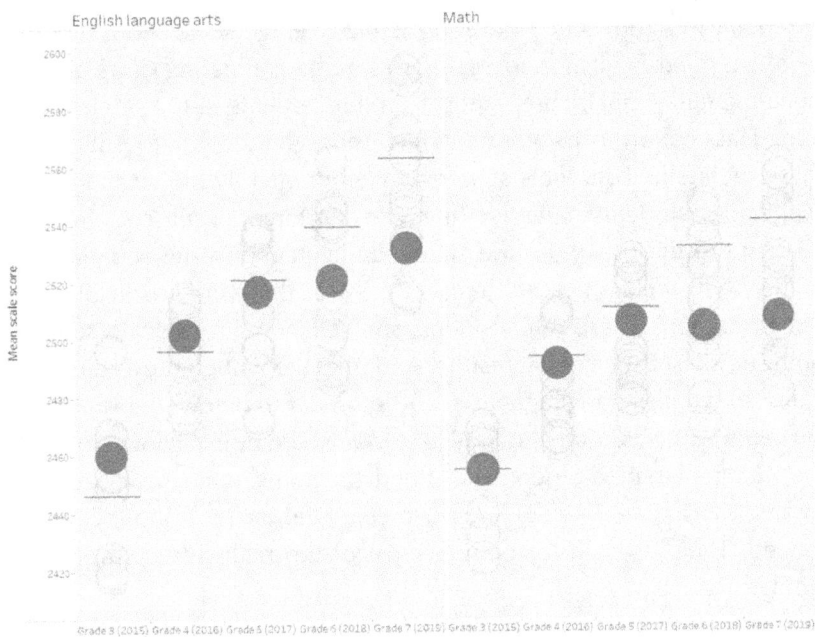

You'll find a link to a live version of this visualization at the following web page: https://www.k12measures.com/ch5/#fig5.4

Figure 5.4 Class of 2024, ELs reclassified as fluent-English-proficient students over five years: Smarter Balanced test results, Napa Valley USD and 15 similar districts

Source: K12 Measures. © School Wise Press

what you see. English language arts results on California's version of the Smarter Balanced tests are in the panel to the left. Math results are to the right. Scale scores are the unit of measurement. The black horizontal bar represents the average scale score statewide for reclassified students in the graduating Class of 2024 in each of five years. Just 85 students are accounted for in third grade, 174 in fourth grade, 275 in fifth grade, 330 in sixth grade and 363 in seventh grade. So, this entity is not composed of the same students each year. Rather, it is composed of students who share one key factor: they were all reclassified English learners. But this gives us relevant evidence needed to answer the question of how well this district is serving its reclassified, English-learner students. If those who are reclassified aren't showing reasonable progress, then it's time to stop the train and figure out what's wrong with the locomotive.

What this shows in Figure 5.4 is the average scale score attained by reclassified-English-learner students in the graduating Class of 2024 in Napa Valley USD, compared to similar students in the same graduating class cohort in 15 other districts. Through third and fourth grades, these reclassified students scored as well or slightly higher than other reclassified students statewide (the black bar) in both subjects. In grade 5, they scored just under the statewide average in both subjects, but higher than reclassified students in most of the comparison districts. But in grade 6, these 330 students showed no gain in scale score in both subjects. Pancake flat results. And in grade 7, they showed modest gains in English language arts but scored far below the statewide average for reclassified students (31 scale score points short). In math, the 363 reclassified students attained the same scale score attained by the 275 reclassified students two years earlier—a troubling signal, indeed. They also fell far behind most of the reclassified students in similar districts.

Let's return to the question of whether their slower reclassification rate and continued academic support enabled them to attain mastery of either math or English language arts subject matter, relative to reclassified students in highly similar districts. The answer is "no."

Next, let's ask whether reclassified students were able to do as well as their English-only fellow students. The scatterplot in Figure 5.5 depicts the 2019 test scores in math of English-only students and reclassified EL students who have now attained English fluency. The results of students in grades 3 through 8 are grouped together to minimize the chance occurrence of oddities in one grade level. The test metric is the percentage of students meeting or exceeding the math standard. English-only students' scores can be read from the vertical axis, and the scores of reclassified English learners can be read from the horizontal axis. Each dot is a district, and the diagonal line represents the point where the scores of both groups of students are identical.

The diagonal line represents the zero-gap line. If reclassified and English-only students scored the same, their results would fall right on that line. The districts to the right of that line are districts where reclassified English learners scored higher in math than their English-only peers.

Logic errors when identifying English learners

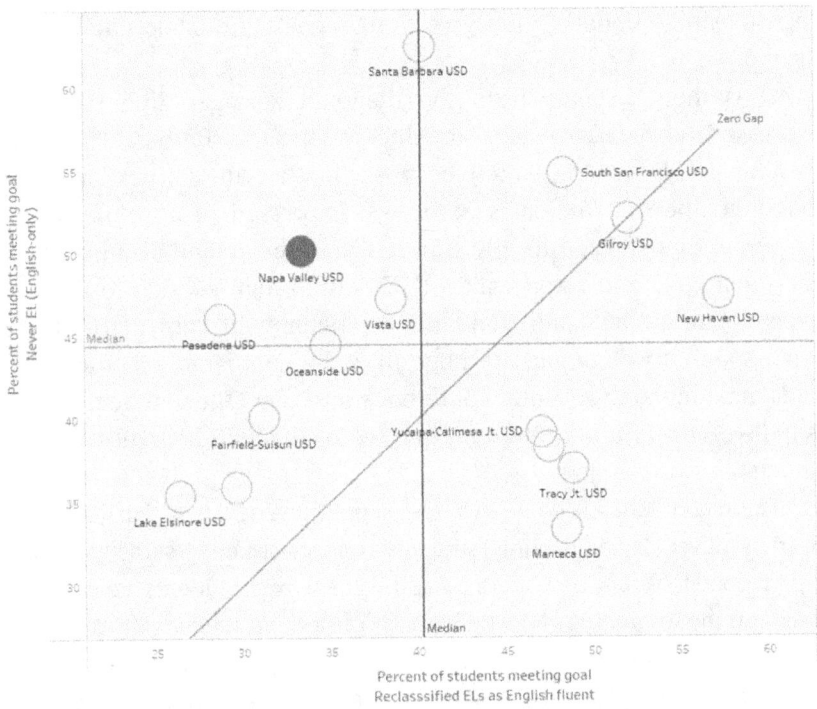

You'll find a link to a live version of this visualization at the following web page: https://www.k12measures.com/ch5/#fig5.5

Figure 5.5 Never EL (English-only) and reclassified English-fluent students' scores on SBAC, math 2019, grades 3–8

Source: K12 Measures. © School Wise Press

Let's put Napa Valley USD's math results for these students into words. Thirty-three percent of the 1,361 students in grades 3 through 8 who were reclassified English learners met the California math standard that year. If you look at their position relative to the vertical median line, you'll see that they were a bit to the left of it (by 7 percentage points). But in rank position, they were fourth lowest among other reclassified-English-learner students. (Count dots from left to right.) Fifty percent of the 4,130 never EL, English-only students met the math standard. If you look at their position relative to the horizontal median line, you'll see that they were a bit above that line (by 6 percentage points). Compared to other English-only (never

Logic errors when identifying English learners

English learner) students, they were fourth highest. (Count dots down from the top.)

It is their distance from the diagonal zero-gap line that best expressed their *relative* gap. Together with Santa Barbara USD and Pasadena USD, it's the largest because they are the farthest from the diagonal line that indicates zero gap. Expressed in *absolute* terms, 17 percent more English-only students than reclassifed EL students in Pasadena USD and Napa Valley USD scored high enough to meet or exceed California's math standard. The benefits of knowing both the relative and absolute gap are huge. It is the comparative context that adds meaning to the absolute difference in scores. The practical benefit is that you can put both findings into words that will help most people understand your point.

Figure 5.6 depicts the 2019 test scores in English language arts of districts' never EL (English-only) students and reclassified EL students. Scores are mapped to values on horizontal and vertical axes. Students are in grades 3–8, and the test metric is the percentage of students meeting or exceeding the English language arts standard. English-only students' scores can be read from the vertical axis, and the scores of reclassified English learners can be read from the horizontal axis. Each dot is a district, and the diagonal line represents the point where the scores of both groups of students is identical.

Let's see if their English language arts scores differed. Note that in the districts to the right of the diagonal line, a higher percentage of reclassified-English-learner students met the English language arts standards than did English-only (the same as never-EL) students. Napa Valley USD, however, sits on the left side of that line. Fifty-one percent of Napa Valley's 1,631 students in grades 3 through 8 who were reclassified English learners scored high enough to meet the California English language arts standard. If you look at the vertical median line, you'll see that they were a tiny bit to the left of it (just 1 percentage point). Sixty percent of this district's never EL (English-only) students in grades 3 through 8 scored high enough to meet the standard. If you look at their position relative to the other districts, they were second highest, far above the horizontal median line.

Describing the gap separating these two groups of students is now possible in both *absolute* and *relative* terms. True, 9 percent more English-only, never EL students scored high enough to meet the English language arts

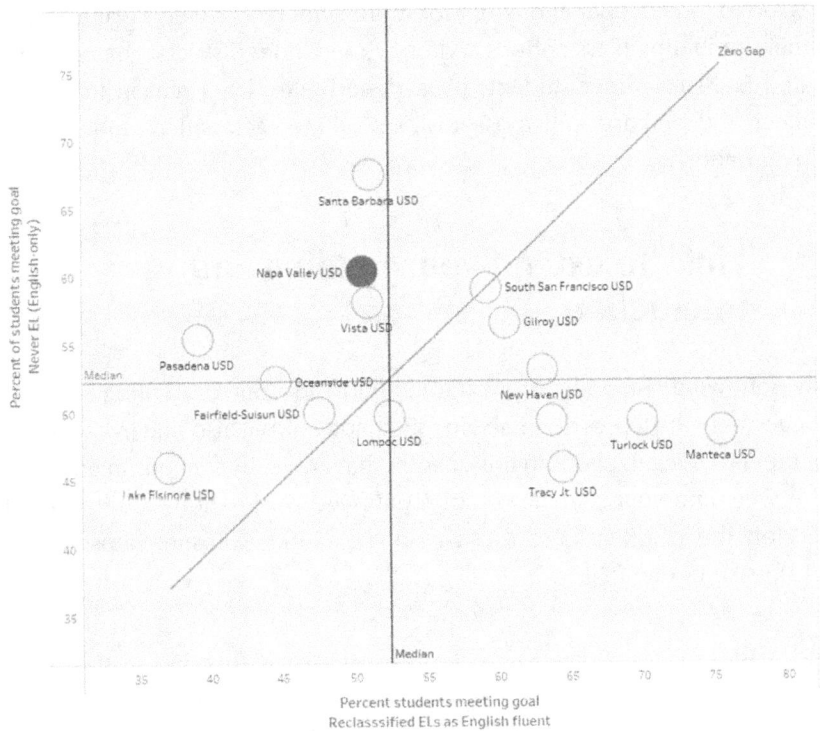

Figure 5.6 Never EL (English-only) and reclassified English-fluent students' scores on SBAC, English language arts, 2019, grades 3–8
Source: K12 Measures. © School Wise Press

You'll find a link to a live version of this visualization at the following web page: https://www.k12measures.com/ch5/#fig5.6

standard than did reclassified EL students. That's the absolute gap measure. But relative to other districts with highly similar students, you could say they were third farthest from the "zero gap" line. But you could also ask why a higher proportion of reclassified EL students in highly similar districts nearby were meeting the standard.

Let's step back and relate this evidence to what we've seen earlier in Figures 5.2 and 5.4. We also see from Figure 5.4 that middle school is where the results of reclassified students flatten out in both English language arts and math. Is that a reason to slow down even further the pace of reclassification, or to bring more support to them once they're reclassified? It's not sufficient evidence to make that decision, but it is a

Logic errors when identifying English learners

reason to look deeper and wider for more evidence, including analysis of other graduating class cohorts. When we see other districts where reclassified English learner students have done better, it's a reason to pause, reflect and perhaps call those districts where reclassified students are doing better.

Links to extend your reading and interaction

The following link will carry you to additional resources, writing and dialogue about the topics discussed in this chapter. You'll also find live versions of the data visualizations in this chapter that are ready for your interaction. We welcome your comments and continued exploration. You'll find all this on the chapter specific page on the book's website: https://www.k12measures.com/ch5.

Questions to spark a conversation

District leaders

1. Do you know the cost to your district of bringing students who are truly English learners to a state of English fluency sufficient to reclassify them? If you were to include only the cost of recruiting, induction, plus current salary and benefits for properly qualified teachers who are prepared to teach second-language learners English, you'd only need to know the average number of students one teacher can serve, and the average number of years it takes a student to be reclassified. Knowing that cost, you know the cost of overidentifying students whom you mistakenly believe to be English learners. Now, given the number of English learners in your district, how much could you save if you reduced your EL identification rate by just 10 percent? Figure that cost not over one year, but over the number

of years those students would have been trapped in the EL category before being reclassified.

2. Discuss the cost of better screening to identify true English-learners more accurately. An accurate screening is one that results in a lower rate of misidentification. What would that better screening look like? How does that investment in more accurate screening compare to the cost of overidentification errors?

Site leaders

3. What goals have you set in your site's annual plan for advancing your second-language learners to mastery of academic English, and reclassification? What grade-level progress markers have you established to share the work of advancing ELs toward those goals? Do you believe that your teaching staff is reevaluating second-language learners on a reasonably uniform basis?

4. Have you assigned each grade-level team a share of responsibility for advancing your second-language learners toward English fluency? Can you see the degree to which your grade-level teams are delivering results? Does your visibility of those results rest on one test result, or on two or more measures?

School board trustees

5. Does your board have a policy for supporting second-language learners after they are reclassified? If you have a policy, how can you tell if the support you call for is being delivered? Does your district expect reclassified students to attain teacher-assigned grades and achieve scores on your state's assessment similar to their English-only peers?

6. What is your board's policy on reclassification? How many conditions must an English-learner meet to be reclassified? How much discretion do you give to teachers? Discuss whether

> your district's conditions, and the logic rules that students must meet, are likely to result in reclassification decisions too soon or too late. Do your policies consider a student's first-language literacy? Do your policies effectively require second-language learners to become more competent as writers or readers than their English-only peers?

Notes

1. The *Lau v. Nichols* decision in 1974 by the U.S. Supreme Court established a clear standard: "Any system employed to deal with the special language skills needs of national origin minority group children must be designated to meet such language skills needs as soon as possible and must not operate as an educational dead-end or permanent track."

2. Kristin Bialik, Alisa Scheller and Kristi Walker, "6 Facts about English Language Learners in U.S. Public Schools," Pew Research Fact Tank, October 25, 2018, www.pewresearch.org/fact-tank/2018/10/25/6-facts-about-english-language-learners-in-u-s-public-schools/.

3. Institute for Education Science, National Center for Education Statistics, "English Language Learners in Public Schools," (website), accessed May 2021, https://nces.ed.gov/programs/coe/indicator_cgf.asp.

4. Katie Stokes-Guinan and Claude Goldenberg, "Use with Caution: What CELDT Results Can and Cannot Tell Us," *CATESOL Journal* 22, no. 1 (2010–2011): 189–202. https://eric.ed.gov/?id=EJ1111981.

5. Ibid., p. 197.

6. California Department of Education, "California English Language Development Test: A Comparison Study of Kindergarten and Grade 1 English-Fluent Students and English Learners on the 2010–11 Edition of the CELDT," October 25, 2011, www.cde.ca.gov/be/pn/im/documents/imadaddec11item02a1.pdf.

7. Peggy Estrada and Haiwen Wang, "Making English Learner Reclassification to Fluent English Proficient Attainable or Elusive: When Meeting Criteria Is and Is *Not* Enough," *American Educational Research Journal* 55, no. 2 (April 2018): 207–42.

8. Estrada and Wang, "Making English Learner Reclassification," p. 223.

9. Education Commission of the States, "50 State Comparison: What Measures Do States Use to Reclassify Students as English Proficient?" (website), November 2014, http://ecs.force.com/mbdata/mbquestNB2?rep=ELL1407.

10. Kenji Hakuta, Yuko Goto Butler and Daria Witt, "How Long Does It Take English Learners To Attain Proficiency?" Stanford University and The University of California Linguistic Minority Research Institute, January 2000, https://eric.ed.gov/?id=ED443275.

11. Laurie Olsen, "Reparable Harm: Fulfilling the Unkept Promise of Educational Opportunity for California's Long Term English Learners," Californians Together, 2010, https://web.stanford.edu/~hakuta/Courses/Ed330X%20Website/Olsen_ReparableHarm2ndedition.pdf.

12. Manuel Buenrostro and Julie Maxwell-Jolly, "Renewing Our Promise: Research and Recommendations to Support California's Long-Term English Learners," Californians Together, October 2021, https://californianstogether.org/wp-content/uploads/2021/10/Renewing_Our_Promise_to_LTELs.pdf.

13. Michael J. Kieffer and Karen D. Thompson, "Hidden Progress of Multilingual Students on NAEP," *Educational Researcher* 47, no. 6 (August/September 2018): 391–8. https://doi.org/10.3102/0013189X18777740.

References

Bialik, Kristin, Alisa Scheller, and Kristi Walker. "Six facts about English Language Learners in U.S. Public Schools." Pew Research Fact Tank, October 25, 2018. www.pewresearch.org/fact-tank/2018/10/25/6-facts-about-english-language-learners-in-u-s-public-schools/.

Buenrostro, Manuel, and Julie Maxwell-Jolly. "Renewing Our Promise: Research and Recommendations to Support California's Long-Term English Learners." Californians Together, October 2021. https://californianstogether.org/wp-content/uploads/2021/10/Renewing_Our_Promise_to_LTELs.pdf.

California Department of Education. "California English Language Development Test: A Comparison Study of Kindergarten and Grade 1

English-Fluent Students and English Learners on the 2010–11 Edition of the CELDT." October 25, 2011. www.cde.ca.gov/be/pn/im/documents/imadaddec11item02a1.pdf.

Education Commission of the States. "50 State Comparison: What Measures Do States Use to Reclassify Students as English Proficient?" (website), November 2014. http://ecs.force.com/mbdata/mbquestNB2?rep=ELL1407.

Estrada, Peggy, and Haiwen Wang. "Making English Learner Reclassification to Fluent English Proficient Attainable or Elusive: When Meeting Criteria Is and Is *Not* Enough." *American Educational Research Journal* 55, no. 2 (April 2018): 207–42.

Hakuta, Kenji, Yuko Goto Butler, and Daria Witt, "How Long Does It Take English Learners to Attain Proficiency?" Stanford University and The University of California Linguistic Minority Research Institute, January 2000. https://eric.ed.gov/?id=ED443275.

Institute for Education Science, National Center for Education Statistics. "English Language Learners in Public Schools." (website). Last modified May 2021. https://nces.ed.gov/programs/coe/indicator_cgf.asp.

Kieffer, Michael J., and Karen D. Thompson. "Hidden Progress of Multilingual Students on NAEP." *Educational Researcher* 47, no. 6 (August/September 2018): 391–8. https://doi.org/10.3102/0013189X18777740.

Olsen, Laurie. "Reparable Harm: Fulfilling the Unkept Promise of Educational Opportunity for California's Long Term English Learners." Californians Together, 2010. https://californianstogether.box.com/shared/static/kjawx856onlpyhtmtc6ajf3x971jko3r.pdf.

Stokes-Guinan, Katie, and Claude Goldenberg. "Use with Caution: What CELDT Results Can and Cannot Tell Us." *CATESOL Journal* 22, no. 1 (2010–2011): 189–202. https://eric.ed.gov/?id=EJ1111981.

 Mistaken ways of measuring money, buildings and people

In 2019, Mark Schneider, the director of the Institute of Education Sciences, fired a flare of caution into the sky warning of leaders' lack of clarity and candor about the cost of educating kids. "As a field, we have been way, way behind the curve in terms of telling people how much things cost."[1] One test of Mr. Schneider's assertion is to look at some of the best authors' writing about school improvement and examine the place of economic analysis in their works. Let's look at two: the Carnegie Foundation team that has championed continuous improvement, and John Hattie who has advanced the cause of making learning visible through comparative measures of impact.

If there's one book that is the bible of continuous improvement for K–12 educators, it is *Learning to Improve: How America's Schools Can Get Better at Getting Better*.[2] It ranks 12th in Amazon's ranking of education administration books, a notable achievement. All four of its authors—Anthony S. Bryk, Louis M. Gomez, Alicia Grunow and Paul G. LeMahieu—are leaders within the Carnegie Foundation for the Advancement of Teaching. Certainly, in a book this influential, written by four people as highly esteemed, you'd expect to see economic analysis used somewhere in its pages. Yet nowhere could I find even a reference to economic analysis. Not in the index. Not in the glossary. Not in the body of the book and its ample real-world examples. This is a book I've read and value highly. It has advanced the cause of smarter management. Some of our clients have gone through the Carnegie Foundation training in California and praise *Learning to Improve* highly. Yet what does it say about the profession of education management when a book this highly regarded disregards the cost-consequences of improvements?

DOI: 10.4324/9781003272915-7

Rather than rush to judgment, I looked at another book that is on the "must read" list for those studying school improvement: *Visible Learning* by John Hattie.[3] He dared to do what no one had done before: compare the relative effect of over a hundred different approaches to improving student learning. He found over 800 studies and used meta-analysis methods to find a common denominator of effect size to estimate the impact of each. Since the book came out in 2008, Hattie has written well over a dozen spin-off books, each of them applying his comparative effectiveness method to specific domains within K–12 (e.g., early literacy, math, special education, etc.). *Visible Learning* soared in popularity and now ranks 188th on Amazon's education administration best-seller list. But does the *cost of achieving gains* appear in this book? In its 392 pages, it appears only in passing. Yet it is central to the decision-making that faces every education leader. It is an obvious constraint. What's the "bang" that they'll obtain for every "buck" they spend? This is a universal and unavoidable question.

Why is this money-related blind spot especially relevant to those who embrace the ideas of continuous improvement? Because waste is the inevitable result of making improvements with unmeasured resources that are of unknown effectiveness. Wasted time—both teacher time and student time—is costly and can be expressed in dollars. If you are wasting time on "solutions" of unknown cost and effect, and which cannot be compared to treatments that may be more effective, aren't you destined to be wasting money? So, let's heed Mark Schneider's warning and look with fresh eyes at the ways that money is accounted for, the ways that land and buildings are used and the ways that people are managed.

Money

When school boards and district leaders talk about money, it is usually *budgets* they discuss. Not cost-effectiveness. Not return on investment. If the board is asking district leaders why they chose this reading program over that one, you will be unlikely to hear a discussion of the cost-benefit of that choice. The problem is that too many district business leaders don't even speak in these economic terms. This restricted vocabulary is a sign of a weak conceptual link between money and the effects of spending it. The effects are for the most part not measured. Now let's look at some of the consequences of looking at money only through the lens of the budget.

Many public agencies develop operating ratios that are an expression of productivity or utility. Many libraries measure the number of items checked out at each branch over a year, as well as the number of cardholders. This enables them to say,

> We increased the number of card-holders by five percent last year, and they borrowed eight percent more items. Because we ran our branches with the same staff head count and budget as we did last year, we're proud to have done so at lower cost-per-cardholder served.

Transportation agencies favor a measure of cost-per-passenger-mile. Running buses or rapid-transit systems efficiently means moving the most people to the places they want to go, at the time they want to get there, at the least cost.

Inside the district office, the leadership too often believes that only the business office team and the chief academic officer need to know a district's financial facts. In California, when district planning teams invite us to run measurement workshops, we have often heard people say that this is the only time of the year when everyone discusses money matters. We have observed that the language spoken by those on the business side of the district is often incomprehensible to those on the instructional side. So not only is the vocabulary of the business leadership team limited to budget-speak, but those in education services and curriculum-and-instruction departments are often unprepared to discuss how to evaluate big purchasing decisions. Budget-speak is fine for discussing whether the purchases are affordable. But economic thinking—especially notions of cost-benefit and cost-effectiveness—are needed when leaders sit down together to plan.

Seeing the per-student cost of educating different students

Education leaders who measure the varied costs of creating different kinds of opportunities to learn for different students can see something that budgets don't reveal. When those opportunities to learn are offered to different students, it becomes possible to estimate how much a district invests in educating students who pursue each path. Marguerite Roza has been an effective advocate for this way of calculating per-student expenses, and her book *Educational Economics: Where Do [$]chool Funds Go?* has been a clarion call for seeing district spending from the students' point of view.[4]

The virtues of this approach are easy to see. In fact, districts have been doing this with special education students for decades. They have calculated the cost-per-student of educating students in the general education program and compared that to the cost-per-student of educating students with learning disabilities. This has helped districts communicate to their public that funds for special education students may be three or four times more per student than funds for general education students. Marguerite Roza asks, why not do this for everyone?

She also argues for looking at the cost of offering specialized classes and programs that are used by small numbers of students: ceramics classes, AP calculus, classes in foreign languages few students care to take. If the cost of those classes is known, then dividing those costs by the number of students who take them results in a clear estimate of the cost-per-student of delivering those classes. Think how differently the course offerings and teaching assignments might look in a high school if these costs-per-student were on the table in the light of day. This view should be part of a fuller review, of course, one which includes the benefit that results from this investment, however pricey on a per-student basis. A costly expenditure could make you wince on a per-student basis but cause you to smile on a cost-benefit basis.

Think, too, of how more fully districts could respond to accusations of inequitable distribution of opportunities to learn. Districts would know, student by student, course by course, school by school, where their investment has gone and who has benefited. In fact, federal legislation required that school districts calculate the actual school-by-school cost of delivering education, based on real teachers' salaries (not the usual average cost-per-FTE). This finding started appearing in schools' accountability report cards, starting in 2018. If you haven't looked at the difference in funding between least costly and most costly school site (on a per-student basis), I urge you to do so. Those costs may vary for entirely defensible reasons, of course. Knowing those reasons will help you when questions about unequal funding percolate to the surface.

The per-student view also leaves open the question of how to value management and support services. These resources are indirectly related to the classroom—everyone from payroll clerks to principals, from janitors to maintenance crews. The resources that support students are a little easier to cost out per-student. Counselors and coaches can be more easily measured on a cost-per-student basis, and their contribution valued as benefits to students. So, cost-per-student is not equally useful across all job responsibilities.

The notion that some students are more expensive to educate than others is not new. It is the basis for categorical funding that has been part of federal funding formulas since the passage of the Elementary and Secondary Education Act in 1965. Just one example is Title I, Part A, of that law, which allocates federal funds to districts based mainly on the number of school-age children from low-income families they serve. Many states have their own categorical funds. Two things make weighed student formula funding different. First, weighted student formula is based on a range of characteristics of students in a school, not just one factor: parents' declared household income. Second, *districts* decide how much funding each school site is allocated based on the characteristics of each student in the school. Many of those districts using this as a budgeting method are larger urban and suburban districts.

Dr. Roza's research team studied 19 districts that have used weighted student formulas to allocate funds; according to her estimates, this approach is now used in districts serving about 10 percent of America's K–12 students. A blog post she wrote in 2019, published by the Institute of Education Sciences that funded the research, provides a handy overview of the phenomenon.[5] In 2020, her team at the Edunomics Lab published the findings of their three-year study and summarized them in a 10-page paper titled, "Lessons Learned: Weighted Student Funding."[6] Their research questions include a look at outcomes, at whether achievement gaps are narrowing more in districts that use weighted student funding and the degree to which those districts are spending more on at-risk students than districts using conventional funding allocation methods.

☞ **Tip:** here's how you can begin to look at your school's or district's differing costs to deliver high school classes to students. Start with the cost of current salary of each teacher. We'll leave aside the benefits and deferred compensation of pension payments, even though that's considerable. Look at the classes each teacher delivers. Divide each teacher's actual salary and benefits by the number of classes, and you have the cost-per-class for that teacher. Then look at the average class size for each of those classes and divide the cost per class again by the number of students who take each of those classes. That yields a cost-per-student for each class. The smaller the enrollment in a class, the higher the cost-per-student to deliver that class. A high school teacher who teaches five sections of math a day, and who earns $95,000 a year in salary and benefits, has a cost-per-class of $19,000. If all those classes have 25 students enrolled, the cost-per-student to deliver those classes is $760. But if one of those classes is an AP calculus class, and it has 15 students enrolled, the cost-per-student for that class is $1,267. This is simply a dollar-based expression of what is easy for everyone to see—the students in the smaller AP calculus class get more of the teacher's time and attention than the students in the other four classes. Of course, that hypothetical high school teacher earning $95,000 a year in salary and benefits has considerable seniority. If that teacher were a newbie, his total compensation might be 60 percent of that. In this analysis, the actual cost of teachers is what counts—not the average cost.

This cost-accounting omits a lot of other factors, of course. It doesn't count the cost of providing a classroom, heating, air-conditioning and cleaning. It doesn't count the cost of maintaining the building, nor does it count the cost of paying the interest on the bonds floated to build the building. Nor does it count the amortization of the value of the square footage in that classroom since buildings have a life span and each year it gets shorter. Nor does it count teachers' pension costs, or the cost of health care for their dependents. Nor does it count the cost of any professional development invested in that teacher. Nor does it count the cost of licensing the AP calculus curriculum from the College Board, or the cost of the AP tests that come with it. But that's okay for a first-round analysis. You should, however, factor in those indirect costs on a second pass. Be aware that indirect costs are many, and they are not inconsiderable. Equally important, those per-student costs get you only part of the way to estimating the cost-effectiveness of that expenditure.

You'll also discover another benefit to denominating revenues and expenses per student. You can easily compare your funding to those of other districts. This is useful if you're asking your community to boost their property taxes to fund your district more fully. The clearer your evidence, the more persuasive your case will appear to voters. If your district has a higher proportion of students with learning disabilities, your instructional costs will be higher overall than that of districts with lower proportions of learning-disabled students. But comparing your instructional costs *per student* for special education and general education separately will make for a fairer comparison, and one that is easy to communicate. But don't be surprised if this leads to other questions you didn't intend to explore. Some districts intentionally serve students with learning disabilities, at much higher cost. Other districts offer before- and after-school care, which may set them apart. Smaller districts usually carry a higher per-student cost for administrative overhead than larger districts. This may lead citizens to question whether your district manages financial resources prudently.

Cost-effectiveness measures and knowing what results from your district's spending

Cost-effectiveness is simply a way to evaluate the cost of achieving an effect. It's used by us daily as we make mundane decisions. For example, what's the least expensive way to travel to visit a relative. Traveling costs both time and money, and it entails other variables like comfort. So, if you're short of time, a cost-effective way for you to visit that relative may be one that takes the least time in transit. But if you've got a lot of time on your hands, you may value the least expensive method even if it takes somewhat longer. If you're physically impaired, the most cost-effective option will provide for the greatest comfort and safety at the lowest cost.

In districts, an analysis of cost-effectiveness belongs on the table when choosing among instructional programs designed to achieve the same effect. For example, consider two competing elementary school math programs. Program A has a cost of $400 per student, and research on it has led to students showing a 20 percent boost in their level of mastery of math (an effect size of .6 standard deviations). Let's presume that this research is third-party research, conducted over a large number of students and that demographically they are fairly similar to your district's students. Program B, the alternative program, has a cost of $200 per student. Its research shows a boost of about 10 percent (an effect size of .3 standard deviations). Which program is most cost-effective? Neither. They produce an identical effect for an equivalent cost: an effective boost of about 5 percent (a .15 standard deviation of gain) for every $100-per-student spent. The purchasing officer thinks Program B is a bargain because it costs half as much per student. But the district's program evaluator says it's a toss-up. If your district heeds your program evaluator's views, you can select the program whose features are more desirable, or the one that proves to be more popular with teachers and students. But you'll do so, knowing that cost is not driving your choice, but rather your cost-effect ratio, or "bang-per-buck."

Education is not the only sector that has a hard time relating spending to outcomes. Health care has been one area where America's sky-high spending and river-bottom health status has led to many debates. But for a long time, health care outcomes and costs weren't thought about in relation to each other. As the fields of health economics and public health matured, the connection between spending and outcomes became more and more clear. The Dartmouth Atlas of Health Care Project advanced the cause further by looking at micro-regional variations in medical needs, costs, resources, frequency of procedures and outcomes. They discovered, using a national database of Medicare data, that health care costs and outcomes often had little relation to each other. Even after applying risk-adjustments to the outcome data, they found that hospitals varied enormously in the quality of the care they delivered and the range of fees they charged for identical procedures. Equally controversial was their discovery that the frequency of some procedures was at times five or six or seven times higher in some micro-regions. What they discovered was that it was supply, the sheer availability of doctors, that was driving higher frequency of certain procedures.

One scholar of economics who has helped lead educators to the promised land is Henry Levin, now retired from Teachers College, part of Columbia University in New York City. He was coauthor of the leading textbooks for administrative leaders, *Economic Evaluation in Education Cost-Effectiveness and Benefit-Cost Analysis*[7] and *Cost-Effectiveness Analysis 2nd Edition: Methods and Applications*.[8] I met him when he was at Stanford University's Graduate School of Education, and when I asked him if he'd join my company's advisory board, he said he would if I read his book first. His generosity enabled me to learn much. I also came to appreciate the challenges he faced bringing economic thinking into the education profession. The preface to the third edition of *Economic Evaluation in Education Cost-Effectiveness and Benefit-Cost Analysis* conveys a hint of the size of those barriers. "The first edition of this volume was published in 1983 and the second in 2001. Unfortunately, over this long period, there was mostly a lot of talk about costs-effectiveness analysis, but there was not very much action."

Evidence of Henry Levin's observation that economic thinking hasn't led to much action is ample. Indeed, administrative credential courses still teach just one dimension of economics to those preparing for the superintendency: budgeting. Chief business officers take a deeper dive, but do their credentialing programs cover cost-benefit, cost-effectiveness or return on investment? If anyone in a district office is ready to think about the relation of costs to benefits, it's likely to be someone responsible for program evaluation. So, if you're looking for anyone in your district who can bring economic thinking to your side, you may enjoy better luck knocking on the door of a program evaluator.

When Teachers College persuaded Henry Levin to leave the oak and palm tree landscape of Stanford University for the streetscape of New York City, he created a center dedicated to this cause. He named it the Center for Benefit-Cost Studies in Education and went to work recruiting graduate students and faculty to produce research, publish papers and advise school districts. That Center is still busy today under the direction of Fiona Holland, advancing the cause of measuring the value of what education dollars buy, and you can find their "Cost Out" toolkit and resource "ingredient" list on their website.[9]

The inability to see the relation of spending to any measured effect is nearly universal. I've seen districts respond to this knowledge void in two ways. Either decision-makers have given up trying to relate money spent and educational outcomes. Or at the other extreme are districts that expect to see a magical cause-and-effect between every dollar spent and expected improvements. I've witnessed dozens of times the district planning process in California, where planning teams are accustomed to the annual ritual of guessing how big a boost to their students' test scores will result from an investment of $250,000 in math coaches or professional development workshops. The projections in these plans are reviewed by county office leaders and then passed to school boards for discussion and a vote. I've seen plans where the projected improvements are expressed to the tenth of a decimal point, as if the planning team possessed big computer models that could deliver precise predictions. The charade of projecting results is repeated year after year, yet the reconciliation of projections to actual outcomes rarely occurs. In public, this planning process is highly praised. In private, I've heard superintendents volunteer deeply critical comments.

If you are a new board member, a new administrator, or an active parent new to the school world, speak up when you expect the costs of improvements to be considered. This is a blind spot shared by advocates and researchers, as well. What's "good for kids" is often what they champion. But good for *which* kids, and to *what degree* and at *what cost?* Many scholars also share this blind spot. I have been to enough meetings of the American Education Research Association and read enough volumes of their research journals to tell you that studies of the effect size of a treatment on student learning or graduation rates almost never includes a measure of the cost of attaining that effect.

Cost-benefit enables you to find your way around zero-sum dilemmas

Think how frequently a district must decide what to invest in. When planning time arrives, every program, every school, every activity is potentially competing for funding. Everyone will have ideas for how to put new funds to work to improve their program or team. One factor that can guide leaders into this difficult moment is cost-benefit analysis. If you can quantify in dollars the size of the benefits that result from investments in different people and programs, and if you can measure their costs, you have a way to make the best use of your district's scarce dollars. For example, if you have evidence that your four high school counselors have, in addition to carrying case loads of 500 students, guided 120 seniors to file FAFSA applications who would otherwise not have done so and prevented 40 kids from dropping out, you can assign a dollar value to those two accomplishments. The dollar value equivalent of those accomplishments was achieved at the cost of the salary and benefits of those four counselors. Now you could ask, "If we added one more counselor to their team, how many more seniors would have completed FAFSA applications, and how many more kids would have not dropped out?" You could compare the cost of those benefits to the cost of adding another math teacher and the ensuing benefit of reducing average math class sizes from 32 to 28. Reducing class size may benefit some students to a certain degree and cause some math teachers to feel less stressed. If you can turn those benefits into dollars, you can compare the cost and benefit of adding a counselor to adding a math teacher. Where would the district's dollars produce the greatest benefit, and for whom?[10]

Valuing benefits or results is admittedly complicated. Not all results can, after all, be reduced to their equivalent in dollars (thank goodness). But there are methods of estimating benefits that have a long history of use in other fields. The field of medicine puts a value on a year of extended life in good health, and a different value on that year if the patient is alive but in compromised health. Baseball puts a value on the lifespan of a pitcher's arm, and this has led to a cap on the number of pitches that a starter will be allowed to throw. Even if a pitcher remains strong and in control, today's managers will bring in a relief pitcher after most starters throw about 100 pitches. Consider the methods of valuing benefits summarized in the book Henry Levin coauthored:

- Contingent valuation method, based on what someone will pay to buy that benefit;
- Hedonic method, based on the perceived value of school quality baked into home prices;
- Defensive expenditure method, based on what people will pay to avoid its opposite; and
- Earnings, based on the gain in earnings that is likely to result from someone attaining a degree or diploma or other expression of educational attainment.[11]

There are ways to make these estimations, and if your district team includes a program evaluator, that person should be well-prepared to help. You are likely to find help outside your business office staff if you ask for help from your board, parents, companies in your community or your local college.

Consider this simpler example of cost-benefit thinking. Your district is feeling the pain of enrollment declines, and you learn from exit interviews that a sizable portion of families are leaving the district to enroll their kids in neighboring school districts and are not leaving the community. Two themes emerge from these discussions. First, parents of elementary age children have heard that your middle schools are rough and that bullying is common. Second, parents of middle school age kids tell you that their kids feel school is all work and no play. Too much homework, too much pressure are frequent themes. You're the school board president, and you meet with the superintendent and ask for her ideas. You tell her that you're ready to tackle the public relations problem if she's willing to change the climate in middle school. The superintendent comes back to you with a list of three things to do. No costs are associated with any of them. You ask her to estimate the costs of all three, and then add a fourth: school marketing.

You also tell her that you will help estimate the value in dollars-per-student of retaining a student for all 13 years and return with a measure of the cost of lost enrollment over the total number of lost enrollment-years. To spark the enthusiasm of the superintendent, you share one quick observation. Since the district gets $15,000 per student per year in total revenue, the loss of one student who leaves middle school before seventh grade is a loss of $90,000. In losing a family with three kids enrolled, each of whom has four, six and eight years left in the district, that's a loss of future revenue that totals $270,000 in current dollars. Suddenly, the value of retaining a family in the district has changed the superintendent's view. Now, fixing these problems with the middle school is more urgent, and the benefit of school marketing now appears to be worth investing in.

Long-term consequence of deferred liabilities

There are two moments when school boards and district bargaining teams wrestle with decisions that have consequences that may last 20 or 30 years, or even longer. One of those moments is the decision to take on debt for the purpose of buying land or building new schools. The other moment occurs during collective bargaining, when labor asks for improvements to employees' salaries or retirement benefits (pensions or health benefits). Both moments are high pressure, high visibility events. Both moments enable a district to make people happy today, at the cost of imposing cost burdens on citizens years later.

Winning a bond election is tough. It requires that the leaders who champion the bond measure take the temperature of their community's voters, understanding how much additional tax on their property they'd accept, while still voting "yes" on the bond measure. This delicate balancing act leads districts to shop for bond terms that may impose lighter tax burdens on citizens in the early years, and increasingly heavier burdens in the later years. Or leaders may ask their citizens to approve several bonds, spread over the years, in more bite-sized portions.

To be sure, the bond rating agencies understand the longer-term consequences. They know the value of the property in that community, the degree to which it is already encumbered, the financial solvency of the district and much, much more. Does the district have an equally complete understanding? But just as important, has the district forecast the cost of debt service and principal repayment as far out as the life of the bonds? The district takes a risk when it borrows, hoping the community's growth can help carry the cost of repayment more easily over time. But those dollars will ultimately be provided by residents, or if the bonds are long-term, by their children.

The pension and health benefit decisions of years ago are now looming larger as retirees live longer than actuarial accountants expected. In fact, the burden is so high that some major metropolitan districts—among them Chicago and Los Angeles—are facing the possibility of financial insolvency due largely to the cost of unfunded retirement benefits. By 2019, Chicago Public Schools' pension benefits consumed one-fourth of their budget.[12]

How did this happen? Many district bargaining teams granted overly generous concessions for deferred compensation in labor agreements when budget cuts were imposed during the economic crises of 2001–2002 and 2008–2009. These commitments may have been considered an unavoidable risk by the bargaining teams. But when those leaders calculated the cost of honoring those improved benefits, they certainly knew that somebody else would be on the board and in the superintendent's seat when the costs came due.

The Government Accounting Standards Board (GASB) only revised the reporting requirements for pensions and other employee benefits in 2013 and 2014, with GASB Statements 67 and 68. They did so in the wake of private sector debacles with underfunded pension funds, and with the hopes that public sector organizations would not be blindsided by deferred liabilities that don't appear in full on their books. Districts would have benefited from an improved reporting requirement had it occurred a decade sooner. But now that districts have to carry the burden of those future obligations more fully on their current books, these deferred liabilities have devoured sizable shares of districts' instructional funds.

The action you can take when exploring the financial condition of your district is to read beyond the budget. Look at assets and liabilities and pay special attention to deferred liabilities for pension and health obligations. Keep your eyes wide open and fasten your safety belt. You are likely to be in for a wild ride.

Land and buildings

Almost all the discussion among educators about money is about the budget, expenses or revenues. This misses not just liabilities, but also assets, and the two that are likely to be most valuable are land and buildings.

School districts usually own their land and buildings. Once they've made an acquisition, they open school and shift to maintenance mode. If the operating cost of maintaining the buildings and grounds is in line with that of neighboring districts, the board is satisfied, and parents and teachers are happy. But what is it worth, and might the district realize fuller value from that land by doing something else with it?

The Government Accounting Standards Board revised their rules on public agency reporting of fixed assets, requiring that public agencies start accounting for fixed assets between 1999 and 2003, with a declaration called GASB-34. Their motivation was to draw attention to the value of land and buildings and other fixed assets that any public sector agency had invested in. Their intent was to draw more attention to the value of land and buildings, adjusted for depreciation and throw light on what had been a rather hidden area of public investment. The value of keeping older buildings well maintained, for example, is more easily justified if you can show that the building will be worth less if it depreciates faster. This turned a common-sense value—it's cheaper to fix the roof today than repair the damage from leaks next year—into a dollars-and-sense value. But the sunlight that GASB-34 shined on districts also led in many cases to worthwhile discussions. "Is our district likely to benefit from moving our old warehouse off this valuable land zoned for retail, to less valuable land on the outskirts of town, so we can lease or sell that property to someone?" With GASB-34 requiring public sector agencies to reevaluate the condition of their infrastructure assets every three years, districts had yet one more reason to keep their buildings in good shape.

The second question is whether the district is fully utilizing the value of its land and buildings. Lawyers will often advise the board to lock up the playground when school is not in session to minimize risk of litigation. And for similar reasons, districts close school buildings by five o'clock, so they can save on utility costs. This tradition helps keep costs down, but does it encourage a district to get the most value from their investment in the land and buildings?

The benefits of a cooperative and enterprising spirit

In many communities, especially small towns, an ethos of cooperation among public sector institutions prevails. Playgrounds may sit inside the school's property lines. But they are there for everyone to use, so gates are left unlocked and community use is welcomed. In cities with a shortage of baseball fields, more enterprising high schools rent their fields to private schools and leagues for use. In some communities, schools are built as community centers and designed for multiuse. The flexibility of smaller communities results in fuller use of schools' resources. Why not measure the use to which these resources are put in relation to the cost of maintenance?

But not all schools own their land and buildings. Charter schools in Los Angeles, for example, faced with a scarcity of suitable spaces, rely on both leases and purchases to acquire school sites. The scrappy charter school operators of Los Angeles stepped outside the tradition of owning the school site, and instead, adapted a building for their use, paying rent instead of bond interest and principal. The resourceful but cash-poor Catholic school in my prior neighborhood sold one-fourth of their land to a developer to raise much needed operating funds. Many opportunities await those who are ready to stretch.

It is, in fact, the moments when districts have to stretch that they discover underutilized resources, including their land and buildings. Waste in these moments suddenly becomes visible. The 180-day school year results in buildings underutilized. Universities repurpose many campus facilities in the summer months. Why couldn't school districts? A California district, Coronado USD in San Diego County, helped pay for an Olympic-scale swimming pool by renting it to private swim clubs and the city's park and recreation department.

Resource sharing works two ways. When the Los Angeles USD began closing school libraries under the duress of the economic downturn of 2000–2001, the city's library system refocused their resources on the schools. This led to school libraries, in some cases, becoming housed in the neighborhood library. In other cases, it meant that city libraries reorganized their children's collections to match the curriculum and reading lists that teachers were assigning their students. It also led to changes in library staffing schedules, hiring and new reading programs hosted in the libraries. Necessity is the mother of invention, and in this case, city librarians spared students much of the loss they would have otherwise suffered.

Does your district value fuller use of school buildings by the community at large? Or do they see fuller use as a risk to be avoided? If you care about fuller utilization, you'll need to create a measure to express it. Perhaps you'll find a way to generate revenue from that wider utilization, in which case you can use dollars to express the benefit of fuller utilization. But dollars aren't the only way to account for this. (In the pandemic era, of course, risks of a new sort would have to be considered.)

Putting a value on the quality of resources

If you care about the quality of the physical classrooms and playgrounds you provide, perhaps you should find a way to measure it. All states should have regulations that define minimal standards of maintenance for public buildings. But that's just a floor level threshold. A quality measure of habitability might include the number of school days when the temperature inside classrooms exceeded or fell below levels your district felt were reasonable. In the pandemic, many districts measured the rate at which fresh air circulated through classrooms. Lighting or access to window light may be a concern in your district. In other districts, the quality of water or cleanliness may be more important factors. Perhaps your local concern is the quality of playground space. All these are measurable.

In California, public interest lawyers representing a group of students sued the state of California over substandard education services and the condition of schools. The building standards that emerged from this 2004 case, known as the Williams Settlement legislation, defined adequate school buildings as the absence of problems.[13] This was a good start, but defining adequacy is a far cry from measuring quality. Architectural firms know what quality looks like—quality of plans, materials, craftsmanship, lighting, interior design—and how to measure it. They know the lifecycle of materials, the cost of flexible space design, the acoustical nature of materials and so much more. If you're defining quality measures in your district, you'd be better served by seeking advice from architects and others who create quality spaces for a living.

People: teachers and principals

How do you evaluate teaching? This question is far from being answered. Yet its answer is central to the management of teaching talent, as is the recruitment of the most promising teacher candidates. The problem at the center of our attention isn't so much the mismeasurement of teaching, but the *absence of measures* altogether. The keenest observers of this problem, The New Teacher Project, stated the problem boldly in their 2009 paper, "The Widget Effect." In the introduction to the second edition, the authors wrote:

> A teacher's effectiveness—the most important factor for schools in improving student achievement—is not measured, recorded, or used to inform

decision-making in any meaningful way. . . . school districts fail to acknowledge or act on differences in teacher performance almost entirely. When it comes to officially appraising performance and supporting improvement, a culture of indifference about the quality of instruction in each classroom dominates.

While the report is mainly a critique of the emptiness of most districts' teacher evaluations, the report probes for the roots of this nearly universal problem.

[I]nfrequent teacher dismissals are in fact just one symptom of a larger, more fundamental crisis—the inability of our schools to assess instructional performance accurately or to act on this information in meaningful ways. This inability not only keeps schools from dismissing consistently poor performers, but also prevents them from recognizing excellence among top-performers or supporting growth among the broad plurality of hard-working teachers who operate in the middle of the performance spectrum. Instead, school districts default to treating all teachers as essentially the same, both in terms of effectiveness and need for development. . . . school districts must begin to distinguish great from good, good from fair, and fair from poor. Effective teaching must be recognized; ineffective teaching must be addressed.[14]

Sure, you can take stock of who is teaching by age, gender, ethnicity and experience. You can look at the level of education your teachers bring to the classroom. But describing teachers' demographic attributes has no relation to measuring teaching. Yet these are the statistical artifacts that districts possess, so that's what districts report in their school accountability report cards, as called for by federal law. When it comes to teaching effectiveness, we are left with an error of omission. The evidence is in most districts simply missing in action. Yet the opportunity to build evidence is in every district's hands.

The emptiness of teacher evaluations

Teacher evaluations are a litmus test of a district's view of teaching quality. If a district's evaluation method doesn't reveal the differences among teachers, it reveals the district's refusal to look at teaching. Yes, principals do indeed evaluate teachers. But based on the findings of "The Widget

Mismeasuring money and people

Effect," those evaluations are universally positive. Looking at surveys from about 15,000 teachers in 12 districts in four states, the authors of the report were able to construct a disturbing portrait of district disinterest in the differences among teachers. In those districts that used the crudest evaluation metric—either satisfactory or unsatisfactory—more than 99 percent of teachers were evaluated by principals to be satisfactory. In districts that used a more reasonable rubric of five categories, 94 percent of teachers received one of the top two ratings. Less than 1 percent were rated unsatisfactory—the same proportion reported by the two-category districts.

In a subset of districts, districts asked teachers to evaluate their own instructional performance. On a scale from 1 to 10, about 43 percent rated themselves at level 9 or 10. The report's authors conclude that, "These teachers are not irrationally inflating their estimate of their teaching performance; they are simply responding to an environment in which all are assumed to be superior performers." Yet teachers also expressed dissatisfaction with the lack of feedback. About three out of four teachers revealed that they received no specific feedback in their most recent evaluation. Fifty-seven percent of teachers in their first four years of teaching were told they had no need to improve in any area.

Adding to the demoralization of teachers is the inability of districts to identify either exemplary teachers or those with serious performance problems. One teacher from Akron, Ohio, commented in the survey conducted by The New Teacher Project, "Poorly performing teachers are rated at the same level as the rest of us. This infuriates those of us who do a good job." Despite Akron's use of a five-category rubric, 60 percent of their teachers were evaluated as "outstanding." This was not far from what the principals of Cincinnati Public Schools did with their teacher evaluations: 58 percent rated as "distinguished" (top level). Nor was it far from how Chicago principals evaluated their teachers: 69 percent "superior" and 25 percent "excellent." This would be hard to believe even if students were all getting into four-year universities. But in the face of students' results in these districts, it's evidence only of the inability of these districts to look squarely and honestly at the work of their teachers.

The mismeasurement of schools' vital signs is inescapable as long as school districts choose to ignore teacher effectiveness. Districts that are ready to take stock of their condition would be wise to start with teacher evaluations. Indeed, distinguishing good teaching from poor teaching should be at the center of professional competence. Those districts that are able to identify their best teachers and have credible evidence to support their conclusions should emerge as leaders.

HR directors and the human resources team

To evaluate teaching, you need a network of human reconnaissance, led by a great HR director. This network includes site leaders who have their eyes and ears wide open and who will share what they observe. It should include students' observations of teachers, as well as those of parents (assuming you value diplomacy and favor a customer service ethos). Your direct observations must be in the network, of course. But every district's director of human resources is your chief people person. She sets the tone, an attitude that echoes throughout the entire district. If you're a superintendent or cabinet-level leader, you are likely to want an HR director whose antennas are acutely attuned to identifying teaching talent. But how do you know if your HR director has that quality? You can observe her in action, of course. But to discover her beliefs, you'll want to ask a lot of questions like these. Try asking her what a successful year looks like. If her answer is about filling positions as early as possible, at the lowest cost possible, you'll have learned that issues of quantity and cost are top of mind. If your HR director hopes for a year free of union grievances and other forms of labor friction, you'll have learned that she places the highest value on harmony. If you hear about improved retention without reference to the quality of teachers who are retained, you'll have learned that your HR director is most focused on making her numbers. If you hear little about the quality of teacher evaluations, you'll have another clue.

What you're looking for are the values that drive your HR leader. If you're lucky, they'll be in line with those of the organization and what you think it needs most. But if you're not lucky, you've unfortunately got company. Far too many district HR directors think of teachers as interchangeable parts, detached from their ability to stimulate student learning and building skills. It's the HR director's detachment from the effect of teachers on students that is the blind spot that makes it hard for districts to manage teacher talent more effectively. All too often, the district's collective bargaining agreement reinforces that blind spot, formally blocking both leaders and teachers from making the best match of teachers to students and subject matter. But the contract doesn't create the blind spot.

The range of talent and skill that a strong HR director will command is vast, of course. These brief comments are not intended to reduce the key elements of HR down to teacher evaluations. Rather, I hope to stimulate your thinking about the impact your HR director should have in the management of teacher talent.

Internal measures your HR team could create

The laws, rules, regs and contract clauses that define the relationship of the district as employer to staff are daunting. It's no surprise, then, that the HR director is too often thought to be an administrator of rules, rather than a leader of people. This often leaves HR directors paying too much attention to signs of friction: grievances, complaints, arbitration hearings, dispute resolutions. The signals of things going well aren't as visible. But they are there, nonetheless. How might you make them visible?

The practice of human relations outside the K–12 world is full of new ideas on this topic, some of them in an area now called "people analytics" or "workforce analytics." Wikipedia offers a brief introduction to the concept.[15] Its history in this century is well presented in Josh Bersin's book, *The Training Measurement Book*.[16] In 2013, the idea was bandied about as the "datafication" of human resources. This was the moment when data scientists were first discovering HR data warehouses. In February 2015, Bersin wrote an article for *Forbes* whose title describes a new stage of the field's development: "The Geeks Arrive in HR: People Analytics is Here."[17] If your HR director is not abreast of these developments in the HR field, your district is missing feedback loops, paths of information about people that could be helping you boost the quality of their efforts.

What vital signs might a modern-minded HR leader develop, beyond authentic evaluations? Opportunities abound. The following list is comprised of examples we've gleaned from our discussions with HR leaders and colleagues, both inside and outside the K–12 world, and readings.[18] This list is intentionally brief and is followed by two cases of more fully formed opportunities: teacher assignments and student surveys.

- *Recruiting*. Emerging from schools of education, new teachers range in talent, of course. That talent is evident in many forms: letters of reference; scores on licensing exams; observation of student teaching;

demonstration lessons during the interview process. Might one of your district's top three sources of new teachers be sending you better prepared reading teachers of early elementary students? Is a different college sending you teachers who are better at teaching math and science to middle schoolers? By relating the effect of new teachers to the college where they earned their credential, could you improve the quality of your new recruits and place them more wisely? The cost of recruiting new teachers is also easy to gather.

- *Retention of new recruits*. But tracking each year's crop of new recruits could be measured in many dimensions. What proportion of them are still working in your district after two years? Are the ones who stay the ones you want to retain the most? Teacher satisfaction surveys could reveal if they believe they've been on-boarded well, placed wisely and supported properly. This feedback is actionable.

- *Investment in professional development*.[19] What investment is your district making in professional development on a per-teacher basis? How do you know it's the right investment? What impact on teacher effectiveness results from this professional development? To what extent does it affect the self-reported job satisfaction of teachers? When you ask teachers their appraisal of the relevance of this investment to their practice, what do they tell you? How many teachers who have received professional development in the last three years are still working in your district? Have you factored the dollar-value of that lost investment into the cost of attrition?

- *Retention of the best teachers*. Keeping your best teachers happy requires knowing who your best teachers are. That's no small feat. Knowing how to retain them requires knowing what they're seeking, and then delivering it. It also involves knowing why teachers are leaving. Exit interviews could be the responsibility of an HR department, and the quality and quantity of reconnaissance gathered could become a valuable resource. Comparing your district's overall retention rate to that of similar districts might be one place to start this analysis. Open channels with the leadership of your teachers union might help, if you are lucky enough to have labor leaders who share your concerns.

- *Underperforming teachers*. Knowing who is underperforming rests on the most difficult of foundations: authentic evaluations. But once you know who's not up to your district's standards, you must either bring them up to par, or guide them to exit. In some districts, where labor–management relations are solid, paving the path to the exit door is possible. But in other districts, that may be a rocky road that requires different exit paths.

- *Measures of the effect of teaching.* The effect of teaching on students is much bigger than test scores can capture. If you put aside the controversy about including value-added estimates of teacher effect in evaluations, so much more evidence remains. Much of it can be discerned by surveying students about their attitudes toward reading, their estimates of their own capabilities or their comments about how helpful their teachers have been in advancing their knowledge and skills.

Licensing exams

Lacking other kinds of information about teachers, what are HR directors to do? In those states where teacher candidates must pass licensing exams, HR directors can ask to see candidates' scores. Rather than accept the limited disclosure of whether a candidate passed or failed the licensing exam, why shouldn't HR directors ask for the actual results of all four components of the multiple subject licensing exam? Why not also ask the prep programs themselves to provide their institutions' track records of their graduates' first-time pass rates?

In too many states, however, teacher licensing tests have fallen out of favor. Kate Walsh, who leads the National Council on Teacher Quality (NCTQ), coauthored a seminal report in 2019, "A Fair Chance,"[20] which pulled together evidence from over 800 colleges that revealed that many prep programs fail to deliver instruction of core content knowledge. The result: more than half of the candidates taking licensing exams fail to pass on the first round. NCTQ based their analysis on the Praxis Elementary Education: Multiple Subjects test fielded by Educational Testing Service. It is one of the tests required in 18 states and optional in five more when deciding whether to license elementary teacher candidates. It's composed of four sub-tests in the subjects they'll be expected to teach: reading/language arts, mathematics, science and social studies. The national pass rates for first-time test-takers on each test, respectively, is 77 percent, 74 percent, 66 percent and 66 percent. Just 46 percent of candidates passed all four tests the first time. (The first-time pass rate for nurses, for comparison, is 85 percent.) Teacher candidates can retake sub-tests, and when candidates did so, the final pass rate reached 72 percent.

The final composite pass rate was vastly different for teacher candidates of different ethnicities. White candidates' final composite pass rate was 75 percent, Latino/Hispanic candidates' 57 percent and Black candidates' 38 percent. It's this spread in pass rates that has led to debates about bias in the exams themselves and driven calls for states to either abandon use of licensing exams or drop their standards for passing. In the face of this, Kate Walsh defended teacher licensing exams in a blog post she wrote in November 2020,[21] calling for states to follow the lead of Massachusetts and improve them. Her organization has been in the vanguard of defending the professionalization of teaching, and she's challenged many of the obsolete traditions and dogmatic beliefs that weigh down teaching quality. She has criticized the teacher unions, to be sure. She has criticized the waste inherent in poor quality professional development. Perhaps most daring, Kate Walsh's organization has evaluated teacher prep programs with a critical eye and published their findings for all to see. She notes with dismay that between 2015 and 2020, the number of states requiring applicants to teacher prep program to pass a test in reading, writing and math dropped from 25 to 15. As of September 2021, 35 states lacked a basic skills test that new teachers must pass before they get a job and start teaching. She notes that the decline in the past five years is due in large part to the belief that these tests are biased.

> Based upon what I'm hearing, there appear to be three primary rationales for reducing or eliminating licensing tests: the tests are biased, due to the fact that much higher percentages of Black and Hispanic candidates fail the test than white candidates; the tests don't predict whether a teacher will be effective, so why require them; and, there's an urgent need to diversify the profession that should take priority over any other considerations, given the profound benefits of matching teacher and student race.
>
> If true, each of those alone provides a compelling argument to lessen the weight of licensing tests. Considered as a group, it is no wonder the future of the tests is teetering on the edge.

> The problem for me (and plenty of others, I imagine) is that not one of the three is unequivocally, demonstrably true. In the laudable, appropriate pursuit of a more diverse workforce, it's tempting to overlook the shaky ground on which some of these rationales rest, that the rightness of this cause is so great that the risks are worth it. And by risks, I refer to deep harm to teacher quality from allowing underprepared teachers into the classroom, something we can ill afford to inflict on children whose lives depend on their access to great teachers.[22]

Part of her defense of teacher licensing exams rests on research from the highly respected CALDER Center that documents the success of Massachusetts's approach.[23] Their state's licensing exam successfully predicted the effectiveness of a teacher. The students of new teachers who did really well (scoring in the top 84 percent of test-takers) learned at *about double the rate* of students taught by an average first-year teacher. Rather than blame the licensing exams for bias due to the higher rates of failure among non-white teacher candidates, Kate Walsh faults the teacher preparation programs. If those programs did a better job of preparing their emerging teachers, then more of them would pass the licensing exams. Faulting the test, in her view, is just blaming the messenger.

A different view of licensing exams was shared with me by Tony Wold, a 30-year veteran of several school district executive cabinets in California. He believes that licensing exams also screen out some teacher candidates who are simply poor test-takers but who could be great teachers. In an environment like today, in the winter of 2021, when teachers are in short supply, he argues that districts could find good candidates who might have had trouble passing all four parts of their licensing exam, but who could demonstrate their qualifications in other ways, such as a performance lesson. Enabling them to show what they know, and then coaching these beginning teachers, could help districts groom new talent.

Enabling elementary teachers to teach their best subject all day long

Proof of the benefit of matching teachers carefully to the subjects they know best, and to the students they are most effective teaching, was developed by a brilliant researcher, John Schacter, who saw this as a "best fit" riddle. He developed a solution to this riddle for the Catholic archdiocese of Indianapolis, Indiana, and in 2009 wrote up his findings together with two coauthors.[24] With a little more than 13,000 students tested in grades 3 through 10, this was a big district by any measure. Schacter applied value-added analysis methods to the math and English language arts scores of students in grades 3, 4 and 5, looking at the differences among schools, and more important, among teachers. The test used in the schools was the Indiana Statewide Test of Educational Progress (ISTEP), a test well suited for comparing results of students over successive grade levels.

Schacter focused on this question: Could he see with reasonable precision with which students and in which subjects teachers generated the greatest gain score? The answer was "yes" if he could aggregate close to 100 students' results for each teacher. His study also included asking teachers what subjects they believed they taught best, and which types of students they believed they were most effective teaching: slow, medium or fast learners. The teachers' responses almost always matched the gain scores that Schacter and his team derived. The conclusion was startling. If teachers could teach their best subject all day and work with just the students they were most effective with, they would see their students' rate of learning *more than double compared to their students' gain scores in the other subjects combined*. This story had a happy ending. The archdiocese leadership persuaded teachers in the late elementary grade levels to switch to single-subject classrooms, so they could teach their best subject all day long. This required reorganizing elementary schools in the process. Students' test scores soared.[25,26]

This discovery of Schacter's rested on a simple premise. If you know your teachers' strengths and place them where they're likely to do their best, their students will learn at their fastest pace. The recognition that elementary teachers who usually teach all subjects to all students are stronger by far in their best subject than in all the rest is a big leap. Add to that the recognition that teachers are often best with students who are either behind, at grade level or above. All districts know about their students' place on that spectrum. But very few districts know about their teachers' strengths and weaknesses. If they did, they would be stepping into the modern world where other professions in knowledge and information fields live. And they could show great gains by doing what the Catholic archdiocese of Indianapolis did, with John Schacter's help.

Surveying students about their teachers

If your district surveys students, you may have a treasure chest of insights in hand. These surveys may reveal the degree to which students feel welcomed by their teachers, how effectively they believe their teachers have taught and more. In some states, questions like these are part of school climate surveys. They are likely to reveal clues to the human chemistry between students and teachers. Survey information is provided by students anonymously, so comments are candid. The best way to interpret this type of evidence is by comparing results against a benchmark school or district whose students are very much like your own.

In higher education, student evaluations of faculty are a tradition. In many colleges, they contribute to tenure decisions. They certainly are taken seriously by faculty, whose courses rise or fall in popularity due, in part, to students' comments published online. If college students' comments are considered of high value to both administrators and fellow students, why are high school students' views of their teachers given so little attention?

Are students' evaluations of teachers really a credible source of information? The research literature says emphatically "yes." It includes affirmation of the validity and fairness of students' views of the quality of their teachers, even down to the elementary level. Ten studies conducted since 2012 explore the question, and while their findings naturally differ to some degree, on the questions of validity and fairness of student opinions, they agree. The use of what have been termed student perception surveys was rare at the turn of the 21st century. But the value of students' views was given a boost by the Measures of Effective Teaching (MET) project, funded by the Bill and Melinda Gates Foundation. That large-scale project won the participation of about 3,000 teachers and enlisted dozens of scholars to explore the results. Three approaches to measuring teacher effectiveness were included: observational studies, value-added measures of the growth of students' test scores and student perception surveys. The soundness of students' views of their teachers became visible through studies that used all three points of reference. In addition to dozens of journal articles, the MET project led to a book, *Designing Teacher Evaluation Systems*, which included 15 articles that should be of interest to anyone responsible for managing teacher talent.[27]

As of 2015, 25 states allowed student perception surveys to be used as part of teacher evaluations, and seven states required them to be used: Alabama, Alaska, Hawaii, Iowa, Massachusetts, Mississippi and Utah. By 2019, this had changed very little. This stable acceptance of a relatively new way to evaluate teachers is notable, especially when contrasted to the declining acceptance of value-added measures of teacher effectiveness over the same period. The demand from these states is met by six firms that provide K–12 student perception surveys. They differ in survey scope, quality of questions, report output and cost. Two scholars wrote a useful article in 2017, comparing their features and costs, and it was published in 2019.[28] It would serve as a useful starting point for any district considering taking students' views into the teacher evaluation process.

Ronald Ferguson's survey, known as the Tripod Survey, is perhaps the most studied of the six in the field. As an economist with a PhD from Massachusetts Institute of Technology, who joined the faculty of Harvard University in 1983, he was exceptionally well prepared to develop it wisely. Ferguson first fielded student surveys in 2001, and by 2012, nearly a million students had completed it. In a 2012 article in *Phi Delta Kappan* titled "Can Student Surveys Measure Teaching Quality?," Ferguson shared his powerful findings.[29] The success of the survey method led him to become cofounder of Tripod Education Founders in 2014.

The method that Ferguson used in the Tripod Project's survey turns out to be both conceptually and empirically compatible with the Framework for Teaching developed by the highly respected educator of educators, Charlotte Danielson. In fact, Ferguson and Danielson coauthored a significant article, "How Framework for Teaching and Tripod 7Cs Evidence Distinguish Key Components of Effective Teaching," which affirms the reliability and validity of the Tripod survey in view of Danielson's framework.[30] A more recent 2021 study pressed harder to explore the validity of student perceptions of their teachers using the seven-dimension framework that Ferguson created and reached positive conclusions.[31] It's heartening to see empirical evidence in the light of day that supports the value of student perceptions of their teachers.

When compared to classroom observations by professional evaluators, students' observations turned out to be *more reliable predictors of students' test score gains*. Another MET study in 2010 found that math teachers who were ranked by their students in the top quartile of teachers attained four to five months of learning more than students whose math teachers were in the bottom quartile of student evaluations. This parallels the findings of Ferguson's team that students of teachers with higher ratings tend to learn considerably more than students of teachers with lower ratings.[32]

When dead ex-employees get paychecks, position control is out of control

Knowing who's working where, and when, is what administrators call "position control." Paying teachers for the work they perform requires the ability to confirm that someone had come to work and taught their classes. This seems simple. But it's fraught with opportunities for bad actors. In California, when Oakland USD hit the financial skids in 1999, and a state administrator, Randy Ward, took over, he suspected that the district office had a loose hand on position control. To test that hunch, he asked every teacher to come in to pick up their paychecks in person. At the end of the payroll cycle, 160 checks remained unclaimed. As it turns out, they were checks made out to teachers who had died. Their relatives or friends had been cashing those checks, taking full advantage of the HR department's blind spot. A similar case of blatant theft was exposed in 2003 in New Orleans's district when Supt. Anthony Amato was digging up a range of corrupt practices. He directed employees to show their ID when picking up their paychecks. At the end of the pay cycle, about 1,500 checks remained unclaimed.[33] Like Randy Ward, Supt. Amato went to work with a bodyguard and at times, a flak jacket. Both endured death threats as a result of their bold defense of district resources.

Where other useful data about teachers may be buried

You should have no trouble learning about your teachers' education (degrees held and credit units attained), years of experience and employment in your district, age, credentials and if they are secondary-level teachers, their subject area authorizations. (Some of this is visible to the public in your school accountability reports, as well as on GreatSchools' website.) You may be able to see if they're on probationary status, tenured, or are long-term substitutes. In addition, you should be able to see their course and grade-level assignments, and the number of students enrolled in each. From your district, you should certainly learn about the compensation of your teachers, and their distribution across the step-and-column table of experience and education.

A well-run teacher and student information system should also enable you to see teachers' retention and attendance rates, their participation in professional development, the rates at which they assign Ds and Fs, and the rates at which they refer students for discipline. An intrepid analyst can do much more by relating at the teacher level factors that are not often associated, for example, a matrix of teacher-assigned grades juxtaposed against students'

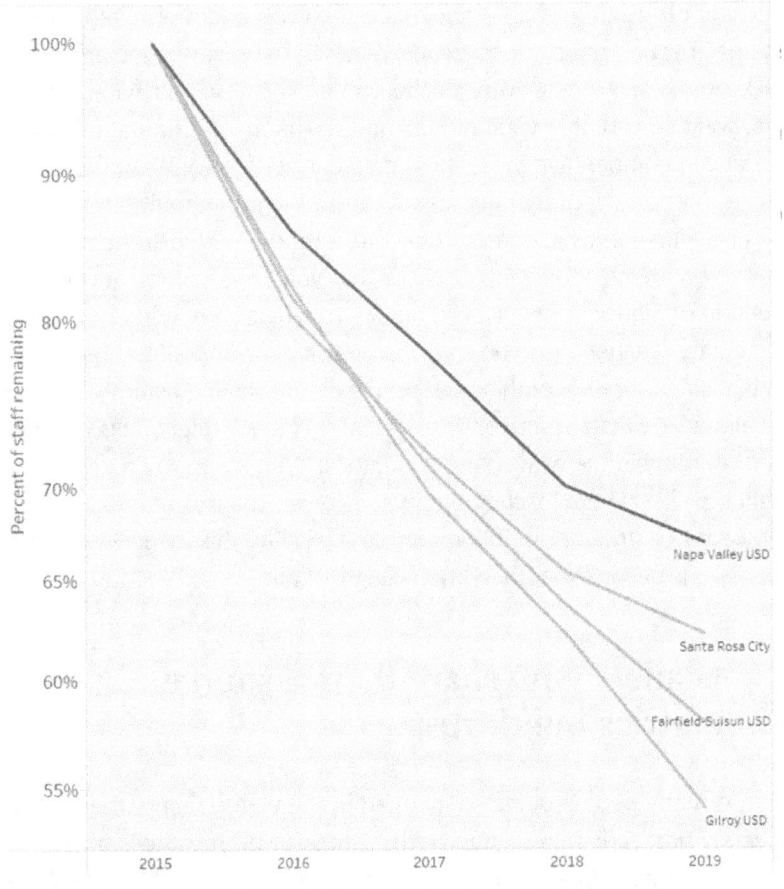

You'll find a link to a live version of this visualization at the following web page: https://www.k12measures.com/ch6/#fig6.1.

Figure 6.1 Teachers retained at district since 2015

        Shows the cumulative, declining rate of retention of teachers within each of four districts, from 2015 through 2019. The base year is 2015.

Source: K12 Measures. © School Wise Press

scores on end-of-year standardized tests. The meaning of this may not be self-evident. But this evidence may become relevant when considering teachers for recognition or promotion. At the site level, it may be relevant in gauging differences in teacher morale, especially if you can add this evidence to teacher-completed climate surveys.

Comparing retention rates can offer a window on morale. Teacher and principal turnover is something you can measure within your district and your schools. But once you know it, how do you interpret it, other than by looking at your organization's trend over time? If, however, you are in a state that keeps track of where every teacher works every year and that shares those data, you can compare your attrition and retention with similar schools and districts. In comparative form, these data can serve as a proxy indicator for teacher and principal morale. Ideally, you'd want the ability to control for planned retirements, maternity leave and extraordinary disruptions like the COVID pandemic. You may discover that you have comparatively higher retention of high school teachers, but lower retention of middle school and elementary teachers. Or you may discover that your younger teachers are exiting at a faster clip, or that your principals are staying within your district at a higher rate than in similar districts. This evidence might help you review your salary schedule or working conditions. Within your own districts, you might see sites where teacher retention is lower. That might indicate leadership issues or student discipline concerns. Having this evidence, whatever it reveals, is better by far than not having it at all.

Leaders who share their resource metrics build trust

With so many people being so invested in the well-being of their schools, leaders who spark a fresh approach to measuring resources and sharing them publicly are likely to earn praise from all quarters. This simple act of measurement, and the sharing of that in full view of staff and the public, can do much to build trust, confidence and respect. In a district where the quality of water is uncertain, isn't it prudent to measure water quality and share the results? In a district where taxpayers are resistant to any effort to raise taxes, isn't it just a sign of respect to show you are prudent in measuring the cost-effectiveness of resources? In a district where deferred maintenance has taken a toll on the expected lifespan of the roof of the high school gym, isn't it easier to generate support for raising operational funds by showing citizens the damage and demonstrating that continued neglect would eventually compromise the building's integrity?

Leading a school or district, or daring to sit on the school board, requires making choices that bring resources to some, and limiting resources to others. These are unavoidably difficult moments. But they become less painful when they can be defended with sound economic analysis in hand. At the beginning of all this is making things visible. Many dimensions of our lives have remained invisible until they become important enough to measure: carbon in the atmosphere, temperature increases of the oceans, vaccination rates of kids in school and adults in our communities. Those measurements sometimes require a little creativity and courage to do something new. Student perception surveys were used in just 5 percent of districts at the turn of century. Now they're part of the new normal in many places. The successful introduction of students' voices to the evaluation of teachers is an encouraging precedent. What else do you care about that you'd like to understand better? You could start by measuring it.

Links to extend your reading and interaction

The following link will carry you to additional resources, writing and dialogue about the topics discussed in this chapter. You'll also find live versions of the data visualizations in this chapter that are ready for your interaction. We welcome your comments and continued exploration. You'll find all this on the chapter specific page on the book's website: https://www.k12measures.com/ch6.

Questions to spark discussion

District leaders

1. Your district has just published your schools' accountability reports, and they now reveal that one of your middle schools gets about 25 percent more funding per student than your

other middle school. The two schools serve students who have equivalent educational needs: similar proportion of learning-disabled students, a similar proportion of English learners and similar after-school programs. Your board has asked you for recommendations about how to equalize that funding. What ideas are you ready to offer them? And what evidence do you want to review before you make those recommendations?

2. You are eager to recruit better quality teachers to your district, especially middle and high school math teachers. You have asked your HR director for suggestions about how to do that, and she has said, "Tell me the attributes of a high-quality math teacher, and I'll go find them." You ask her to research this question, starting with interviews of the schools of education that provide most of your teacher candidates. You turn to the math department chairs at your middle and high school and ask them to identify their best math teachers. They answer, without hesitation. You validate their answers by talking with students who took their classes. Imagine that you have the funds to recruit more actively than before. How might you build on what you've learned and draw more talented math teachers to your district? How might you retain the better math teachers you already have and encourage the weaker instructors to find other employment?

Principals

3. You are a high school principal, and your district has asked you to prepare a plan for a year of cutbacks in the range of 5–10 percent. For the first time, they have shared with you all the expenses for your site over the past three years. The district's chief business officer has opened the door and offered to answer any questions. You select one teacher leader and one parent and sit down with a ton of new information. Before you start looking at programs to cut, you start looking at the cost-per-student to deliver specialized classes and discover those classes cost two to three times more than the common classes with larger class

sizes. What new approaches to budget cuts are you ready to explore with this new analysis in hand?

4. You are about to write your school's site plan. This year, with one-third of your teachers having less than three years' experience, you believe that providing coaching or mentoring to them could pay off in faster development of their teaching skills. How might you estimate the value of that improvement? How might you construct the evidence and measure its progress? Where would you go for mentors or coaches? What would they cost? You know you have terrific senior-level teachers on your staff already. How could you lighten their teaching schedule to free them up to coach or mentor younger teachers? Prepare a cost-benefit argument for this reorganization that could work with only a modest boost in funding from the district.

School board trustees

5. You are about to start your campaign for reelection to the school board, a public commitment you've made for the past eight years and enjoyed. But this time you face opposition by a local organization that opposes raising taxes. They oppose your reelection because you've made the case that local support of schools is among the lowest in the county. But the value of taxable property in your district is also among the lowest in the county. So, your critics say you want to tax them at a higher rate than districts in other towns like yours, who happen to benefit from a base of more valuable property. You'd like to come up with a new approach, one that not only shows the need for stronger funding, but which also doesn't raise the property taxes across the board. See if you can come up with a creative alternative.

6. You are concerned that your district's teachers have commanded too large a share of the district's payroll and benefits. Class sizes are among the smallest in the county, and teacher-student ratios are also among the lowest. You believe high school counselors are needed. The counselors in your high school already carry a

> case load of 525 students, well over your state's average of 340. Before your district enters collective bargaining, you want to establish a board policy that rebalances staffing positions more in line with the state staffing ratios for administrative, classified and certificated positions. How might you build an argument that persuades your fellow board members to join with you to create that policy? And how might it read so that the rationale is clear and persuasive to teachers?

Notes

1. Sarah Sparks, "More Education Studies Look at Cost-Effectiveness," *Education Week*, April 10, 2019, www.edweek.org/ew/articles/2019/04/10/more-education-studies-look-at-cost-effectiveness.html.

2. Anthony S. Bryk, Louis M. Gomez, Alicia Grunow and Paul G. LeMahieu, *Learning to Improve: How America's Schools Can Get Better at Getting Better* (Cambridge: Harvard Education Press, 2015).

3. Hattie, *Visible Learning*.

4. Marguerite Roza, *Educational Economics: Where Do [$]chool Funds Go?* (Washington, DC: Urban Institute Press, 2011).

5. Marguerite Roza, "Weighted Student Funding Is on the Rise: Here's What We're Learning," Institute of Education Sciences, Inside IES Research (blog), accessed May 9, 2019, https://ies.ed.gov/blogs/research/post/weighted-student-funding-is-on-the-rise-here-s-what-we-are-learning.

6. Marguerite Roza, "Lessons Learned: Weighted Student Funding," Seattle: Edunomics Lab, October 2020, https://edunomicslab.org/wp-content/uploads/2020/11/WSF-Lessons-Learned.pdf.

7. Henry M. Levin, Clive R. Belfield, Patrick J. McEwan, Robert D. Shand and A. Brooks Bowden, *Economic Evaluation in Education: Cost-Effectiveness and Benefit-Cost Analysis*, 3rd edition (Thousand Oaks, CA: SAGE Publications, 2017).

8. Henry M. Levin and Patrick J. McEwan, *Cost-Effectiveness Analysis 2nd Edition: Methods and Applications* (Thousand Oaks, CA: Sage Publications, 2001).

9. The "Cost Out" toolkit is available from www.cbcse.org/costout.

10. Levin and McEwan, *Cost-Effectiveness Analysis*, 19. Cost-utility analysis may be more useful when comparing two outcomes of different types. Certainly, it could be used in the example evaluating the benefit to students of an added counselor or two, versus the benefit to students and teachers of an additional teacher or two to reduce class sizes. Levin and McEwan call cost-utility analysis "an evaluation of alternatives according to a comparison of their costs and their utility or value. . . . Unlike CE analysis, which relies upon a single measure of effectiveness (e.g., a test score, the number of dropouts averted), CU analysis uses information on the preferences of individuals in order to express their overall satisfaction with a single measure or multiple measure of effectiveness."

11. Levin et al., *Economic Evaluation in Education*, 204–17.

12. Vincent Caruso, "Chicago Teachers Can No Longer Save 40 Sick Days for Retirement: Now It's 244," Illinois Policy (website), accessed November 19, 2019, www.illinoispolicy.org/chicago-teachers-no-longer-can-save-40-sick-days-for-retirement-now-its-244/.

13. The California Department of Education website contains guidance about evaluating the physical condition of schools that may serve as a useful starting place: www.cde.ca.gov/ls/fa/sf/williams.asp. Pay particular attention to what they call their Facilities Inspection Tool.

14. Daniel Weisberg, Susan Sexton, Jennifer Mulhern and David Keeling, *The Widget Effect: Our National Failure to Acknowledge and Act on Differences in Teacher Effectiveness*, 2nd edition (New York: The New Teacher Project, 2009), 2.

15. "Wikipedia: Analytics: People Analytics," Wikimedia Foundation, accessed November 20, 2021, https://en.wikipedia.org/wiki/Analytics#People_analytics.

16. Josh Bersin, *The Training Measurement Book* (San Francisco: Pfeiffer, 2005).

17. Josh Bersin, "The Geeks Arrive in HR: People Analytics Is Here," *Forbes*, February 1, 2015, https://www.forbes.com/sites/joshbersin/2015/02/01/geeks-arrive-in-hr-people-analytics-is-here/?sh=11ae22a673b4.

18. An excellent resource is an anthology of essays, edited by Dan Goldhaber and Jane Hannaway, *Creating a New Teaching Profession*, published by the Urban Institute Press in 2009. The volume's first part contains five essays that look at human capital systems in other countries and the private sector. Six essays follow in the second part, all

focused on reform ideas. Among the authors are Frederick M. Hess, Paul T. Hill and Eric A. Hanushek. The third part includes five essays on the politics of education reform that comment on contributors' essays. A balance of views emerges from the essays by Joel L. Klein, Randi Weingarten and Andrew J. Rotherham.

19. In a 2015 report titled "The Mirage: Confronting the Hard Truth About Our Quest for Teacher Development," the team at The New Teacher Project discovered that in the three large districts and one charter management organization they studied, the average annual cost of teacher professional development was nearly $18,000. The result of that surprisingly high investment was unknown. The report challenged the widely held notion that professional development leads to improved teaching. https://tntp.org/publications/view/evaluation-and-development/the-mirage-confronting-the-truth-about-our-quest-for-teacher-development.

20. Hannah Putman and Kate Walsh, "A Fair Chance: Simple Steps to Strengthen and Diversify the Teacher Workforce," Washington, DC: National Council on Teacher Quality, February 2019, www.nctq.org/publications/A-Fair-Chance.

21. Kate Walsh, "Are We Done with Teacher Licensing Tests?" (blog), National Council on Teacher Quality, November 23, 2020, www.nctq.org/blog/Are-we-done-with-teacher-licensing-tests.

22. Ibid.

23. James Cowan, Dan Goldhaber, Zeyu Jin and Roddy Theobald, "Teacher Licensure Tests: Barrier or Predictive Tool?" CALDER Working Paper No. 245–1020, October 2020, https://caldercenter.org/sites/default/files/WP%20245-1020_0.pdf.

24. Ron Costello, Peggy Elson and John Schacter, "An Introduction to Value-Added Analysis," *Journal of Catholic Education* 12, no. 2 (December 1, 2008): 193–203, http://doi.org/10.15365/joce.1202062013.

25. Wangui Njuguna, "Value-Added Model Could Improve Teacher Assignments," *Education Daily* 42, no. 40 (March 4, 2009): 2.

26. John Schacter, "The Research on Teacher Effects," a slide deck presented at the California Education Research Association Conference, 2008. Provided by John Schacter to the author.

27. Thomas J. Kane, Kerri A. Kerr and Robert C. Pianta, eds., *Designing Teacher Evaluation Systems: New Guidance from the Measures of Effective Teaching Project* (New York: John Wiley & Sons, 2014).

28. Tray Geiger and Audrey Amrein-Beardsley, "Student Perception Surveys for K-12 Teacher Evaluation in the United States: A Survey of Surveys," *Cogent Education* 6, no. 1 (April 2019), https://doi.org/10.1080/2331186X.2019.1602943.

29. Ronald Ferguson, "Can Student Surveys Measure Teaching Quality?" *Phil Delta Kappan* (November 2012): 24–8. https://doi.org/10.1177/003172171209400306.

30. Ronald F. Ferguson and Charlotte Danielson, "How Framework for Teaching and Tripod 7Cs Evidence Distinguish Key Components of Effective Teaching," in *Designing Teacher Evaluation Systems: New Guidance from the Measures of Effective Teaching Project*, eds. Thomas J. Kane, Kerri A. Kerr, and Robert C. Pianta (New York: John Wiley & Sons, 2014), 98–143, https://doi.org/10.1002/9781119210856.ch4.

31. Sandra Phillips, Ronald F. Ferguson and Jacob F. S. Rowley, "Do They See What I See? Toward a Better Understanding of the 7Cs Framework of Teaching Effectiveness," *Educational Assessment* 26, no. 2 (January 2021): 69–87, https://doi.org/10.1080/10627197.2020.1858784.

32. Kim Marshall, "Fine-Tuning Teacher Evaluation," *Educational Leadership* 70, no. 3 (November 2012): 50–3, https://marshallmemo.com/articles/Ed-Leadership-Nov-2012.pdf.

33. David Osborne. *Reinventing America's Schools: Creating a 21st Century Education System* (New York: Bloomsbury, 2017).

Resources

Bryk, Anthony S., Louis M. Gomez, Alicia Grunow, and Paul G. LeMahieu. *Learning to Improve: How America's Schools Can Get Better at Getting Better*. Cambridge: Harvard Education Press, 2015.

Caruso, Vincent. "Chicago Teachers Can No Longer Save 40 Sick Days for Retirement: Now It's 244." (website) Illinois Policy. Accessed November 19, 2019. www.illinoispolicy.org/chicago-teachers-no-longer-can-save-40-sick-days-for-retirement-now-its-244/.

Costello, R., P. Elson, and J. Schacter. "An Introduction to Value-Added Analysis." *Journal of Catholic Education* 12, no. 2 (2008): 193–203. http://doi.org/10.15365/joce.1202062013.

Cowan, James, Dan Goldhaber, Zeyu Jin, and Roddy Theobald. "Teacher Licensure Tests: Barrier or Predictive Tool?" CALDER Working Paper No. 245-1020, 2020. https://caldercenter.org/sites/default/files/WP%20245-1020_0.pdf.

Goldhaber, Dan, and Jane Hannaway, eds. *Creating a New Teaching Profession*. Washington, DC: Urban Institute Press, 2009.

Jacob, Andy, and Kate McGovern. *The Mirage: Confronting the Hard Truth About Our Quest for Teacher Development*. New York: The New Teacher Project, 2015.

Kane, Thomas J., Kerri A. Kerr, and Robert C. Pianta, eds. *Designing Teacher Evaluation Systems: New Guidance from the Measures of Effective Teaching Project*. New York: John Wiley & Sons, 2014. https://doi.org/10.1002/9781119210856.

Levin, Henry M., Clive R. Belfield, Patrick J. McEwan, Robert D. Shand, and A. Brooks Bowden. *Economic Evaluation in Education: Cost-Effectiveness and Benefit-Cost Analysis*. 3rd edition. Thousand Oaks, CA: Sage Publications, 2017.

Levin, Henry M., and Patrick J. McEwan. *Cost-Effectiveness Analysis 2nd Edition: Methods and Applications*. Thousand Oaks, CA: Sage Publications, 2001.

Njuguna, Wangui. "Value-Added Model Could Improve Teacher Assignments." *Education Daily*, March 4, 2009, p. 2.

Osborne, David. *Reinventing America's Schools: Creating a 21st Century Education System*. New York: Bloomsbury, 2017.

Roza, Marguerite. *Educational Economics: Where Do [$]chool Funds Go?* Washington, DC: Urban Institute Press, 2011.

Schacter, John. "The Research on Teacher Effects." A slide deck presented at the California Education Research Association Conference, 2008. Provided by John Schacter to the author.

Walsh, Kate. "Are We Done with Teacher Licensing Tests?" (blog) National Council on Teacher Quality. Accessed November 23, 2020. www.nctq.org/blog/Are-we-done-with-teacher-licensing-tests.

Weisberg, Daniel, Susan Sexton, Jennifer Mulhern, and David Keeling. *The Widget Effect: Our National Failure to Acknowledge and Act on Differences in Teacher Effectiveness*. 2nd edition. New York: The New Teacher Project, 2009.

Reducing barriers to progress at every level

After spending more than 20 years helping school and district leaders make sense of their numbers, I have become more impatient and yet more hopeful. My impatience comes from my strong belief that some mismeasurement is correctable. That's the part that's due to bureaucratic ineptitude, slothfulness and innocent human errors. But I'm not naïve enough to think it's all correctable without friction among competing parties. Some mismeasurement has evolved because it has served both institutional and professional interests. To take one example of institutional interests, everyone wants students to graduate, so there's an incentive for districts to make it increasingly easy for students to earn a diploma. The bar gets lowered so far in some districts that the value of the diplomas they award become questionable. To take an example of professional interests, consider the state of teacher evaluations. Principals need the cooperation of their teachers. So, principals by and large evaluate teachers without providing critical feedback, believing this wins them a more cooperative staff. The long tradition of teacher compensation that rewards time-in-service and education adds to the ethos of treating all teachers equally, or as "widgets," the key word in the title of the report of the National Center for Teaching Quality. The result: almost no information captured in teacher evaluations about the quality of teaching.

My hopefulness comes from meeting and working with many school and district leaders who are hard at work bringing evidence and empirical methods to the table. My hope also comes from the fact that you're reading this book. If I'm not falling under the spell of premature exuberance, then I have a hunch you have already joined (or are about to join) the small but growing legion of principals, superintendents, school board members, teacher leaders and citizens who are ready to insist that evidence and reason must justify decisions.

Our small band of empiricists is already suspicious when school leaders justify their decisions with "experience" alone. When someone high up justifies her opinion with "tradition" or "common sense," we reply, "Show me the evidence!" Among the "common sense" crowd, most fall into three camps: those who are puzzled or overwhelmed by too much data; those who distrust measurement altogether; and those who believe that wisdom comes solely from experience. Each deserves attention of a somewhat different sort. Each has a reason to undervalue or disfavor empirical paths to knowledge. Persuading colleagues begins with understanding their viewpoint.

Those who are puzzled or overwhelmed are understandably reticent to embrace something as unfamiliar as quantified expressions of human activity. They may see little benefit in doing so. They may see a lot of time and money spent capturing, validating, correcting, communicating and publishing so many numbers. This may seem to them to be a waste of resources. They are likely to consider data to be a cost, not an asset from which valuable evidence can be built.

Those who distrust measurement altogether may be battle-scarred veterans of the accountability wars, who have seen numbers used as weapons against them. This is certainly understandable. The aspirational arithmetic of the No Child Left Behind legislation of 2001 led to many schools getting reorganized, based mainly on their students' low test scores. In some cases, this may have been warranted. But in many cases, it was not. People who saw their schools' principals reassigned, or their teaching staffs turned over, or in the worst case, their schools closed are now likely to be skeptical of claims that sound evidence well analyzed could lead to improved management of school resources or lower rates of student misclassification.

Those who favor experience over analysis have an almost philosophical objection to empirical analysis. They look toward the old-timers to lead, those with the most experience. They value most the judgment of practitioners. They tend to embrace the current state of things, because they have a notion that best practices evolve naturally. This leads them to favor the current state of their schools and champion "best practices" as a way to codify the status quo. And they often favor investment in peer-to-peer networks because this provides for the sharing of experiences by practitioners.

People you know may hold these points of view. I suspect that many districts and schools have placed people in leadership whose views are close to one of these three views. In my experience in California, it is rare to find a district that is governed by a school board whose citizen-members insist on evidence and whose superintendent and cabinet also insist on evidence and reason with care when making decisions. The good news is that many districts and schools contain a small cadre of data mavens. They tend to band together, because they are heavily outnumbered by practitioners for whom "data" is a foreign language. Perhaps you are part of a cadre like this, waging your own campaign to create an appetite for evidence, and a healthy skepticism that leads to a readiness to say "Show me the proof." (I hope the state slogan of Missouri, the "show-me" state, becomes the slogan in more schools and districts.)

By "proof" I do not mean "data," by the way. This is really about reasoning from evidence. It's about empirical methods and bringing more rigorous methods to managing and governing schools and districts. It's about challenging the sloppy thinking that underlies so much mismeasurement of schools' vital signs—the lack of logic, the lack of care in handling the statistical artifacts of so much earnest effort by students and teachers, the lack of effort learning the principles that are the foundation to the meaning of test scores.

If you are already inside the profession of school management, don't you wonder why your own preparation for work—pre-service and in-service—barely touched on quantitative methods, assessment and research methods? By now you've probably been introduced to the idea of continuous improvement, thanks to the initiative of the Carnegie Foundation. Right at the start of their ideas is a set of skills common to many fields: measurement, self-documentation, the building of evidence from observations, and generating hypotheses. It's an applied version of the scientific method. But do you believe that your credential program or your education leadership master's program prepared you to tackle all this?

My hope also rises from the freedom granted by state laws to school boards. So much of what gets measured is prescribed by law, but thankfully it is not *proscribed by law*. School boards are entirely *free to measure what they consider to be most important*. If a board insisted that every student be able to read a chapter book by the end of third grade, board members could pass policies that focus attention on learning to read. Given the heated debates over how to teach reading, they could hire independent evaluators to do a curriculum audit. They could seek a review of the research literature, to make sure their own curriculum is sound. They could direct their district to invest in assessments and evaluations that mark each student's progress. They could monitor the frequency of referrals to Tier 2 reading supports. Boards could require universal screening for dyslexia, starting in kindergarten, so that students who have a biological barrier to associating letters with sounds could be helped as early as possible.

If you are in leadership, you can steer your school or district toward measuring the important things and doing so accurately. For starters, you can require that only higher-quality evidence be considered when making decisions. (Naturally, you'll have to define what makes one body of evidence higher quality than another.) Consider this example of a big question being answered too often with low-quality evidence. "In general, is our district teaching reading effectively? And in particular, what portion of our students are being referred to Tier 2 support, and what portion of our entering third graders are reading at grade level?" The first source some districts turn to is their statewide assessment, which is not designed to answer this particular question. You can reorganize results from your state assessment to get a distant view of part of the answer. But you need internal data at the student level to really answer it correctly. The second questionable source is often the assessment portfolio provided by the same firm that provided the instructional materials. There's a bias of self-interest in what is politely called curriculum-embedded assessment. If a publisher of Balanced Literacy instructional materials has encouraged struggling readers to rely on cues to help students figure out the meaning of words when they can't sound them out, then loads their tests with visual cues, a child who can't sound out words is likely to guess a correct answer from the context provided. If the student answers a multiple-choice question correctly by having guessed the meaning of a word she can't really sound out, the publisher looks good, the teacher looks competent, and the student appears to be reading. But she isn't. *She's guessing*.

If you're reading this final chapter, I have a hunch that you share some degree of my impatience. My hope is that you are now or will soon be in a position to help your school or district or state education agency break the habits of mind that result in mismeasurement, flawed evidence and eventually errors in judgment. Impatience and anger can become the source of energy that carries you to the front of the room or to the conference table to ask simple questions. "How do you know that's true?" "How much imprecision in those test results did you account for when you reached your conclusion?" "What additional evidence should we have before making such a consequential decision?" "What's the rate of false positives and false negatives that results from our method of identifying English learners?"

You may be the only person in the room or at the conference table who is ready to question the evidence. Others may believe that numbers don't lie, that if an assertion is supported by numbers, then the assertion must be true. You know better. You may feel a bit weak in the knees when you stand to raise your questions. But take heart. Outside the room, there are hundreds of thousands of others like you, who are ready to bring higher standards of evidence to the field of education. The legal field has standards of evidence. Data may be presented and those arguing a case expect it to be questioned. Often outside experts are paid to testify to the quality of the data and the validity of the interpretation. Why shouldn't standards of evidence for education decision-makers hold as high a place?

When you raise your questions, you may face others who argue that "common sense" wouldn't support your doubts, or that teacher recommendations or principal judgment is the arbiter of what works. Others may pull out a cookbook of what they call "best practices." Do not surrender. Voice your doubts with conviction. Know that you have more than *Star Trek*'s Spock on your side.[1] You have social scientists at your side who have taken measurement of human activity to new heights. Some of them have developed new methods of analysis that can be applied to the questions of K–12 education, with the help of analytic software. You have data visualization practitioners at your side, as well, some of whom have shared their handiwork for others to use. The user community of Tableau, one of the leading data visualization and analytic software tools now in the market, is huge. It includes some in the education area, whose work may help you advance your own efforts.[2]

You also have at your side allies in many fields close to education. In fact, psychology was a practitioner-dominated profession until 1954, when one of its leaders, Paul Meehl, published a book asserting that statistical analysis was able to diagnose schizophrenia solely from a review of quantified clinical evidence at a higher rate of accuracy than the psychiatrists who were treating the patients themselves. That book, *Clinical vs. Statistical Prediction: A Theoretical Analysis and a Review of the Evidence*, started a heated debate that by most accounts, is far from resolved.[3] No surprise, he questioned the accuracy of clinical judgment, arguing that psychologists and psychiatrists are likely to be biased and pay insufficient attention to the evidence itself. Interestingly, Meehl was elected president of the American Psychological Association in 1962, and in his acceptance speech, delivered a paper that challenged the prevailing theory of the causes of schizophrenia. The dominant theory was that schizophrenia was caused by one's parents. Meehl's thesis was that the cause was primarily genetic. As the science evolved, Meehl's assertion proved to be true.

Perhaps education management is due to enter its own Paul Meehl moment, a quantum leap of evolutionary maturation. If anyone can take it there, it is John Hattie, the New Zealand educator of educators whose book, *Visible Learning*, has distilled evidence from over 800 studies that result in a ranking of relative effectiveness of over 140 education reforms. Hattie calls education an "immature profession" and asks whether it can shift "from opinions to evidence." Perhaps Hattie's critique and James Popham's conclusion after 50 years of teaching that educators suffer from "abysmal assessment literacy" lets us see the size of the barriers we face when we insist that school-related decisions be based upon higher-quality evidence and empirical methods.

Let's take the insights of John Hattie and James Popham to heart. Their calls to action will advance the cause of improving schooling itself. Each participant in the schooling of children has a role to play in this. Here are some practical steps participants might take to accomplish that worthy goal.

Schools of education

From a distance, schools of education may appear to be carriers of the flag of learning, defenders of the intellectual lives of children. But as institutions of higher education, most are lagging in the quantitative disciplines. At the same time that many colleges have eagerly scrambled to meet the rising desire of students to become data literate, and the aspirations of some to become data scientists, schools of education have continued to merge quantitative and qualitative methods into a single course and think that's sufficient. Some schools of education have even refused to raise their graduation standards to ensure that their students are at least capable of passing data literacy and assessment literacy tests. The question that deserves study is whether this is equally true of graduate-level programs, especially those focused on leadership or policy.

The toughest critics of the data-resistant holdouts in these schools of education have been Ellen Mandinach and Edith Gummer. Their book, *Data Literacy for Educators*, includes a review of the way that data and assessment skills are taught to emerging teachers in their credential programs.[4] Their conclusion, based on a review of the syllabi from 208 schools of education in 47 states, is that *data analysis skills are not really taught at all*. They concluded that it is really assessment knowledge that is taught, and in stand-alone courses in just two-thirds of the institutions. Their conclusion was that new teachers are being credentialed who are unprepared to interpret data correctly and consume data critically.

Administrative credential programs

In too many states, this is a case of the blind leading the blind. Too many district leaders, undereducated in assessment fundamentals, lack an appreciation of empirical methods of analytic inquiry. These credential programs tend to perpetuate traditions so candidates can pass a test and earn their credential. No surprise, these programs produce administrators who are all too ready to trust their gut instincts and follow whatever "best practices" cookbook they've been handed.

Every state will have its own spin on the requirements for school and district leaders, and those will be codified into state-specific standards. But in 2016, a group of educators from 37 states, working under the auspices of the National Center for Education Statistics, published the "SLDS Data Use Standards: Knowledge, Skills, and Professional Behaviors for Effective Data Use—Master Standards for School and District Leadership."[5] They created three editions. One was for teachers, another for data leads and a third was specifically for school and district leaders. This straightforward document put forward the knowledge, skills and professional behaviors these educators believed should be expected from those trusted to run schools and districts. The standards articulate the quantitative analysis skills that should belong to every administrator. And they define the proper place for analytic methods in the rhythm of running schools and districts. These standards, in their role-based versions, belong in the hands of those responsible for finding and hiring talented leaders.

The colleges, universities and professional associations that have the power to issue credentials to administrators-in-training must step outside their castles and into the modern world. My guess is that change will come from a generational replacement of older leaders by younger ones who are data savvy *before* they begin their leadership education, and who expect to bring empirical methods to the analysis of evidence when making decisions.

State departments of education

Some state agencies have worked to build empirical thinking skills, analytic methods knowledge and quantitative capabilities among their districts. For example, Oregon's state department of education has supported a smart team that invested in sound reporting of statewide education data and supported site and district leaders with professional development services. They don't just generate reports. They interpret statewide data and publish their findings, a commitment that few states have been willing to make. Minnesota has provided a lot of support staff who have held regional meetings to train district data leads and assessment staff. There's so much value that an enlightened state education agency could provide. Even if the decentralized responsibility for delivering schooling is in the hands of 13,000 plus districts, state agencies could create valuable resources, especially in conjunction with universities. Research partnerships between big urban districts and universities are common. State agencies could look to them as models worth emulating.

Assessment firms

You'd think that companies whose entire business is delivering insights of value from the measurement of student learning would invest heavily in higher-quality reporting. Unfortunately, we've seen scant evidence of that from most of the assessment firms. Part of the problem is that there is insufficient demand for high-quality reporting among the districts and state agencies that comprise the client base. An additional problem is that the bigger testing firms are given specifications by state education agencies that don't invite them to bring their best creative efforts to the table. The request-for-proposal process for statewide assessments is one part of the problem. When the buyer of services (a state education agency) assumes the role of architect of the assessment, and the assessment firm is limited to the builder's role, it effectively blocks the assessment firms from bringing their research and creative talent into the design process.

Standards for communicating the meaning of test results to readers in varying roles have only recently been established. Jenny Rankin's book, *Designing Data Reports that Work*, makes a strong argument that poor design is the cause of a great deal of mistaken conclusions reached by teachers and principals.[6] Rankin's standards are not severe. They are the quality standards you'd expect from a publisher or a public policy research firm. It is time for Rankin's standards to be read widely by those who use student test results. It is time for state departments of education to build these report standards into the specifications they put in bid requests. It is certainly time for districts to expect that ed tech firms at least meet the standards Rankin defined. It is well past the time for assessment firms to ante up and invest in the design talent that could bring their reporting up to the standards that are expected in other fields. The Grow Network's short-lived contribution to McGraw-Hill Education's reporting capability in 2004 enabled them to elevate their report quality. Among the districts that benefitted was New York City's system, and according to a 2009 study, seven researchers found ample evidence that teachers and administers reported high value in the Grow Network's reports.[7] The design expertise that assessment firms seek can readily come from outside their own enterprises.

Districts

Too many superintendents think a good assessment director is a person who can administer tests on time, on budget, without glitches. The people they hire, as a result, have operational, technical and organizational strengths. But why aren't most superintendents looking for analytic talent, research skills and communication abilities when they look for assessment directors? These key people are like navigators on ships at sea. Superintendents are captains of those ships, with their hands on the wheel. But to get to their destinations safe and sound, they need to know where they are. This requires the technical skills to read a map, measure their precise location, anticipate weather and chart a course to their destination. Assessment directors do that and more. But unless their captain, the superintendent, expects this set of rounded talents, districts are unlikely to have a modern-minded assessment director in their team with both analytic and communication skills.

Dr. Ritu Khanna: an assessment director who teaches leaders how to think about test results

By Jill Wynns

When Dr. Ritu Khanna, Chief of Research, Planning and Assessment for the San Francisco Unified School District, took charge of her department, she was prepared to serve not only the 114 school sites, the district leadership and the board. She was prepared to deliver data to a federal judge, William Orrick, who was responsible for monitoring a desegregation consent decree. Because the judge and the NAACP were tracking progress by the numbers, they requested unusually specific data for their analysts to review. At that time, San Francisco USD was one of the few districts that disaggregated data by ethnicity, a practice that would later become universal after the passage in 2001 of No Child Left Behind legislation.

She established a tradition of service to school site teams that remains in effect today. At the heart of that tradition is a start-of-year meeting when Dr. Khanna presents district data to all administrators and leads discussion. Groups of site administrators attend skill-building sessions that teach them how to understand their site-level data. After Dr. Khanna and her staff deliver school site teams their own data, they dedicate six weeks to conferences lasting half a day with each site administrator and their teams. High school teams even include students and parents. Dr. Khanna's goal is to get all participants to own their data, interpret them wisely and create their annual school plans using what they learn.

The concrete result of these sessions is that each school team identifies two or three data patterns of consequence and supports their findings with at least three pieces of evidence. Dr. Khanna believes that patterns are easier to understand and accept than raw data on their own. School data include suspensions and attendance, climate surveys that reflect opinions of students and parents, grades, test results and other indicators of achievement, behavior and attitudes.

For at least the last years 15 years that I was on the board, Dr. Khanna's data presentations were, for me, an important opportunity to learn how our

> schools and the district were doing. They included information that helped me to understand not only the data that we were collecting, but the methodology used, the trends they revealed and the degree to which she was confident of her conclusions. By making the path of her own logic clear, she also deepened my understanding of the challenge of interpreting education data.
>
> Dr. Khanna's charts showed us if we were meeting the state's goals. Naturally, she also extended those comparisons to include other large urban districts in California. We also valued her internal comparisons of groups of schools within the district that shared key characteristics, like schools supported by desegregation funds. Some of Dr. Khanna's analyses were in response to questions asked at committee meetings by board members or the public.
>
> My questions, often of the "What do you think this means?" variety, were always welcomed and answered candidly. Over time, I started to suggest my own interpretations. "Do you think this may suggest . . .?" She always shared her knowledge of additional sources of data, offered to respond to our questions in writing and reminded us that we were always welcome to sit down with her privately to discuss the data in more detail.
>
> A leader like Dr. Ritu Khanna is a huge asset for a school district. Someone who supports board members and managers in their professional growth, as she has, creates a strong foundation of trust and also maximizes the value of the data already in a district's hands.

I have reviewed dozens of "help wanted" job descriptions for assessment directors that emphasize this operational side of the job. In addition, I've spoken with dozens of assessment directors all over California, who have staffed districts large and small, urban and rural. Too many of them were disheartened because of the overemphasis on the operational side of their jobs. They were demoralized because most of them were proudest of their ability to bring meaning out of test results for the purpose of improving instruction. They were proud of their abilities to diagnose misunderstood concepts that were barriers to student progress, to identify students who were way behind grade level and not getting help, and similar judgments that required interpretive skill.

The underinvestment in assessment directors has been matched by the overinvestment in making teachers into analysts. Prior to the year 2000 and the introduction of test-data-management-and-reporting systems, teachers weren't really expected to interpret interim and end-of-year state tests on their own. In that era, teachers turned to their district assessment team for analytic leadership. This skill is uncommon, so districts did what other organizations have done—centralize their analytic talent in one team and task them to communicate their findings to instructional leaders and teachers.

The wishful thinking that software could encapsulate the analytic skill of assessment leaders and put it in the hands of teachers at a quicker pace and at a lower cost has not panned out. That wishful thinking coincided with the business interests of ed-tech firms, whose sales materials promised that assessment knowledge could be turned into stoplights whose red, yellow and green lights would provide clear signals to teachers. Left to their own, teachers appear to be interpreting test results correctly *about half the time at best*, if Jenny Rankin's findings from her 2013 California study are generalizable.[8] If you're in district leadership, you can begin the improvement process by elevating the responsibilities of your assessment director. Then you can continue pushing for progress by:

- Revising the job descriptions of your district assessment leaders to include skills in logical reasoning, analytic methods and data visualization;
- Requiring data analysis and critical reasoning skills tests of current leaders and new hires whose job responsibilities include measurement of student learning;
- Telling your state's professional associations that they need to take the lead in calling for members to elevate their current level of skill in data analysis and assessment interpretation; and
- Telling the higher-ups at the schools of education who send your district teacher candidates that their graduates need to be more assessment literate and data savvy.

School boards

You're sitting in perhaps the most powerful position of all, and you face the fewest barriers to doing the right thing. You have the power to ask questions in public meetings. You have the power to approve your district's budget. You create your district's policies. You have the power and responsibility to review the superintendent annually. All four of these moments are suitable occasions for you to ask district leaders to explain how they arrived at their conclusions. Asking the superintendent to back up, slow down and explain something more fully is likely to lead to discovery of previously unstated assumptions. Consider the power of asking the right person the right question at the right time in these scenarios:

> *Scenario #1: Leadership reports to the board on the meaning of the test results on the state's assessment.* The district's director of research and evaluation is presenting her interpretation of what these results mean. She compares your district throughout her talk to the statewide average results. You could ask:
>
> Why is comparing our students' results to the results of the students statewide a helpful guide? Let's also compare our students' results to those of districts whose students are very similar to our own, or to districts in communities more like ours.
>
> *Scenario #2: The board requests a report on the condition of reading instruction.* The superintendent and the director of elementary education are delivering this report. They've provided a written report to board members, and you've read it and brought your marked-up report to the meeting. You're troubled because it relies too heavily on the results of just one assessment—the one that is provided by the publisher of the reading program. This means it is likely to be biased to reflect well on the program itself. You want to see other evidence. Your list of questions: "Why aren't the reading results from our interim assessments included in your report?" "Could you also show us our students' results on the state assessment that provide evidence about reading mastery?"
>
> *Scenario #3: The district's budget is on the agenda for the board meeting next week.* You have time to prepare, and you've noted that a lot of money is budgeted for teacher professional development. But to what end, and at what cost? You also note a lot of money budgeted for leadership's professional development. But the budget doesn't specify what skill-building should result from that investment. You've not been pleased with the quality of the principals' annual site plans, so you could ask: "Does this professional development investment for our site leadership include skill-building in the areas of data literacy and assessment fundamentals?"

The human drive to connect the dots

Why do we connect the dots? This may not seem like a natural impulse, but indeed it is a deeply human behavior. The connecting of dots was the pleasure of our ancestors, as they gazed at the stars. From the randomness of the night sky, they imagined lions and bears, hunters and hares, bulls and winged horses. They drew pictures of the constellations and gave them names we use today. The itch to make sense of the patterns we see led the soothsayers to read tea leaves, and the priests at the oracle of Delphi to swirl pig entrails in a tray and believe the gods were speaking to them. Children learn to speak by making sense of the pattern of the words and behaviors they hear and see.

Pattern-seeking humans today are also likely to be scientists. They hope that the patterns they detect hold clues of consequence. Unlike our ancestors who named the constellations, scientists choose to study patterns they believe to be the result of phenomena that deserve our attention. Identifying patterns of the outbreak of COVID-19 may indicate its causes and the means by which it spreads. Discovering patterns of the genes that comprise the coronavirus will predict whether mutations will change the virus's contagion factor, its severity and its response to vaccines.

Why do we measure? Measuring is the means by which patterns can be identified. Like scientists, those of us who study the interaction of humans inside organizations called schools also seek to identify patterns of consequence. Discovering consequences, both good and bad, is a step toward identifying their causes. The motivation of most of us who measure human interaction in schools is to discover the causes of bad things so that we can stop them from happening and discover the causes of good things so that we can enable them to persist.

The adversaries of measurement in the school world sometimes paint us to be less in touch with the human qualities, to describe us as technocrats and characterize us as descendants of the Taylor time-motion school of management. This cartoon characterization paints us to be heartless accountants who believe people can and should be reduced to numbers in the interest of efficiency. This is humbug.

Measurement of human activity in schools is one path toward making schools more human. Our work is aimed at identifying the patterns that make school an ordeal for so many. Our belief is that stopping the mismeasurement that's so prevalent and creating wiser measures can provide sounder evidence, so leaders can make schools fit students better. Let's build better evidence using wiser measures and equip people who govern and lead to see that evidence with the clearest, most open eyes possible. The outcome is likely to be a quantum leap over the status quo.

Links to extend your reading and interaction

The following link will carry you to additional resources, writing and dialogue about the topics discussed in this chapter. You'll also find live versions of the data visualizations in this chapter that are ready for your interaction. We welcome your comments and continued exploration. You'll find all this on the chapter specific page on the book's website: https://www.k12measures.com/ch7.

Notes

1. Spock was the part-Vulcan/part-human science officer on the U.S.S. Enterprise, the fleet's command ship in the long-running television series, *Star Trek*.
2. Tableau's user community for K–12 has both a national user group (https://usergroups.tableau.com/K12) and state-based user groups in California and Colorado as of October 2021.
3. Paul E. Meehl, *Clinical vs. Statistical Prediction: A Theoretical Analysis and a Review of the Evidence* (Minneapolis: University of Minnesota Press, 1954), https://doi.org/10.1037/11281-000.
4. Mandinach and Gummer, *Data Literacy for Educators*.
5. Statewide Longitudinal Data Systems Grant Program, *SLDS Data Use Standards: Knowledge, Skills, and Professional Behaviors for Effective Data Use, Version 2*. U.S. Department of Education. (Washington, DC: National Center for Education Statistics, 2015). https://slds.ed.gov/#program/data-use-standards.
6. Jenny Rankin, *Designing Data Reports that Work: A Guide for Creating Data Systems in Schools and Districts* (New York: Routledge, 2016).

7. Cornelia Brunner, Chad Fasca, Juliette Heinze, Margaret Honey, Daniel Light, Ellen Mandinach and Dara Wexler, "Linking Data and Learning: The Grow Network Study," *Journal of Education for Students Placed At Risk* 10, no. 3 (2005): 241–67, https://doi.org/10.1207/s15327671espr1003_2.

8. Jenny Rankin, "Remedying Educators' Data Analysis Errors with Over-the-Counter Data," *CCNews: Newsletter of the California Council on Teacher Education* 24, no. 4 (December 2013): 14–21, http://ccte.org/wp-content/pdfs-newsletters/ccte-news-2013-winter.pdf.

References

Brunner, Cornelia, Chad Fasca, Juliette Heinze, Margaret Honey, Daniel Light, Ellen Mandinach, and Dara Wexler. "Linking Data and Learning: The Grow Network Study." *Journal of Education for Students Placed At Risk* 10, no. 3 (2005): 241–67.

Hattie, John. *Visible Learning: A Synthesis of Over 800 Meta-Analyses Relating to Achievement*. New York: Routledge, 2009.

Mandinach, Ellen, and Edith S. Gummer. *Data Literacy for Educators: Making It Count in Teacher Preparation and Practice*. New York: Teachers College Press, 2016.

Meehl, Paul E. *Clinical versus Statistical Prediction: A Theoretical Analysis and a Review of the Evidence*. Minneapolis: University of Minnesota Press, 1954.

Rankin, Jenny. *Designing Data Reports that Work: A Guide for Creating Data Systems in Schools and Districts*. New York: Routledge, 2016.

Statewide Longitudinal Data Systems Grant Program. *SLDS Data Use Standards: Knowledge, Skills, and Professional Behaviors for Effective Data Use, Version 2*. Washington, DC: National Center for Education Statistics, U.S. Department of Education, 2015.

Index

Note: Page numbers in *italic* indicate a figure on the corresponding page.

absentee rates 6–7
academic fraud 92
Accelerated Schools Project 91
accountability: California accountability dashboard, critique of 23, 33n14, 63–4, 78n14; flaws with accountability metrics xiv; and graduation rate problems 99–101; imprecision of test results affecting school or district accountability status 57; No Child Left Behind federal rules 11, 31n5; principals as casualties 12–13; school accountability reports xii–xiii
"Accountability for Alternative Schools in California" (Velasco and Gonzales) 98
administrative credential programs 73, 203, 239–40
Advocates for Children of New York 89–90
age-and-body-mass index for boys 46, *47*
Akron, Ohio teachers 212
Alabama: student perception surveys 220
Alaska: student perception surveys 220
Aldine ISD, Texas 144–8, *145–7*
algebra 86, 87

Amato, Anthony 222
American Community Survey 167, 168
American Education Research Association 25, 58, 173, 204
American Education Research Journal 173
American Psychological Association 238; Standards for Educational Assessment 38, 58
American Statistical Association: criticism of statistical significance 20, 27, 74
American Statistician, The (journal) 20, 27
analytic software 237
Ánimo Ellen Ochoa Charter Middle School, East Los Angeles 3, 63–5
architectural firms, and quality of physical resources 210
assessment directors: literal-minded 71; recommendation on assessments 73; underinvestment in, and responsibilities of 241–4
assessment firms: recommendation on assessments 74; reducing barriers to progress 240–1; test design errors 41–2

249

Index

assessment illiteracy, in introducing errors 20–1
assessment literacy, from schools of education 238–9
assessments: curriculum-embedded 236; diagnostic and interim 38; Spanish language 39; *see also* Smarter Balanced assessments; state assessments
assets, mismeasurement of 195–232; economic analysis, lack of 195; human resource directors 213–16, 222; land and buildings 207–10; money 196–207 (*see also* money); position control and paychecks to dead teachers 222; teachers (*see* teachers as school district assets)
Associated Press: *Style Guide* 58
attendance statistics 6–7
averages, and blind spot of spread of test results 52–4

Balanced Literacy approach to teaching reading 61, 236
baseball 4, 95, 205
baseball fields 209
Beane, Billy 4, 95
benchmarks 70; in errors of commission 46–51
Bersin, Josh 214
"best practices" approach: explained 25–6; critique of 234, 237, 239
bias: assumption of bias without sufficient evidence 122; confirmation bias 113; gender bias in teachers' grading practices 133–4; identity politics masking barriers to all students' progress 122; proving teacher bias in discipline of students of different ethnic groups 117–20, *118, 120*; *see also* gaps

Bill and Melinda Gates Foundation 220
birth weight, correlated with students' test scores 159n1
Black teacher candidates, and teacher licensing exams 217
Bloomfield School District, Indiana 140–4, *141, 142, 144*
body-mass index for boys 46, *47*
bond measures 206
bond rating agencies 206
Book of Why: The New Science of Cause and Effect, The (Pearl and Mackenzie) 109
Brann, Don 96
Bryk, Anthony S. 195
bubble kids 71
budgets 196–7, 245; *see also* finances
buildings *see* land and buildings
Burton High School, San Francisco 12–13

CALDER Center 218
California: English Language Proficiency Assessments for California 171, 175–6; English learner classification 168, 169, 170–1, 175–6; ever-English learners 178, 180–1; school building standards 210
California Assessment of Student Performance and Progress (CAASPP) 52, *53*
California Department of Education: adoption of growth measure 63–5; graduation requirements of 86–7; information design flaws and logic errors 23; and score imprecision 55
California Dropout Research Project (CDRP) 92–3, 97
California English Language Development Test (CELDT) 169, 170–1

Index

California High School Exit Exam (CAHSEE) 87
Californians Together 175
California School Dashboard 63–4; critique of 23, 33n14, 78n14
California Standards Tests 10
Cannell, J.J. 49
Carnegie Foundation for the Advancement of Teaching 195, 235
categorical funds 199
Catholic Archdiocese Schools, Indianapolis 4, 218–19
causation see multicausal model of influences
Center for Benefit Cost Studies in Education 203
Center for Education Policy Analysis (CEPA) 139
Charlottesville City Public School District, Virginia 148–53, *149–50, 152–3*
charter schools: human cost of mismeasurement 3, 63–5; predictive analytics and graduation rates 96; renting *vs.* ownership of buildings 209
Chicago Guide to Writing about Numbers (Miller) 18, 154
Chicago Manual of Style 18
Chicago Public Schools 207, 212
Chico Unified, California 148–53, *149–50, 152–3*
chronic absentee rates 6
Cincinnati Public Schools 212
classification error rates 71
class size reduction, and cost-benefit analysis 204
Class Struggle: What's Wrong (and Right) with America's Best Public High Schools (Mathews) 94
Clinical vs. Statistical Prediction: A Theoretical Analysis and a Review of the Evidence (Meehl) 33n21, 237

cohort of ninth graders 82–3
collective bargaining 206, 207, 213
College Board, norm tables 46
college-going rates 50, *51*
Colorado: English learner classification 168
commission see errors of commission
Common Core math standards 43
"common sense" for decision-making 234, 237
community centers 209
community cooperative spirit xvi, 208–9
comparative approach in gap analysis 116, 119, 123
comparative effectiveness research (CER) 24–6
confidence, degree of 45
confidence interval (degree of uncertainty) and relation to error margin (degree of imprecision) 57
confirmatory approach in building evidence 112–13
contingent valuation method 205
continuation high schools and graduation rates 84, 97–8
continuous improvement 195–6, 235
Core 40 as tiered diploma 88
core content knowledge 216–17
Coronado USD, San Diego County 209
Cortines, Ramon 86
cost accounting 199–200
cost-benefit analysis 204–6
cost-effectiveness 196–7, 201–4
Cost-Effectiveness Analysis: Methods and Applications (Levin) 202
cost-per-student analysis of expenses 197–201; weighted student formulas 199
cost-utility analysis 227n10
credential programs see administrative credential programs

251

Index

credit recovery and graduation rates 91–3, 100
cross-sectional view of test results 44, 65, 66, *67*, 69, *70*
CTB/McGraw-Hill 170–1
Cult of Statistical Significance, The (Ziliak and McCloskey) 19
Cummings, Amy 92
curriculum-embedded assessments 236
cystic fibrosis 4

Danielson, Charlotte 221
Dartmouth Atlas of Health Care 24–5, 202
data: data mavens' relative scarcity 235; disaggregated by ethnicity 242; quality of 115; in steps to building evidence 14–16; visual representations of 22–3
data analysis training, needed from schools of education 238–9
data-driven decision-making 28
Data Literacy for Educators (Mandinach and Gummer) 239
data visualization: advantages of comparative methods 117–20; design of visual representations of data 22–3; leaderboards 50, 119; scatterplots 60, 139, 143, 148, 186; software suitable for visual analysis 237
DaVinci Science High School 96
decision-making: based on evidence 234–7; data-driven 28
defensive expenditure method 205
deferred liabilities 206–7
Designing Data Reports that Work (Rankin) 241
Designing Teacher Evaluation Systems (MET project) 220

diagnostic assessments 38
diplomas 84–6; tiered 88
discipline, proving teacher bias in discipline of ethnic groups 113–20; building evidence with suspension data 116–17; data on suspensions 115–16; presenting the evidence 117–20, *118*, *120*; questions on equal treatment 114–15
district leaders, guiding questions for; about assessment director responsibilities 75; about credit recovery 102; about gaps in achievement between English-only students and English learners 157–8; about gaps in math achievement between Latino/Hispanic and white students 158; about graduation rate decline 101–2; about mismeasurement 29; about recruiting better quality new teachers 226; about test evidence used to identify English learners 75; about test's single best purpose 75; about the cost consequences of misidentifying English learners 190–1; about unequal funding of school sites 225–6
districts: assessment directors' responsibilities 241–4; evaluation of teachers 211–13; graduation rate dishonesty 89; graduation requirements 86–7, 88–9; policies and dropout rates 94; test scores as proxy for effectiveness 36–7
dropouts, and graduation rates 83, 92, 94, 95–6
Dropping Out: Why Students Drop Out of High School and What Can Be Done About It (Rumberger) 92

Index

dyslexia: and errors in test sensitivity and specificity 43–4; human cost of mismeasurement 2; as influence on learning 110; school boards, screening requirements 236

economic analysis 195–6; see also finances
Economic Evaluation in Education Cost-Effectiveness and Benefit-Cost Analysis (Levin) 202
Educational Economics: Where do [$]chool Funds Go? (Roza) 198
Educational Leadership 36
Educational Opportunity Explorer 139; see also gap measurement, exemplary models of
Educational Testing Service (ETS) 85; Praxis Elementary Education, Multiple Subjects test 216
Education Next 87
Education Week 61, 92, 96, 138
effect size 27
Elementary and Secondary Education Act (ESEA) (1965) 199
emerging bilingual students 166; see also English learners
English Language Proficiency Assessments for California (ELPAC) 171, 175–6
English learners: and errors of commission 39; and errors of omission 8; human cost of mismeasurement 1–2; long-term 175
English learners, logic errors in identifying 165–94; English learners defined 166–72; exiting EL status 172–6; factors in mismeasurement 165–6; Home Language Survey 166, 167–9; lowering the risk of mistaken classification 172; test results, incorrect frequency 170–1; tests to confirm EL identification 169–70
English learners, mismeasurement of progress 176–90; ever-English learners 176–7, 180–1; mismeasurement of reclassification rates 178–9; transient entity problem 177–8; visualization of pace of reclassification 179–90, *181–3, 185, 187, 189*
English proficiency tests of English learners 166, 169–71
equal treatment under the law 114
equity see bias; fairness; gap analysis
error margin (degree of imprecision) 57
errors, introduction of 17–23; assessment illiteracy 20–1; design of visual representations of data 22–3; quantitative illiteracy (innumeracy) 18–20; semantics 17–18
errors of commission 7, 8–9, 37–51; test administration errors 39–41; test design and item construction errors 41–3; test sensitivity and specificity errors 43–4; wrong benchmark or norms 46–51; wrong instrument 38–9; wrong purpose 38; wrong students 39; wrong unit of measurement 44–5
errors of interpretation or judgment 8, 9–10, 62–72; evidence not matched to the question 66–70; excessive certainty 71–2; misleading school dashboard 63–5; scale properties 72; validity 62; wrong vantage point 65–6
errors of omission 7–8, 52–62; averages and blind spot of spread 52–4; challenge of multiple measures 59–62; imprecision blind

253

spot 54–7; uncertainty blind spot 57–8
Estrada, Peggy 173, 174
ethnicity: teacher licensing exams 217; see also Latino/Hispanic students
ever-English learners 176–8, 180–1
Every Student Succeeds Act (ESSA) 32n5, 85
evidence: conflicting, in reading tests 61–2; decision-making based on evidence 234–7; not matched to the question 66–70
evidence, building: with data to prove bias in discipline of ethnic groups 116–17; gap analysis with exploratory and confirmatory approaches 112–13; of gaps in students' test scores 125–7; of gender bias in teachers' grading practices 133–4; for graduation rates 98–9, 101
evidence, methods to minimize risk of misjudging 23–7; comparative effectiveness 24–6; practical benefit 26–7
evidence, steps in building 14–17, 15; drawing inferences 16–17; observing 14; organizing data to build evidence 16; recording data 14–15; viewing data 16
evidence-based medicine 4, 5n1, 28
evidence-based practices, resistance to 27–9
exit exams for high school 38–9, 87
exit interviews of teachers 215
"experience" alone, for decision-making 234
exploratory approach in building evidence 112–13

Fairfield-Suisun USD, California 183, 183–4
fairness, for equal treatment under the law 114
Ferguson, Ronald 221
Figlio, David 159n1
finances: budgets and economic analyses 196–7, 245; deferred liabilities 206–7; property taxes 200; weighted student formulas 199; see also money
Fiske, Edward 49
Florida: English learner classification 168
Fountas & Pinnell 60, 61
Framework for Teaching 221
fraud: academic fraud in credit recovery 92; district dishonesty in graduation rates 89; paycheck theft 222
free-and-reduced-price lunch status see meal subsidies
frequency distribution 52–4, 53
fuzzy factor 54–7, 73
fuzzy graduation rates 88–9, 93–4

gap analysis 106–13; building evidence with exploratory and confirmatory approaches 112–13; design-build in construction 106–7; distortion by home environment and heredity 107–8, 110; influences shaping the gaps 108–10; work on the question first 110–12; see also bias
gap measurement, exemplary models of 139–53; centrality of context when analyzing gaps 139–40; Stanford Educational Opportunity Project 139–40; test score gaps and learning rate gaps 148–53, 149–50, 152–3; test score gaps and levels of test scores 140–4, 141, 142, 144;

test score gaps and socioeconomic profiles 144–8, *145–7*
Gapminder 156
gaps 106–64; challenge of discussing gap measures 155–7; gap analysis 106–13 (*see also* gap analysis); gaps in discipline 113–20 (*see also* discipline, proving teacher bias in discipline of ethnic groups); gaps in opportunities to learn 129–32 (*see also* opportunities to learn, measuring gaps in); gaps in students' test scores 121–8 (*see also* test scores, gaps in); gender bias in teachers' grading practices 132–4; measurement, exemplary models of 139–53 (*see also* gap measurement, exemplary models of); talking and writing about gaps 154–5; visualizing gaps, customary methods of 134–8
Gawande, Atul 5n1
GED Testing Service 85
gender bias in teachers' grading practices 132–4
General Educational Development (GED) program 90
general education diploma 85
general equivalence diploma (GED) 85
Gewertz, Catherine 92
Goldenberg, Claude 170, 171
Gomez, Louis M. 195
Gonzales, Daisy 98
Government Accounting Standards Board (GASB) 207, 208
grade-level norm tables 46
graduation rates 81–105; adjusted cohort rate 84; continuation high schools 84, 97–8; credit recovery 91–3, 100; denominators 81–4; district dishonesty 89; districts' graduation requirements 86–7, 88–9; dropout indicators 95–6; dropout rates 83, 94; five-year rates 85, 100; fuzzy numbers 88–9, 93–4; mobility of students 82–3, 99–100; numerators 84–6; push-outs 89–91, 100; student's point of view 86–7; unusual local circumstances 100–1; vital signs in the right direction 98–101
GreatSchools 222
Green Dot Public Schools 63
Grow Network 241
Grunow, Alicia 195
Gummer, Edith S. 73, 239

Hakuta, Kenji 174
Harrington, Bob xi
Harvard Strategic Data Project 96
Hattie, John 25–6, 28, 74, 195, 196, 238
Hawaii: student perception surveys 220
health benefits for teachers 207
health care *see* medicine
hedonic method of estimating prices 205
heredity as confounding factor in gap analysis 107–8, 110
Higher Order Thinking Skills (HOTS) 91
high school counselors and cost-benefit analysis 204
high school exit exams 38–9, 87
HiSet exam 85
Holland, Fiona 203
home environment in gap analysis 107–8
Home Language Survey 166, 167–9
How Public Educators Cheat on Standardized Achievement Tests (Cannell) 49
human resource directors 213–16, 222

Illinois: English learner classification 168, 174
immigrants, as English learners 167

Index

imprecision: blind spot of 54–7; degree of 45, 57; and excessive certainty 71; standard error of measurement 126
Indiana: tiered diplomas 88
Indianapolis Archdiocese Schools 4, 218–19
Indiana Statewide Test of Educational Progress (ISTEP) 219
Individual Education Plan (IEP) 86, 137
inequality *see* bias
inferences, drawing, as step in building evidence 16–17
inferential errors, reduction of 72–4
influences at work on kids at school, multicausal model of 109–10, *110*, 111
information design 22–3
innumeracy 18–20
Innumeracy: Mathematical Illiteracy and Its Consequences (Paulos) 18
institutional and professional interests, reducing barriers to progress 233
interim assessments, measuring gaps in students' test scores 124–5
interpretation *see* errors of interpretation or judgment
Iowa: student perception surveys 220

James, Bill 4, 95
Just-4-Kids 84

Kaiser Permanente 131
Khanna, Ritu 242–3
Klein, Joel I. 89–90
Korn, Shira 64
K12 Measures *118*, 119, *120*, 180

"Lake Wobegon Report" (Cannell) 49
land and buildings 207–10; community cooperation and resource sharing 208–10; value of quality of resources 210
LAS-LINKS test of English learners 169
Latino/Hispanic students, gaps in test scores with white students 127–8, *128*, 138, *142*, 145, *146*, *152*, *153*
learning barriers 122
learning rate gaps 148–53, *149–50*, *152–3*
Learning to Improve: How America's Schools Can Get Better at Getting Better (Bryk, Gomez, Grunow, and LeMahieu) 195
LeMahieu, Paul G. 195
Levin, Henry 91, 202–3, 205
Lewis, Michael 95
libraries, and resource sharing 209
licensing exams for teachers 216–18
longitudinal measures 45, 68–9, *70*, 82, 128; *see also* quasi-longitudinal view
long-term English learners 175
Los Angeles USD 207, 209
Loveless, Tom 138

Mackenzie, Dana 109
Malkus, Nat 92, 93
Mandinach, Ellen B. 73, 239
Massachusetts: student perception surveys 220; teacher licensing exams 217, 218
master schedule, measuring gaps in opportunities to learn 131–2
math: gap analysis question 111–12; skills deficits and human cost of mismeasurement 2–3; test design errors 41–2
Mathews, Jay 92, 94
Matthews, Leroy 4
McCloskey, Deirdre N. 19–20
McFall, Russell 64

Index

McGraw-Hill: CTB/McGraw-Hill 170–1; Education, report quality 241; LAS-LINKS test 169
meal subsidies 48, 123, 143, 160n4
Measures of Effective Teaching (MET) project 220
medicine: clinical trials, numeracy, and statistical significance 19–20; comparative effectiveness research 24–5; cost-benefit analysis 202, 205; diagnostic assessments 2; evidence-based 4, 5n1, 28; mismeasurement in 1, 74; providing information about doctors 131
Meehl, Paul 33n21, 237–8
"meeting standard" threshold measure 3, 44–5, 71, 154
Merck 19–20
migration of students *see* mobility of students
Miller, Jane E. 18
Minnesota: training of data leads and assessment staff 240
mismeasurement, and the occurrence of 6–34; defined 6–7; frequency of mismeasurement of test results 10–14; human cost of 1–5; introduction of errors 17–23; minimizing risk of misjudging evidence 23–7; resistance to evidence 27–9; steps to building evidence and interpreting its meaning 14–17; types of 7–10
Mississippi: student perception surveys 220
mobility of students and graduation rates *82*, 82–3, 99–100
Moggia, Chris 175
money 196–207; budgets and cost-effectiveness 196–7; cost accounting 199–200; cost-benefit analysis 204–6; cost-effectiveness measures 201–4; cost-per-student 197–201; deferred liabilities 206–7; weighted student formulas 199; *see also* finances
Moneyball (Lewis) 95
Morgan Hill USD 50, *51*, *118*, 119, *120*
multicausal model of influences at work on kids at school 109–10, *110*, 111
multilingual students 178
multitiered systems of support (MTSS) Tier 2 referrals 59

NAACP xi, xvi, 242
Napa Valley USD, California 180–8, *181–3*, *185*, *187*, *189*
National Academy of Medicine 24
National Assessment of Educational Progress (NAEP) 127, *128*; hazards of comparing states' results 137–8; as used by Stanford Educational Opportunity Project 139
National Center for Education Statistics (NCES) 127, 239
National Center for Fair and Open Testing (FairTest) 35
National Center for Teaching Quality 233
National Council on Measurement in Education 21, 58
National Council on Teacher Quality (NCTQ) 216
Nevada: English learner classification 168, 174
New Mexico: English learner classification 168
New Orleans school district 222
New Teacher Project 210, 212
New York: design of test result reports 241; English learner classification 174; tiered diplomas 88

Index

New York State English as a Second Language Achievement Test (NYSESLAT) 174
New York Times 49, 89–90, 139
No Child Left Behind: Adequate Yearly Progress goals 3, 11, 13, 14; disaggregated data by ethnicity 242; error of wrong purpose 38; federal accountability rules xiv, xviii, 11, 31n5; human cost of mismeasurement 3, 234; NAEP and Title 1 funding 127, 137; Program Improvement 13
norms in errors of commission 46–51
norm tables 46, 49
Northwest Evaluation Association (NWEA): Measures of Academic Progress (MAP) 40, 56, 61
numbers, language of 18, 154

Oakland USD 222
Obama administration: Race to the Top 12; waivers for NCLB AYPs 11, 32n5
Ohio: English language proficiency test 169
Olson, Laurie 175
online credit recovery programs 93
opportunities to learn, measuring gaps in 129–32, 156; cost-per-student 197–8; master schedule 131–2; school assignment policies 129–30; teacher assignment across school sites 130–1
Oregon: English language proficiency test 169; reporting of education data 240
Organisation for Economic Co-operation and Development (OECD) 19
Orrick, William xi, 242
Osborne, David 63

Partnership for Assessment of Readiness for College and Careers (PARCC): and score imprecision 55; testing reading skills 59
Paulos, John Allen 18
paycheck theft 222
Pearl, Judea 109
Pearson, SELP (Stanford English Language Proficiency) Test 169
peer-to-peer networks 234
pencil-and-paper tests 40
pensions 207
people analytics 214
people as assets: HR team (*see* human resource directors); teachers (*see* teachers as school district assets)
percentage points *vs.* percent 155
percentages *vs.* ratios 154–5
percent-meeting-standard 69
percent proficient metric 69
Phi Delta Kappa 221
Phi Delta Kappan journal 36
phonics skills, measuring 124–5
playgrounds 208–9, 210
Pogrow, Stanley 26–7, 91
Polikoff, Morgan 64, 138
Popham, James 14, 20–1, 35, 36, 73, 238
position control 222
practical benefit 26–7
Praxis Elementary Education: Multiple Subjects test 216
predictive analytics 95–6
pregnant students 90–1
presentation of evidence, proving bias in discipline of ethnic groups 117–20, *118*, *120*
principals: administrative credential program requirements 73; as casualties of accountability 12–13; of continuation high schools 97;

morale of 224; push-outs, steering lagging students to leave high school 90–1
principals, guiding questions for: about cost-benefit rationale for investing in professional development of teachers 227; about effect of teacher assignments on gaps in student achievement 158; about gender bias in teacher assigned grades 158; about high school principals planning for budget cuts 226–7; about interpreting reading results 76; about mismeasurement 30; about site plan for continuation high 102; about test result interpretation and site plans 76; about when to recommend a struggling high school student to transfer to continuation high 102; site planning goals for reclassifying English learners 191
professional development 215, 245; writing for school accountability report cards xiv
"proficient" level 3, 44–5, 71, 138
program evaluators 203, 205
Program Improvement schools 11, 13
progress *see* barriers to progress, reducing
property taxes 200
ProPublica, on comparative effectiveness research in medicine 24–5
PSAT, norm tables 46
push-outs, and graduation rates 89–91, 100
p-values, critique of 20

quantitative illiteracy (innumeracy), in introducing errors 18–20
quantitative literacy 18, 239
quasi-longitudinal views 66, *69, 70,* 82, 128
questions for analysis, improving in gap analysis 110–12

Rankin, Jenny 10–11, 58, 241, 244
Rasmussen, Steven 41–3
ratios *vs.* percentages 154–5
reading, learning to, and hereditary influence on 110
reading instruction, questions to ask at school board meetings 245
reading remediation 59
reading skills tests 59–62, 123–4
Reardon, Sean xxv, 139, 161n6
reclassification of English learners 179; *see also* English learners
reconstitution 12
recruitment of new teachers 214–15
Regents Diploma (New York) 88
resource metrics, sharing of 224–5
resources, quality of buildings and playgrounds 210
resource sharing between schools and communities 209
response to intervention (RtI) 59
retention of teachers 215, *223,* 224
retirement benefits 207
Rosemount-Apple Valley-Eagan, Minnesota 144–8, *145–7*
Rosling, Anna 156
Rosling, Hans 156
Roza, Marguerite 197–9
Rumberger, Russell 92, 97
running record of students' reading accuracy 61

San Francisco USD xi, xv–xvi, 3–4, 242–3
Schacter, John 4, 218–19

Index

schizophrenia, diagnosis of 33n21, 237–8
Schneider, Mark 195–6
school assignment policies, measuring gaps in opportunities to learn 129–30
school boards: attendance boundaries 129; during NCLB era xviii; budgets 203; freedom to measure what they consider important 235–6; long-term financial impact of deferred liabilities 206; reducing barriers to progress 244–5; school assignment policies 130
school board trustees, guiding questions for: about board policies for when English learners should be reclassified 190; about board policies supporting English language learners after reclassification 190; about college prep curricula for all students 102–3; about equity audits 159; about how to propose to voters that they fund schools more fully 227; about mismeasurement 30; about rationale for hiring of counselors instead of teachers 227–8; about sharing the pain of budget cuts fairly 159; about test result interpretation for evaluating superintendents 76; about test results and accountability sanctions 76–7; about test results and district plans 77; about variation in graduation rates 103
school climate surveys 220, 224
school districts *see* districts
schools of education: as barriers to progress in fostering quantitative literacy 238–9, 244; recommendation on assessments 73;

recruitment of new teachers from 214–15
School Wise Press *118*, 119, *120*
scientific method 235
score creep 49
segregated housing patterns 129–30
SELP (Stanford English Language Proficiency) Test 169
semantics in introducing errors 17–18
signal processing technology 61n5, 124
"SLDS Data Use Standards" (NCES) 239
SLDS (student longitudinal data system) 83
Smarter Balanced Assessment Consortium (SBAC): English language arts test 59; math test 52, *53*
Smarter Balanced assessments: errors in test design for math 41–3, *42*; and imprecision 55–57; visualizing reclassification of English learners 185, *185*, *187*, *189*; visualizing test score gaps in English/language arts 135–7, *136*
socioeconomic profiles and test score gaps *141*, 144–8, *145–7*, 149–50, *152–3*
Sparks, Sarah 96
special education students: cost-per-student of education 198, 201; graduation of 85–6, 91
spread (frequency distribution) of test scores 44
standard deviation 45, 52
standard error of measurement 126
Standards for Educational and Psychological Testing 58, 62
Standards for Reporting Data to Educators (Rankin) 11, 58
Stanford Educational Opportunity Project 139; Educational

Opportunity Explorer 139–40; see also gap measurement, exemplary models of
Stanford Education Data Archive (SEDA) 139
Stanford English Language Proficiency Test (SELP) 169
state assessments: measurement for evidence in making decisions 236; measuring gaps in students' test scores 123–4; questions to ask at school board meetings 245; state-level reporting 137–8
state departments of education: recommendation on assessments 73; reducing barriers to progress 240
state graduation requirements 87
statistical significance: in clinical trials 19–20; critiqued 20; much used, abused, and buried 20, 27, 74
Stokes-Guinan, Katie 170, 171
student longitudinal data system (SLDS) 83, 239
students: accelerating 91; cost-per-student 197–201; surveys of students about teachers 216, 219–21, 225; see also English learners; graduation rates; Latino/Hispanic students
superintendents: analytic skills of assessment directors 241–2; evaluations 76; qualities of human resource directors to be considered 213; see also district leaders, guiding questions for
support services, cost of 198–9
surveys of students about teachers 216, 219–21
suspensions, and proving bias in discipline 115–17, *118*, *120*

Tableau software 237
teacher evaluations 211–13; ineffectiveness of 211–12; value-added analysis of effect of teachers 216, 219; "The Widget Effect" 211–12
teachers: analytic skills of 243–4; assignment across school sites, and opportunities to learn 130–1; detecting gender bias in grading practices 132–4; master schedule 131–2; morale of 212, 224; mistakenly interpreting test results 10–11, 244; paychecks to deceased teachers 222; recruitment and retention of 214–16, *223*, *224*; underperforming teachers 215–16
teachers as school district assets 210–24; data about teachers 222–4; human resource opportunities 214–16; licensing exams 216–18; result of elementary teachers teaching their best subject all day long 218–19; student perception surveys 219–21, 225; teacher evaluations 211–13
teacher satisfaction surveys 215
test administration, errors of 39–41
test design and errors of commission 41–3
test publishers see assessment firms
test results 35–80; ambiguity of 71; debate around testing 35, 72–3; errors of commission 37–51 (see also errors of commission); errors of interpretation or judgment 62–72 (see also errors of interpretation or judgment); errors of omission 52–62 (see also errors of omission); frequency of mismeasurement of 10–14; as proxy for school and

district effectiveness 36–7; reducing inferential errors 72–4; standards for communicating the meaning of 241; teaching as immature profession 74

test scores: above average in every state 48–9; as errors example 8–10; gaps in levels of achievement 140–4, *141, 142, 144*

test scores, gaps in 121–8; building evidence 125–7; presenting the evidence 127–8; questions with learning barriers 121–3; and socioeconomic profiles *141, 144–8, 145–7, 149–50, 152–3*; state assessments and interim assessments 123–5

test sensitivity and specificity, and errors of commission 43–4

test validity 62

Texas: English learner classification 168, 169, 174

theft *see* wrongdoing

threshold boundary measure 45, 69–70

tiered diplomas 88

Tier 2 referrals in MTSS system 59

time, in measurement 70

Title 1 funding: and NAEP 127, 137; Part A 199

Title III funding 177

tradition, as rationale for decision-making 234

Training Measurement Book, The (Bersin) 214

transfer schools (New York) *see* continuation high schools and graduation rates

transient entity problem in defining English learners 177–8

Tripod Education Founders 221

Tripod Survey 221

true measure of test score 57

uncertainty, blind spot, and errors of omission 57–8

units of measurement 44–5; cross-sectional view 44; longitudinal measure 45; standard deviation 45; threshold boundary measure 45

Unlearned Lessons: Six Stumbling Blocks to Our Schools' Success (Popham) 20

U.S. Census Bureau 167, 168

U.S. Department of Education: rules on counting graduates 84–6; Title III funding 177

user experience (UX) engineering 41

user interface (UI) engineering 41

Utah: student perception surveys 220

validity 62, 64

value-added analysis 216, 219

vantage point 65–6, 70

Velasco, Jorge Ruiz de 98

vertical equating of test scores 68, 72

Vioxx 19–20

Visible Learning (Hattie) 25, 28, 74, 196, 238

visualizing gaps, customary methods of 134–8

visual representations of data 22–3

Wainer, Howard 35

Walsh, Kate 216–18

Wang, Haiwen 173, 174

Ward, Randy 222

Warren Consolidated Schools, Michigan 140–4, *141, 142, 144*

Warwick, Warren 4

Washington Post 92, 94

Washoe County School District, Nevada 135–7, *136*
weighted student formulas 199
"what works" approach 25
WIDA screener 169
"Widget Effect, The" in teacher evaluations 210, 211–12, 233
Williams Settlement legislation, California 210
Wiseburn ESD 96

Wold, Tony 218
workforce analytics 214
World-Class Instructional Design and Assessment Consortium (WIDA) 169
wrongdoing: academic fraud in credit recovery 92; district dishonesty in graduation rates 89; paycheck theft 222
Wunder, Matt 96

Ziliak, Stephen T. 19–20

For Product Safety Concerns and Information please contact our EU representative GPSR@taylorandfrancis.com
Taylor & Francis Verlag GmbH, Kaufingerstraße 24, 80331 München, Germany

www.ingramcontent.com/pod-product-compliance
Lightning Source LLC
Chambersburg PA
CBHW052214300426

44115CB00011B/1688